THE MYSTERY OF CHOPIN'S *PRÉLUDES*

Frontispiece: The Carthusian Monastery of Valldemossa.
Photograph by Enric Calafell Alemany

The Mystery of Chopin's *Préludes*

ANATOLE LEIKIN
University of California, Santa Cruz, USA

ASHGATE

© Anatole Leikin 2015

All rights reserved. No part of this publication may be reproduced, stored in a retrieval system or transmitted in any form or by any means, electronic, mechanical, photocopying, recording or otherwise without the prior permission of the publisher.

Anatole Leikin has asserted his right under the Copyright, Designs and Patents Act, 1988, to be identified as the author of this work.

Bach musicological font © Yo Tomita

Published by
Ashgate Publishing Limited
Wey Court East
Union Road
Farnham
Surrey, GU9 7PT
England

Ashgate Publishing Company
110 Cherry Street
Suite 3-1
Burlington, VT 05401-3818
USA

www.ashgate.com

British Library Cataloguing in Publication Data
A catalogue record for this book is available from the British Library

The Library of Congress has cataloged the printed edition as follows:
Leikin, Anatole, 1946- author.
   The mystery of Chopin's Preludes / by Anatole Leikin.
       pages cm
   Includes bibliographical references and index.
   ISBN 978-1-4094-5224-9 (hardcover)—ISBN 978-1-4094-5225-6 (ebook)—
   ISBN 978-1-4724-0681-1 (epub) 1. Chopin, Frédéric, 1810-1849. Preludes, op. 28. piano. I. Title.

   ML410.C54L35 2015
   786.2'18928092--dc23
                                                                    2014026189
ISBN 9781409452249 (hbk)
ISBN 9781409452256 (ebk – PDF)
ISBN 9781472406811 (ebk –ePUB)

Printed in the United Kingdom by Henry Ling Limited,
at the Dorset Press, Dorchester, DT1 1HD

Contents

List of Figures		*vii*
List of Music Examples		*ix*
Preface		*xiii*
1	The Traditions, the Innovations, and the Predicaments	1
2	Lamartine's *Les Préludes*: The Lyrics and the Milieu	13
3	The Mallorca Factor	23
4	Lamartine's *Les Préludes* and Chopin's *Préludes*	43
5	Deciphering the *Préludes*	67
6	Further Thoughts	145
Appendix: Alphonse de Lamartine, *Les Préludes* (with English translation by Tamah Swenson)		*161*
Bibliography		*179*
Index		*187*

List of Figures

Frontispiece: The Carthusian Monastery of Valldemossa.
Photograph by Enric Calafell Alemany

3.1	The cemetery at the Carthusian monastery. Drawing by J.B. Laurens	33
3.2	A corridor in the Carthusian monastery. Historical photograph by Charles W. Wood, as found in his book *Letters from Majorca*	34
3.3	The ceiling in Chopin's cell. Photograph by Maria Ezerova	36
3.4	Gothic chair in Chopin's cell. Photograph by Maria Ezerova	37
3.5	A corridor at the Carthusian monastery at night. Photograph by Maria Ezerova	38
3.6	The Carthusian monastery in winter. Photograph by Enric Calafell Alemany	39
5.1	Chopin's manuscript, Prelude 1, mm. 29–34	70

List of Music Examples

1.1	Hummel, Prelude 1 from *24 Preludes*, Op. 67	5
1.2	Hummel, Prelude 2 from *24 Preludes*, Op. 67	5
4.1	Bach, *The Well-Tempered Clavier*, Book II, Prelude and Fugue in G♯ minor, (a) Prelude, m. 50, (b) Fugue, mm. 1–2	49
4.2	Bach, *The Well-Tempered Clavier*, Book I, Prelude and Fugue in E♭ major, (a) Prelude, mm. 63–70, (b) Fugue, mm. 1–2	50
4.3	Bach, *The Well-Tempered Clavier*, Book I, Fugue in E♭ major, m. 37	50
4.4	*Dies irae*, stanzas 1–4, with an English translation	57
4.5	*Dies irae* motifs written separately	58
4.6	*Dies irae*, inner motivic structure	60
4.7	(a) Kirnberger, *Die Kunst des reinen Satzes in der Musik*, (b) Cherubini, *Cours de contrepoint et de fugue*	61
4.8	*Dies irae*, a complete chart of all the motifs	62
4.9	Beethoven, Piano Sonata, Op. 7, No. 3, movement 4, (a) mm. 87–89, (b) mm. 106–108	64
5.1	Chopin, Prelude 1 from Opus 28	69
5.2	Kirnberger, *Die Kunst des reinen Satzes in der Musik*	70
5.3	(a) Chopin, Prelude 1, mm. 28–34, (b) Prelude 2, mm. 1–4	71
5.4	(a) Chopin, Prelude 1, mm. 1–9, (b) Prelude 1, mm. 21–34, (c) Prelude 2, mm. 1–7	72–3
5.5	Chopin, Prelude 2, mm. 1–8 in George Sand's copy	74
5.6	Chopin, Prelude 2	75
5.7	Chopin, Prelude 3, imitation between LH and RH, (a) LH, m. 1, (b) RH, mm. 3–6	79
5.8	(a) Chopin, Prelude 3, mm. 1–10, (b) Prelude 3, mm. 16–26	80–81
5.9	Chopin, Prelude 3, mm. 26–33	82
5.10	(a) Chopin, Prelude 4, mm. 1–12, (b) Prelude 4, mm. 20–23	83
5.11	Bach, Crucifixus, mm. 1–4	84
5.12	Chopin, Prelude 4, mm. 1–10 (LH)	84
5.13	Bach, Crucifixus, mm. 5–14 (chorus reduction)	84
5.14	Chopin, Prelude 4, mm. 1–23 (Crucifixus motifs)	86
5.15	(a) Chopin, Prelude 4, mm. 7–9 (RH), (b) Prelude 4, mm. 17–23	87
5.16	Chopin, Prelude 5	88
5.17	Chopin, Prelude 6	91
5.18	Chopin, Prelude 7 (modified)	92

5.19	Chopin, Prelude 7, eight sequential patterns	93
5.20	Chopin, Prelude 7	94
5.21	Chopin, Prelude 8, mm. 1–4	95
5.22	Chopin, Prelude 8, mm. 9–19 (RH)	96
5.23	Chopin, Prelude 8, mm. 22–24 (RH)	96
5.24	Chopin, Prelude 8, mm. 27–34	97
5.25	Chopin, Prelude 9	99
5.26	(a) Chopin, Prelude 10, mm. 1–8, (b) Prelude 10, mm. 15–18	102
5.27	(a) Chopin, Prelude 11, mm. 1–5, (b) Prelude 11, mm. 10–15, (c) Prelude 11, mm. 20–27	103
5.28	Chopin, Prelude 11, mm. 18–19	104
5.29	Chopin, Prelude 12, mm. 1–16	105
5.30	Chopin, Prelude 12, mm. 18–40	106
5.31	Chopin, Prelude 12, mm. 47–81	107
5.32	Chopin, Prelude 13, mm. 1–20	109
5.33	Chopin, Prelude 13, mm. 22–28	110
5.34	Chopin, Prelude 13, mm. 36–38	111
5.35	(a) Chopin, Prelude 14, mm. 1–5, (b) Prelude 14, mm. 9–19	112
5.36	(a) Chopin, Prelude 15, mm. 1–4, (b) Prelude 15, mm. 8–13, (c) Prelude 15, mm. 16–20 (RH)	114
5.37	(a) Chopin, Prelude 15, mm. 28–35, (b) Prelude 15, mm. 60–64, (c) Prelude 15, mm. 75–76	115
5.38	Chopin, Prelude 15, mm. 84–89	116
5.39	(a) Chopin, Prelude 16, mm. 1–6 (Paderewski edition), (b) Prelude 16, mm. 1–30, (c) Prelude 16, mm. 35–36	117–21
5.40	Chopin, Prelude 17, mm. 65–67	122
5.41	(a) Chopin, Prelude 17, mm. 1–10 (RH), (b) Prelude 17, mm. 24–31	122
5.42	(a) Chopin, Prelude 17, mm. 43–50, (b) Prelude 17, mm. 51–61	123
5.43	Chopin, Prelude 17, mm. 80–90	124
5.44	(a) Chopin, Prelude 18, mm. 1–4, (b) Prelude 18, mm. 9–13, (c) Prelude 18, mm. 14–21	126
5.45	(a) Chopin, Prelude 19, mm. 1–8, (b) Prelude 19, mm. 13–26, (c) Prelude 19, mm. 29–32	128–30
5.46	Chopin, Prelude 19, mm. 43–71	131
5.47	Chopin, Prelude 20, mm. 1–8	133
5.48	Chopin, Prelude 21, mm. 1–16	134
5.49	Chopin, Prelude 21, mm. 17–32	135
5.50	Chopin, Prelude 21, mm. 33–59	136
5.51	(a) Chopin, Prelude 22, mm. 1–9, (b) Prelude 22, mm. 12–15	138
5.52	Chopin, Prelude 22, mm. 17–24	138
5.53	(a) Chopin, Prelude 23, mm. 1–5 (RH), (b) Prelude 23, mm. 14–16	139
5.54	Chopin, Prelude 23, mm. 19–22	140
5.55	(a) Chopin, Prelude 24, mm. 1–14, (b) Prelude 24, mm. 42–43	141
5.56	Chopin, Prelude 24, mm. 60–62 (RH)	142

5.57	Chopin, Prelude 24, mm. 73–77	143
6.1	(a) Chopin, Ballade, Op. 38, mm. 3–10, (b) Ballade, Op. 38, mm. 38–42	146
6.2	(a) Chopin, Ballade, Op. 38, mm. 177–182, (b) Ballade, Op. 38, mm. 157–166	147
6.3	Chopin, *Polonaise-fantaisie*, Op. 61, mm. 24–31	148
6.4	Chopin, *Polonaise-fantaisie*, Op. 61, mm. 166–168	148
6.5	Schubert, *Winterreise*, 'Gefrorne Tränen,' (a) mm. 22–24, (b) mm. 26–28	149
6.6	Schubert, (a) 'Gute Nacht,' (b) 'Erstarrung,' (c) 'Der Lindenbaum,' (d) 'Auf dem Flusse,' (e) 'Rückblick,' (f) 'Irrlicht,' (g) 'Einsamkeit,' (h) 'Täuschung'	150
6.7	(a) Octatonic scale (diatonic tetrachords), (b) Dorian scale, (c) Octatonic scale (chromatic tetrachords)	151
6.8	Schubert, *Winterreise*, 'Gute Nacht,' (a) mm. 10–11, (b) mm. 22–23	152
6.9	Schubert, *Winterreise*, (a) 'Gefrorne Tränen,' (b) 'Rückblick,' (c) 'Die Krähe,' (d) 'Letzte Hoffnung,' (e) 'Im Dorfe,' (f) 'Mut'	153
6.10	Schubert, *Winterreise*, (a) 'Erstarrung,' (b) 'Der Lindenbaum,' (c) 'Die Wetterfahne'	154
6.11	Schubert, *Winterreise*, (a) 'Der greise Kopf,' (b) 'Mut'	154
6.12	Schubert, *Winterreise*, 'Der Leiermann'	155

Preface

In recent years I have become more and more intrigued by Chopin's set of preludes, Opus 28. I heard something that was hidden in this set, which I could sense but not describe—something that made the whole collection sound far more meaningful and substantial than the mere sum of its parts. So I began looking into it in earnest. As I was digging more deeply and widely, and playing the preludes myself over and over, a growing host of nagging questions kept surfacing. A quest for answers turned out to be full of surprises, with newly emerging lines of inquiry—and entirely unforeseen results.

My research, as well as the preparation of this book, has been supported by grants from the Academic Senate, the Division of the Arts, and the Arts Research Institute of the University of California, Santa Cruz, for which I am deeply appreciative. I also wish to thank the welcoming and helpful staff of the Chopin Museum in Valldemossa, Mallorca, Spain.

Quite a few people have contributed to this project, and I owe a great debt of gratitude to all of them. Tamah Swenson translated Alphonse de Lamartine's poem *Les Préludes* and on many occasions counseled me on the finer points of French poetry. Jonathan Bellman reviewed the initial book proposal that I had submitted to Ashgate Publishing and offered numerous, detailed, and highly valuable suggestions.

Jordi Aladro-Font communicated on my behalf with the Council for Culture of the municipality of Valldemossa and connected me with two of my main sources of information regarding the Royal Carthusian Monastery there: Rosa Capilonch Ferrà and Concepció Bauçà de Mirabó. Dr Bauçà de Mirabó was particularly generous with her time, giving me long tours of both the monastery and the village and sharing with me her vast historical expertise.

Mark Woodworth and Mark Rhynsburger, a duo of uncompromising and fiercely nitpicking copyeditors, did absolute wonders with the text of the book, adroitly and tenaciously whipping it into shape. Beth Ratay spent many weeks preparing the musical examples as Sibelius music-notation files.

Maria Ezerova rendered her astute advice and unflagging support, along with a few photographic contributions. The singularly talented Valldemossa photographer Enric Calafell Alemany graciously allowed me to use some of his images of the Carthusian monastery. Finally, Peter Harris, with his characteristic flair, prepared all the illustrations for publication.

Two places have been particularly stimulating during my analysis and writing: Valldemossa itself, and West Cliff Drive in Santa Cruz. Being in the poetic Valldemossa (and listening to Bauçà de Mirabó's fascinating talks there) provided priceless insights into the circumstances of Chopin's life during the winter of 1838–1839. Similarly, many ideas presented in this book occurred to me during my morning runs on West Cliff, a spectacularly scenic path alongside the Pacific Ocean.

I employ a few standard abbreviations in the book: mm. for 'measures,' RH for 'right hand' and LH for 'left hand.' The word *Préludes* indicates the original French title of the entire set. Individual pieces from Opus 28 are referred to as 'Prelude in C major' and so forth, while the word 'prelude' is applied as a generic term.

Chapter 1

The Traditions, the Innovations, and the Predicaments

'Preludes to What?'

When Chopin's 24 *Préludes*, Op. 28 were first published in 1839, many of his contemporaries did not quite know what to make of them. In some respects, Opus 28 still remains an enigma today.

It was not the lack of fugues or any other subsequent pieces in Opus 28 that compelled a perplexed Schumann to describe the *Préludes* as 'strange pieces,' 'sketches' and 'ruins,' 'a wild motley' containing 'the morbid, the feverish, the repellent.'[1] André Gide's famous bafflement is a much later development: 'I admit that I do not wholly understand the title that Chopin chose to give these short pieces: *Préludes*. Preludes to what? Each of Bach's preludes is followed by its fugue; it is an integral part of it.'[2] In this twentieth-century view, Chopin was a trendsetter who dropped the main dish (the fugue) and kept only the appetizer, blazing a trail for the sets of preludes by Debussy, Scriabin, Rachmaninov, Shostakovich, and many others. Chopin's contemporaries, however, were not in the least bothered by the absence of fugues or any other larger compositions in Opus 28. They knew perfectly well that Chopin's book of preludes had been preceded by dozens of prelude collections by other composers.

The concert practice of improvising short piano preludes before larger works was common in the late eighteenth through the early twentieth centuries. Preludes were routinely improvised, even on monophonic instruments, such as the flute, and not only before an entire composition but also, quite often, before each movement of a sonata.[3] Many concert reviews of that time mentioned extemporaneous preludes, which Franz Liszt, Hans von Bülow, Anton Rubinstein, and others played before the programmed pieces during their concerts.[4] Unfortunately, since preludes were improvised on the spot, there is no documentary evidence left of how

---

[1]   Quoted in the critical edition of the Preludes, ed. Thomas Higgins, Norton Critical Scores (New York: W.W. Norton, 1973), p. 91.

[2]   André Gide, *Notes on Chopin*, trans. Bernard Frechtman (New York: Philosophical Library, 1949), p. 32.

[3]   See Leta Miller, 'C.P.E. Bach and Friedrich Ludwig Dülon: Composition and Improvisation in late 18th-Century Germany,' *Early Music*, 23/1 (February 1995), pp. 67–8.

[4]   Kenneth Hamilton, *After the Golden Age: Romantic Pianism and Modern Performance* (Oxford: Oxford University Press, 2008), pp. 105–7; V.V. Krutov and L.V.

these preludes sounded. One notable exception is some preludes played by Clara Schumann before the compositions she performed in concerts. At her daughters' request, she wrote a few of them down, even though she complained that writing the preludes was difficult since she played them differently every time.[5]

Clara Schumann's written preludes are short, between eight and 40 measures. Several of them are rather all-purpose improvisational studies, with no discernible connections to presumed pieces to follow. Four preludes, however, are conceived as specific introductions to Robert Schumann's works: 'Des Abends' and 'Aufschwung' from *Fantasiestücke*, Op. 12, 'Schlummerlied' from *Albumblätter*, Op. 124, and the slow movement of the F-minor Sonata.[6] In each of these four preludes, C. Schumann not only sets the key and the mood of an ensuing composition, but also introduces its thematic material.[7] These preludes, as well as her concert programs and published reviews of her performances, make it abundantly clear that improvised introductions were played before both large-scale compositions and shorter works (including individual sonata movements).

Historical evidence of improvised preludes in public concerts can be found as late as 1945. In the live recordings of Josef Hofmann's Golden Jubilee Concert at the Metropolitan Opera House on 28 November 1937, and at Carnegie Hall on 24 March 1945, the pianist improvised short preludes before programmed works. The latter included both shorter and larger piano pieces, as well as Hofmann's own *Chromaticon* for piano and orchestra.[8]

In the late eighteenth and early nineteenth centuries, when the piano became immensely popular and the number of children and adults studying the instrument grew exponentially, piano methods and instructional books of piano exercises proliferated. One of the main new outgrowths of the piano boom was the etude (or study). Thousands of etudes aimed at the development of piano technique at every level appeared during these decades. The prelude, related to the etude through its purpose of warming up one's fingers as well as its predisposition for fast passagework, was another flourishing offshoot of the piano's upsurge.

In response to the public's hunger for more preludes, numerous prelude collections appeared in print. Many method books offered detailed instructions on prelude improvisation and included numerous sample preludes in various

---

Shvetsova-Krutova, *Mir Rakhmaninova: temy i variatsii* [*Rachmaninov's World: Themes and Variations*] (Tambov: Shusharin Y.M., 2004), vol. 1, p. 402.

[5] Valerie Woodring Goertzen, 'Setting the Stage: Clara Schumann's Preludes,' in Bruno Nettl and Melinda Russell (eds), *In the Course of Performance: Studies in the World of Musical Improvisation* (Chicago: University of Chicago Press, 1998), pp. 242–3.

[6] Ibid., 242–4.

[7] Ibid., 249–51.

[8] The entire Golden Jubilee concert was released on a two-LP set by I.P.A. in the 1970s, and then re-released on two compact discs in 1992 by VAI Audio (VAIA/IPA 1020–22). Only a portion of the Carnegie Hall concert has been found so far; this portion is included in the two-disc set by VAI Audio. I thank my graduate student Colin Hannon for drawing my attention to the Golden Jubilee concert.

keys. Students, amateur pianists, and even professional pianists of modest improvisational abilities could either modify or memorize these preludes and then perform them in front of an audience before main pieces.

The piano prelude collections published in the nineteenth century prior to Opus 28 consist of preludes written either in the most common keys or in all the keys:[9]

André Ernest Modeste Grétry, *Méthode Simple pour Apprendre à Préluder* (1801).

James Hewitt, *Il Introduzione di Preludio, being an easy method to acquire the art of playing extempore upon piano-forte, interspersed with a variety of examples, showing how to modulate from one key to another, and from which a knowledge of the science of music may be acquired* [1810?].

Philip Antony Corri, *Original System of Preluding. Comprehending instructions on that branch of piano forte playing with upwards of two hundred progressive preludes in every key and mode, and in different styles, so calculated that variety may be formed at pleasure* (1810).

Muzio Clementi, *Preludes and Exercises in all major and minor keys* (1811).

Johann Nepomuk Hummel, *Vorspiele vor Anfange eines Stükes* [sic] *aus allen 24 Dur und mol Tonarten zum nützlichem Gebrauch für Schüler*, Op. 67 (ca. 1814).

Johann Baptist Cramer, *Twenty-Six Preludes or short Introductions in the Principal Major and Minor Keys for the Piano Forte* (1818).

Tobias Haslinger, *XXX Vorspiele in den gebräuchlisten Dur und Moll Tonarten* (1818).

Maria Szymanowska, *Vingt Exercices et Préludes* (1819).

Wilhelm Würfel, *Zbiór exercycyi w kształcie preludyów ze wszystkich tonów major i minor* (1821).

Ignaz Moscheles, *50 Preludes in the Major and Minor Keys, intended as short introductions to any movement and as preparatory exercises to the authors' studies*, Op. 73 (1827).

Frédéric Kalkbrenner, *Twenty-four Preludes for the Piano Forte, in all Major and Minor Keys, being an Introduction to the Art of Preluding* (1827).[10]

---

[9] I do not list here some late eighteenth-century publications containing preludes that were not intended specifically for piano, such as August Friedrich Christopher Kollmann's *An Introduction to the Art of Preluding and Extemporizing in Six Lessons for the Harpsichord or Harp*, Op. 3 (London: R. Wonum, 1792).

[10] See Jean-Jacques Eigeldinger, 'Twenty-Four Preludes Op. 28: Genre, Structure, Significance,' in Jim Samson (ed.), *Chopin Studies* (Cambridge: Cambridge University Press, 1988), p. 172; Valerie Woodring Goertzen, 'By Way of Introduction: Preluding by 18th- and Early 19th-Century Pianists,' *The Journal of Musicology*, 14/3 (Summer 1996): pp. 300–309; Andreas Boelcke, 'Chopin's *24 Préludes*, Opus 28: A Cycle Unified by Motion between the Fifth and Sixth Scale Degrees' (DMA thesis, University of Cincinnati, 2008), pp. 33–5; Aaron Berkowitz, *The Improvising Mind: Cognition and Creativity in the Musical Moment* (Oxford: Oxford University Press, 2010), pp. 21–4.

4 *The Mystery of Chopin's* Préludes

Carl Czerny, with his characteristic fecundity, produced a staggering quantity of preludes that far outstrips the number of preludes written by any other early nineteenth-century composer: *Präludien, Cadenzen und kleine Fantasien im brillanten Style*, Op. 61 (1823); *48 études en forme de préludes et cadences dans tous les tons majeurs et mineurs*, Op. 161 (1829); *Systematische Anleitung zum Fantasieren auf dem Pianoforte*, Op. 200 (1836); *Die Kunst des Präludirens in 120 Beispielen*, Op. 300 (ca. 1834); and *24 préludes dans les tons les plus usités*, Op. 501 (1830s).

It goes without saying, of course, that Czerny also provided detailed instructional rules on how to use and improvise preludes. In his textbook on improvisation he described three types of preludes. One is 'quite short, as though through only a few chords, runs, passagework and transitional materials, one were trying out the instrument, warming up the fingers, or arousing the attention of the listeners. These must conclude with the complete chord of the principal key of the work performed.' The second type is 'longer and more elaborate, just like an introduction belonging to the following piece; therefore, even the thematic materials from the latter can be introduced therein.' The preludes of this kind, according to Czerny, should end on the dominant seventh chord of the following piece. Yet another style of preluding, Czerny writes, is 'completely unmeasured, almost like a recitative.'[11]

Only some of the printed preludes were intended for specific companion pieces mentioned in the prelude title; these preludes usually incorporated thematic ideas from the following main piece. The vast majority of published preludes were thematically neutral. Czerny, Hummel, and others did recommend, however, that pianists should modify the text of the preludes taken from published collections and individualize the preludes by inserting melodic ideas from the following main pieces.

Another example of this rather indulgent attitude toward the text of a prelude can be seen in Jan Dussek's *Trois Sonates* [for pianoforte, flute, violin, and cello] *et Trois Préludes Pour le Piano*, Op. 31 (ca. 1812), which consists of Sonatas in B♭ major, D major, and C major. The three short piano Preludes, in identical keys (B♭ major, D major, and C major), are not intrinsic parts of the Sonatas, as one would expect. In the score, the individual Preludes do not precede each of the three Sonatas. Instead, all three Preludes are grouped together as an addendum to the score of the Sonatas. There is no verbal instruction by the composer regarding possible connections between the Sonatas and the Preludes or even the order of performance, yet the implicit meaning is not difficult to understand. The pianist is presumed to perform a Prelude before each Sonata, as the custom suggests, but Dussek's Preludes, discreetly attached at the end, are apparently optional. The pianist may choose to extemporize an introduction

---

[11] Carl Czerny, *A Systematic Introduction to Improvisation on the Pianoforte* [*Systematische Anleitung zum Fantasieren auf dem Pianoforte*], Op. 200, trans. and ed. Alice L. Mitchell (New York: Longman, 1983), p. 23.

Example 1.1 Hummel, Prelude 1 from *24 Preludes*, Op. 67

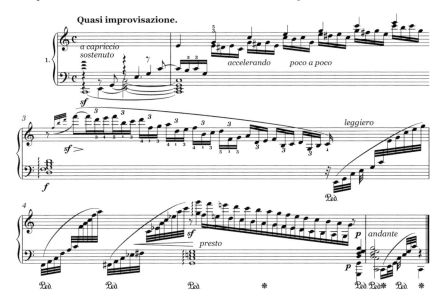

Example 1.2 Hummel, Prelude 2 from *24 Preludes*, Op. 67

before a Sonata; or, lacking improvisatory skills, he or she may simply pull from the addendum the Prelude in an appropriate key and play it instead.

The casual treatment of the published preludes—one could change the text, add to it, supplant parts of it, even replace an entire piece—bespeaks their humble ranking among other, more artistic musical genres early in the century. The numerous nineteenth-century pre-Chopin preludes, in spite of their textural variety (arpeggios, scales, occasional intricate passageworks or polyphonic passages, block chords and broken chords, octaves, and instrumental recitatives), had one central trait in common: they were all utterly unremarkable and unmemorable (if pleasant), just as the two Preludes in Examples 1.1 and 1.2.

The Preludes in Examples 1.1 and 1.2 happened to be written by Hummel (as part of his collection of 24 preludes), but they could just as easily have been jotted down by any other composer listed above, or even improvised by a competent pianist.[12] Within this historical context we can better understand George Sand's statement that Opus 28 was 'modestly entitled *Préludes*.' It must be noted that she did not define Chopin's *Préludes* per se as modest; on the contrary, she described them as 'the most beautiful' pages of music, and 'masterworks.'[13] To us, the title Prelude does not sound any more modest than, for example, a Nocturne, an Impromptu, or an Intermezzo. Yet public perception was quite different back in 1839, as at that time 'preludes' were merely utilitarian, didactic pieces with an optional observance of the printed text.

'A Riddle Wrapped in a Mystery Inside an Enigma' Underneath a Conundrum

What, then, was Chopin's innovation? Definitely not the absence of fugues. Chopin's contemporaries never posed the question 'Preludes to what?' At that time, everyone knew that published preludes served as models for improvisation and as a bank of ready-made (or, more specifically, half-ready-made) introductions that pianists were supposed to pick out and turn into preludes to larger compositions they performed. Chopin's collection of preludes in all 24 keys, arranged in pairs of relative major and minor keys ascending through the sharps and descending through the flats, was not new, either. Hummel used this particular tonal layout of 24 preludes in 1814 (see Examples 1.1 and 1.2), although his preludes, just like those by other nineteenth-century composers before Chopin, were never meant to be played as independent concert pieces, whether singly or in groups.

Yet, from the moment Chopin's preludes were presented to the public, it became obvious they differed strikingly from their immediate precursors. As Franz Liszt put it, 'Chopin's Preludes are compositions of an order entirely apart; they are not merely, as the title would indicate, introductions to other *morceaux*.'[14] Lamentably, Liszt neither elaborated his point further nor provided any details

---

[12]   Bach's preludes are a notable exception. First, he was apparently incapable of penning anything unremarkable and forgettable. Second, his preludes form an unbreakable whole with the subsequent fugues and suites. Even his *Kleine Präludien*, conceived solely as exercises for beginners, are musical gems.

[13]   George Sand, *Histoire de ma vie*, trans. Dan Hofstadter (New York: Harper & Row, 1979), p. 231.

[14]   Chopin, Fryderyk, *Preludes, Opus 28*, ed. Thomas Higgins. Norton Critical Scores (New York: W.W. Norton, 1973), pp. 91–2.

The Traditions, the Innovations, and the Predicaments

explaining Chopin's innovation. Despite the lack of verbal elucidation, Chopin's new, albeit undefined, concept of the prelude has become vastly popular. From that point onward, the fully emancipated prelude has meant a self-sufficient character piece rather than an auxiliary preamble.[15]

The import of the newly created genre was widely accepted. Nobody at the time expressed the desire to use Chopin's preludes as introductions to other compositions, quite unlike the preludes of his predecessors. We know of two documented cases when two preludes from Opus 28 were turned into introductions to other pieces, and they both took place long after the composer's death. In 1885, a student at one of Liszt's master classes prefaced Chopin's C-minor Nocturne, Op. 48 with Chopin's C-minor Prelude, No. 20. A few decades later, in 1922, Busoni recorded Chopin's Etude in G♭ major, Op. 10, No. 5, placing Chopin's A-major Prelude, No. 7, before the Etude as an introduction. He then improvised a bridge between the two pieces with a short modulation from A major to G♭ major.[16]

Jeffrey Kallberg suggests that Chopin might have performed at least one of his preludes as an introduction to an Impromptu. The printed program from Chopin's concert in Glasgow on 27 September 1848 lists 'Andante et Impromptu' as the opening number. Kallberg's assumption is that the 'Andante' in question could have been the F♯-minor Prelude, No. 8, even though the tempo of this Prelude is indicated as Molto agitato rather than Andante. The 'Impromptu,' he continues, could have been Op. 36 in F♯ major.[17]

Kallberg does not consider the opening 'Andante' to be the *Andante spianato*, Op. 22, primarily because of key differences. In his view, it would be more logical to deem the F♯-minor Prelude rather than the G-major *Andante spianato* as an introduction to the F♯-major Impromptu. William Atwood, however, refers to a surviving copy of the original program with opus numbers added in ink. The handwritten opus numbers were probably added by John Muir Wood (1805–1892), a Glasgow pianist, impresario, and amateur photographer, who organized that particular concert.[18] His son Herbert kept an annotated copy of the program. According to the notation on the program, the 'Impromptu' was indeed Op. 36, and the 'Andante' was definitely from Op. 22.[19]

---

[15] Jim Samson, *The Music of Chopin* (London: Routledge & Kegan Paul, 1985), p. 79; Jim Samson, *Chopin* (New York: Schirmer Books, 1997), p. 158.

[16] Hamilton, *After the Golden Age*, pp. 101–2.

[17] Jeffrey Kallberg, 'Small "Forms": In Defence of the Prelude,' in Jim Samson (ed.), *The Cambridge Companion to Chopin* (Cambridge: Cambridge University Press, 1992), pp. 137–8; also in Jeffrey Kallberg, *Chopin at the Boundaries: Sex, History, and Musical Genre* (Cambridge, MA: Harvard University Press, 1996), pp. 150–52.

[18] Chopin traveled with Wood in the same train carriage from London to Edinburgh in 1848, according to Chopin's letter of 19 August 1848 to his family in Warsaw (*Selected Correspondence of Fryderyk Chopin*, trans. and ed. Arthur Hedley [New York: McGraw-Hill, 1963], p. 336).

[19] William G. Atwood, *Fryderyk Chopin: Pianist from Warsaw* (New York: Columbia University Press, 1987), pp. 179, 281.

In Opus 22, the *Andante spianato* is conjoined with the *Grande polonaise brillante*. Chopin, nonetheless, had no problem detaching the Andante from the Polonaise and placing it in front of other pieces. He often used the *Andante spianato* as a program opening that introduced another composition in a different key. The key unity was not an issue from the start, since the Andante and the Polonaise were written in two different keys—in G major and E♭ major, respectively—with a short modulating bridge inserted in between.

Thus, the program from Chopin's concert in Paris on 21 February 1842 listed the G-major *Andante spianato* as a preamble to the Third Ballade in A♭ major. The program of his London concert on 7 July 1848 began with 'Andante Sostenuto et Scherzo (Op. 31).' If there is any question as to what piece introduced the B♭-minor Scherzo, a concert review in the *Examiner* clarified that the opening 'Andante Sostenuto' was Opus 22, and that it had been additionally preceded by a slow, most probably improvised preamble in G minor, not mentioned in the printed program.[20] Chopin then repeated the *Andante spianato* as an introduction to the same Scherzo at a concert in Manchester, on 28 August 1848.[21] Most likely, Chopin improvised a modulating bridge from G major of the *Andante spianato* to the key of a subsequent piece, in the same manner as he wrote it down in the original tandem of the *Andante spianato et Grande polonaise brillante*, Op. 22 (G major—E♭ major).

But if no one, including the composer, intended to pluck single preludes out of the collection and play them as introductions to other works, then performing solitary preludes in a concert program presents another problem. Most of the preludes are very short. The C-minor Prelude originally was even shorter than its final version, consisting of only the first two phrases (nine measures total). Chopin decided to repeat the second phrase as a concession to the publisher of Opus 28, Camille Pleyel, who 'must have felt that the piece was outrageously short, too much so to be published.'[22]

The brevity of Cramer's, Moscheles's, or Hummel's preludes (Examples 1.1 and 1.2) was never disputed in terms of their publication or performance, since these short introductions were not designed as self-standing compositions. Chopin's preludes, by contrast, were treated from the outset as independent works rather than utilitarian, no-frills prefaces to longer, more important, artistic compositions. Why? Did Chopin discuss this new quality of his preludes with Pleyel (or anyone else) before or during their composition, or even after they had been completed?

The miniature dimensions of most of Chopin's preludes are not, of course, an aesthetic shortcoming, despite a once-common conviction that small forms were not sufficiently complex and were therefore inferior to large-scale works. This judgmental notion has been dispelled by later writers, most recently by Jeffrey Kallberg.

---

[20] Ibid., pp. 140, 170, and 247. Both of Hofmann's performances of the *Andante spianato et Grande polonaise brillante*, Op. 22, in 1937 and 1945, also started with improvised preludes.

[21] Ibid., pp. 174, 280.

[22] Eigeldinger, 'Twenty-Four Preludes,' p. 178.

The terseness of Chopin's preludes creates, however, a different kind of predicament—a pragmatic rather than aesthetic or structural one. Although Kallberg urges audiences 'to accept the possibility of a work like the A-major Prelude ... standing alone in performance,'[23] the prospect of having the audience settle down after applauding a previous number, then listen to the A-major Prelude for 37 seconds (or to the C♯-minor Prelude for 30 seconds, or to the E♭-minor Prelude for 20 seconds) and to applaud again is not realistic. It is indeed difficult to imagine a real-life concert program, apart from beginner student recitals, featuring a single, stand-alone composition that would last a minute or less.

To be sure, like any other piece, a longer prelude may appear as a separate item on a concert program, and Chopin did publish such a prelude, Opus 45. The size as well as the mood of Prelude, Op. 45 is nevertheless comparable to those of a full-scale nocturne. The only attribute that may distinguish this Prelude from a nocturne is the lack of fully developed melodic phrases and its incessant modulations, which collectively impart a strong improvisatory character to the piece.

Not all the Preludes in Opus 28 are tantalizingly short. A few of them are quite extensive: Prelude 15 (D♭ major), for example, lasts for about five minutes and is more than ten times longer than the C♯-minor or E♭-minor Preludes. Such proportional discrepancies present yet another puzzle. No other collection of pieces of the same genre (excluding the earlier didactic preludes) before and during Chopin's time are so seemingly unbalanced in terms of their size. In Chopin's books of etudes, some etudes run shorter or longer than others, but not by a tenfold differential. The same can be said of Chopin's dance and nocturne opuses. Among all of Schumann's suites, only *Papillons*, Op. 2 and *Carnaval*, Op. 9 include comparable proportional discrepancies. These suites, however, ostensibly differ from Opus 28, as they are integrated suites bonded by unifying programmatic ideas, and the sharply varying durations of individual numbers are justified by the extra-musical meaning they carry.

When Chopin performed Opus 28 in public concerts, according to the surviving program listings, he played the preludes not as single pieces but in groups. One can see a few reasons why several preludes were strung together in the composer's performance. First, as I mentioned before, introducing a single number that sounds for less than a minute would fracture a concert program. Second, grouping several preludes together in performances may heighten the Romantic sense of yearning, when the opening prelude, without reaching its presumed goal, is followed by another prelude, then by yet another prelude, and so forth. Of course, it still remains to be determined how much the popular Romantic sentiment of unfulfilled desire meant to Chopin, given his seeming lack of interest in lofty Romantic ideals and in most contemporaneous instrumental music.

But was there yet another, more profound, reason for Chopin to link several preludes in concerts? Does Opus 28 contain underlying motivic and conceptual ties that connect individual preludes, as do Schumann's programmatic suites?

---

[23] Kallberg, *Chopin at the Boundaries*, p. 158.

The opinions concerning the existence of such ties are sharply divided. As Kevin Korsyn points out, 'Some analysts are convinced—indeed, passionately certain—that the twenty-four preludes in Op. 28 form a unified multimovement suite or cycle; others are equally adamant that they constitute no such thing.'[24]

Thus, Lawrence Kramer maintains that 'the most immediately striking features of the preludes are those that undermine their coherence as a group. Chopin does not link the different pieces motivically, as Schumann does in suites like *Carnaval*, and he does not arrange them on the basis of any dramatic or expressive logic.' Furthermore, continues Kramer, 'taken as a gestural sequence, the twenty-four preludes sound like an exaltation of … random association. … The preludes are not a work at all, but simply an aggregation, … a wild motley of pieces.'[25]

Similarly, Kallberg does not consider Opus 28 to be a set unified through either motivic or harmonic connections. Instead, he regards the preludes as self-standing concert pieces, appropriate for performance either separately or before other larger works.[26] Jeffrey Kresky likewise concludes that motivic recurrences are lacking across the Chopin preludes.[27]

From another quarter, Jim Samson refers to Opus 28 as 'a unified cycle of independent pieces.'[28] He also points out a two-note trill-like motif that recurs in some of the preludes.[29] Jósef Chomiński observes that a melodic figure consisting of two adjacent pitches (G-A), established in the first Prelude, runs like a thread through many other preludes as well.[30] Andreas Boelcke particularizes this gesture as a persistently iterated motion between the fifth and sixth scale degrees that unify the *Préludes* into a cycle.[31] Another approach binds Opus 28 into a cycle on the basis of tuning, that is, 'the temperament of Chopin's piano' and a melodic cell that derives from it, an ascending major sixth followed by a descending major second. As Jean-Jacques Eigeldinger summarizes, 'In the final analysis, what governs op. 28 and makes it a cycle is the logic of its temperament.'[32]

---

[24]   Kevin Korsyn, *Decentering Music: A Critique of Contemporary Musical Research* (Oxford: Oxford University Press, 2003), p. 101.

[25]   Lawrence Kramer, *Music and Poetry: The Nineteenth Century and After* (Berkeley: University of California Press, 1984), pp. 99–100.

[26]   Kallberg, 'Small "Forms,"' pp. 135–43.

[27]   Jeffrey Kresky, *A Reader's Guide to the Chopin Preludes* (Westport, CT: Greenwood Press, 1994), p. xvii.

[28]   Samson, *The Music of Chopin*, p. 79.

[29]   Ibid., p. 74.

[30]   *Preludia Chopina* (Cracow: PWM, 1950), pp. 300–333.

[31]   Boelcke, 'Chopin's *24 Préludes*.'

[32]   Eigeldinger, 'Twenty-Four Preludes,' p. 184. For a more detailed discussion of two opposing views on Opus 28, either as a collection of independent pieces or as a unified cycle, see Korsyn, *Decentering Music*, pp. 101–23.

The Traditions, the Innovations, and the Predicaments 11

The quandaries surrounding Opus 28 are compounded by yet another intriguing remark. In the concert review in which Liszt stated that Chopin's preludes are unique compositions and not merely introductions to something further, he went on to say that these pieces are 'poetic preludes similar to those of a great contemporary poet,' clearly alluding to Alphonse de Lamartine's poem entitled *Les Préludes*. In another review of that very concert by Chopin, published on the same day as Liszt's review (2 May 1841) but in a different newspaper, *Le Ménestrel*, an anonymous critic suggested that to understand Chopin one must read Lamartine.[33]

Regrettably, these fleeting remarks were not followed by further clarifications. It is also unclear how Liszt and the anonym arrived at their conclusion. Did they hear the parallels between the pieces and the poem, either jointly or independently from each other, or did the composer himself mention it to the reviewers? And if he did not, did he approve of these statements after they had appeared in the press? In any event, Chopin voiced no objections in the manner that he vigorously protested attempts to attach programmatic contents or titles to his other works. In the end, however, it matters little which scenario prompted these particular assertions: in either case, Chopin's *Préludes*, unlike their precursors, were heard as being inspired by and related to Lamartine's poetic masterpiece.

Chopin's 24 *Préludes* remain as mysterious today as when they were newly published, which is why Winston Churchill's famous description of Russia, quoted earlier in the subtitle of this section, not only suits Chopin's *Préludes* to a tee but warrants a rhetorical extension as well.

There are several focal issues we have to deal with to unravel the mystery of Opus 28: What prompted Liszt and others to consider Chopin's *Préludes* to be compositions in their own right, rather than introductions to other works? What specifically set Chopin's *Préludes* so drastically apart from their forerunners? What were 'the morbid, the feverish, the repellent' elements that Schumann heard in Opus 28, in this 'wild motley' of 'strange sketches' and 'ruins'? What is the source of the huge proportional discrepancies between the shortest and the longest preludes? If we accept the assertion that Lamartine's *Les Préludes* served as an inspiration for Chopin, how did the poem affect the structure and the thematic contents of Chopin's *Préludes*? Why did Chopin choose such a deliberately unassuming title, *Préludes*, for Opus 28? And, lastly, are the *Préludes* a random group of short pieces or a cohesive cycle?

All these questions are, in fact, closely interrelated. Furthermore, it is Lamartine's poem *Les Préludes* that holds the key to a fuller understanding of Chopin's *Préludes*.

---

[33] Atwood, *Fryderyk Chopin*, pp. 233, 236.

Chapter 2

Lamartine's *Les Préludes*: The Lyrics and the Milieu

The Poem and Its Imagery

Alphonse Marie Louis de Prat de Lamartine (1790–1869) was a French poet, writer, and statesman. The popularity of Lamartine's poetry in the nineteenth century was enormous; he is credited with revitalizing French lyrical poetry.[1] Since the 1820s, the 'new poet' in France was not Victor Hugo—it was Lamartine.[2] Not surprisingly, Lamartine was in the midst of French cultural life, enjoying friendly relationships with many fellow artists.

He was part of Chopin's circle of artistic friends, along with Hugo (1802–85), Heinrich Heine (1797–1856), and the Polish poets Adam Mickiewicz (1798–1855) and Juliusz Słowacki (1809–49). Lamartine was a regular feature in Parisian literary and musical salons, where many poets, including himself and Hugo, read their latest works, while composers and pianists were asked to play. Chopin, who frequented these salons, sometimes played almost until dawn. Lamartine also visited Sand and Chopin at their Square d'Orléans apartments (along with Hugo, Balzac, and Heine).[3]

Lamartine wrote the poem *Les Préludes* in 1822 and published it the next year as part of the collection *Nouvelles méditations poétiques*, which came out three years after the success of the earlier *Méditations poétiques*. *Les Préludes*, dedicated to Hugo, consists of 11 sub-poems, or cantos, which have no individual titles or numbers and differ vastly in length (for convenience, I will number the individual cantos I–XI).[4] The length of the cantos ranges from 4 lines (Cantos II and IV) to 116 lines (Canto VIII).

---

[1] Charles M. Lombard, *Lamartine* (New York: Twayne Publishers, 1973), pp. 108, 111.

[2] Francis Claudon, 'Chopin et Lamartine ou l'élégie moderne,' in Irena Poniatowska (ed.), *Chopin and His Work in the Context of Culture* (Cracow: Musica Iagellonica, 2003), vol. 2, p. 189.

[3] Tad Szulc, *Chopin in Paris: The Life and Times of the Romantic Composer* (New York: A Lisa Drew Book/Scribner, 1998), pp. 11, 74, and 274.

[4] I am deeply indebted to Tamah Swenson for her invaluable help with the French text of Lamartine's *Les Préludes*. Her translation of the poem, along with the original French text, can be seen in the Appendix.

14 *The Mystery of Chopin's* Préludes

Although the poem may appear whimsically irregular, it is actually tightly organized. Lamartine ties together Cantos I and II, IV and V, VII and VIII, and, finally, X and XI:

1. In Canto I, the protagonist decries his languishing soul and implores a heavenly spirit (the Genius) to come down, comfort his heart, and inspire him; 'prelude as you like!' pleads the hero. The spirit descends in Canto II.
2. In Cantos IV and V, the Genius conjures up a vision of a terrifying storm at sea. Canto IV heralds the advancing tempest; in Canto V the storm rages in full force.
3. Cantos VII and VIII bring forth another fantastic image: a powerful clash of two huge armies. Canto VII warns that a battle is about to begin; Canto VIII portrays a horrifying encounter between the combatants.
4. The protagonist, who is shocked and deeply saddened by the frightening visions, begs the spirit for consolation and peace. In Canto X, the caressing wind gently touches the hero's lyre as the last vision unfolds in Canto XI: a depiction of his rustic homeland; the Genius then ascends.

As Table 2.1 shows, Lamartine structured *Les Préludes* in such a way that Cantos I, IV, VII, and X function as introductions, or 'preludes,' to the subsequent cantos. Cantos III, VI, and IX separate the pairs from one another, acting as interludes. The first two interludes, Cantos III and VI, are reflections upon the preceding pairs of cantos. The last interlude, Canto IX, is a plea to the Genius for a calming song before its departure.

Table 2.1   The inner structure of Lamartine's *Les Préludes*

I/II   III   IV/V   VI   VII/VIII   IX   X/XI

The poem contains the most appealing Romantic images of the strange, the alluring, the mysterious, and the horrifying. The reader finds in the poem bucolic scenes, various states of love (from blissful passion to a 'gentle smile of happiness' to overwhelming ecstasy to sorrow and tears), nocturnal scenes, peculiar visions induced by a supernatural force, delightful landscapes with murmuring streams, seawater ripples, raging winds, and dreadful storms.

Furthermore, the poem overflows with musical images. Except for Canto V, every canto is replete with expressive references to musical instruments: a 'vibrating string,' the 'obedient harp,' a 'blood-soaked string,' 'the joyful cymbal,' an 'angry string,' a 'bronze bell ringing from the clock tower.' The text of the poem also mentions music of nature, music of the soul, and music of the heavenly spheres, as well as other highly poignant musical evocations. Marius-François Guyard declares that Lamartine's secret of success is music—that is to say, the rhythm, melody, and harmony of Lamartine's verse. The poet himself defined *Les Préludes* as '*une sonate de poesie*' ['a sonata of poetry'].[5]

Among the sundry images of the poem, there is one, however, that is the most powerful and omnipresent: death. This theme appears in Canto III, in which the hero laments how 'life flees with each breath we take' (III, 34–5). In the same canto, the hero contemplates the inevitable (III, 41–5):

> All is born, all proceeds, all arrives
> At the unknown hour of its fate:
> To the Ocean the plaintive wave,
> To the winds the fugitive leaf,
> The dawn to evening, man to death.

In the following pairs of cantos—IV/V, VII/VIII, and X/XI—every second canto (that is, V, VIII, and XI) portrays a certain manifestation of death. In Canto V, the hero spies a storm that splits the ocean into liquid valleys and imagines himself on a ship without masts that is thrown around helplessly, up and down, from cresting waves into a black abyss. From this image, the hero draws the conclusion (V, 31–6):

> Alas! such is my fate and the fate of mankind!
> Our fathers have traveled along the same paths.
> Burdened with the same fate, our sons will take our places.
> Those who are not yet born will find their footprints there.
> Everything wears away, perishes, passes: but, alas!
> Except for mortals, nothing changes here!

Before Cantos VII and VIII, the hero ruminates in Canto VI that death is frightening to all mankind, and the best way to deal with it is: 'Let us forget, let us forget: this is the secret of living' (VI, 14). But as soon as he pronounces this, a new, deeply disturbing vision assails him. The battle scene in Canto VIII is the bloodiest and deadliest scene in the entire poem. A hundred thousand soldiers march 'like a single man toward the chasm of death' (VIII, 11–12). The two armies collide; the cannons spit forth death; dazzling young cavalrymen and old warriors perish as 'death flies at random.' Lamartine paints horrible scenes of carnage, crammed with mutilated and dead bodies.

After this apotheosis of death, in Canto IX, the protagonist pleads the 'Spirit of fire' to sing a consoling song, filled with peaceful tones and soothing images. And a picture of his tranquil homeland appears in Canto XI. But even then, as he relishes the bucolic landscapes, he muses that, while this rustic life is enjoyable and carefree, days follow days and pass irretrievably 'for those who must die.'

---

[5] Alphonse de Lamartine, *Méditations poétiques*, ed. Marius-François Guyard (Paris: Editions Gallimard, 1981), p. 17.

The Gothic Allure

There are two questions that can only be answered in a broader cultural context. Is Lamartine's preoccupation with the macabre unusual for early nineteenth-century literature? Who is the Genius and how can we explain his appearance in the poem? Interestingly enough, it was Chopin's A♭-major Prelude from Opus 28 that provided a clue to better understanding of the cultural and literary background of Lamartine's poem.

In the last 26 measures of the Prelude, the bass strikes 11 times *sf*, while the top voices are played pianissimo and sotto voce (see Examples 5.40 and 5.43). This conclusion may seem a bit odd, but in Chopin's conversation with his student Camille Dubois (who later recounted the story to Ignacy Paderewski), the composer revealed that he based his Prelude 'on the sound of an old clock in the castle which strikes the *eleventh* hour' (emphasis by Dubois, italics by Paderewski).[6]

Now, the question is, what does 'the *eleventh* hour' mean? There are only two possibilities: an hour before noon or an hour before midnight. Taking into account the strong emphasis on '*eleventh*,' a premonition of midnight seems more fitting than anticipation of lunch.

I queried a few professors of French literature about the significance of midnight in nineteenth-century French fiction; their response was that there is none. It took me some time to eventually realize—not as a scholar but as a reader—that an old clock, a castle, and looming midnight are typical trappings of a certain literary genre: Gothic fiction. And this realization immediately put both Lamartine's *Les Préludes* and Chopin's *Préludes* in an entirely different light.

Gothic literature has a rich genesis and an even more fertile history. It began with Horace Walpole's novel *The Castle of Otranto: A Story*, published in England under a pseudonym on Christmas Day of 1764. The novel instantly became so popular that it was reprinted the following year under Walpole's name and with a different subtitle: *A Gothic Story*. The success of Walpole's novel impelled several other authors in England to follow in his footsteps and to publish novels with 'Gothic' in the title, including Clara Reeves's *The Old English Baron: A Gothic Story* (1778), Richard Warner's *Netley Abbey: A Gothic Story* (1795), and Isabella Kelly's *The Baron's Daughter: A Gothic Romance* (1802).

Other literary titles at the time did not include the word 'Gothic,' yet the term eventually became a common reference to this type of literature, particularly in the twentieth century. In the late eighteenth and nineteenth centuries, Gothic stories were more often called 'romances,' to set them apart from 'realist' novels.[7] *The Castle of Otranto* introduced many dramatic paraphernalia that recurred in

---

[6] Eigeldinger, *Chopin: Pianist and Teacher as Seen by His Pupils*, p. 83.

[7] E.J. Clery, 'The Genesis of "Gothic" Fiction,' in Jerrold E. Hogle (ed.), *The Cambridge Companion to Gothic Fiction* (Cambridge: Cambridge University Press, 2002), pp. 21–2, 28; Steve Clark, 'Graveyard School,' in Marie Mulvey-Roberts (ed.), *The Handbook to Gothic Literature* (New York: New York University Press, 1998), p. 107.

Lamartine's Les Préludes: *The Lyrics and the Milieu*   17

subsequent tales of horror: a rambling ancient castle with deserted wings and damp corridors, darkness, death, madness, the supernatural, ghostly apparitions, and so forth.[8]

Walpole's first Gothic novel had predecessors, however. Walpole himself, in the preface to the second edition, pays homage to Shakespeare, drawing parallels between *Hamlet* and the novel. Not only Walpole but other Gothic writers as well revered several scenes from Shakespeare, particularly the Witches' scenes from *Macbeth* and the Ghost's scenes from *Hamlet*, as originary.[9]

Another influential force was a group of poets who emerged in England in the eighteenth century. The impetus for a new poetic movement was inaugurated in 1721, when the poem *A Night Piece on Death* by Thomas Parnell (1679–1718) was published posthumously. The poem was soon followed by many other poetic works written in the same vein, among which we find Edward Young's *The Complaint: Or, Night-Thoughts on Life, Death, & Immortality* (1742–45), Robert Blair's *The Grave* (1743), James Hervey's *Meditations Among the Tombs* (1746–47), and Thomas Gray's *Elegy Written in a Country Church-Yard* (1751).

All these poems, as evident from their titles, were filled with mournful reflections on the brevity of life, terror, loneliness, darkness, and ruins. The poets of this movement meditated on these topics deep into the night, usually amid tombs at a graveyard, which earned this movement the name 'graveyard school.'[10] Many graveyard poets were clergymen who interspersed their thoughts of death with religious ponderings.

The graveyard poets gained vast popularity in England and were translated throughout Europe. Lamartine read them in translation, and their 'brooding about man's existence,' death and destruction, 'the origin of the soul, and other weighty questions'[11] are present in Lamartine's poetry, as well. Indeed, it is quite conceivable that the titles of his two poem collections, *Méditations poétiques* and *Nouvelles méditations poétiques*, could be traced back to Hervey's *Meditations Among the Tombs*.

Early Gothic writers in England eagerly absorbed and expanded the themes and the moods of the graveyard school. The dramatic paraphernalia of Gothic tales included rambling old castles and abbeys; supernatural manifestations and apparitions; stark contrasts between pastoral landscapes at daytime and hair-raising graveyard settings at night; characters consumed by love and haunted by

---

[8]   Howard Phillips Lovecraft, *Supernatural Horror in Literature* (New York: Dover Publications, 1973), p. 25.

[9]   Peter Cochran, 'Byron Reads and Rewrites Gothic,' in Peter Cochran (ed.), *The Gothic Byron* (Newcastle Upon Tyne: Cambridge Scholars Publishing, 2009), p. 3.

[10]   Clark, 'Graveyard School,' in *The Handbook to Gothic Literature*, p. 107; Alexandra Maria Reuber, 'Haunted by the Uncanny – Development of a Genre from the Late Eighteenth to the Late Nineteenth Century' (PhD Dissertation, Louisiana State University, 2004), pp. 20–21.

[11]   Lombard, *Lamartine*, pp. 22, 104.

18   *The Mystery of Chopin's* Préludes

death; mysterious occurrences and dreadful hallucinations. English readers met new Gothic fiction with delight and a growing demand for more, and the genre flourished. After Walpole's *The Castle of Otranto*, the throng of authors included Ann Radcliffe (*The Castles of Athlin and Dunbayne*, 1789, and *The Mysteries of Udolpho*, 1794), Matthew Lewis (*The Monk: A Romance*, 1796), and Charles Maturin (*Melmoth the Wanderer*, 1820), along with many others.

Gothic fiction thus became an integral part of Romantic literature. Anne Williams insists that 'Gothic' and 'Romantic' are not two but one poetic tradition.[12] And indeed, one of the most prominent Romantic authors in England who thrived on the Gothic thread was Lord Byron (1788–1824). He read in depth a great number of Gothic novels, including those by Horace Walpole and Ann Radcliffe, and reused their notions ingeniously. Byron's *Manfred* and *Childe Harold* IV both teem with Gothic details.[13] As Peter Cochran asserts,

> The Gothic literary tradition meant a lot to Byron in his writing as well as in his leisure activities. He derived from it a template for his more mysterious, alienated, sociopathic characters, and an encouragement for his preoccupation with ruins, and the inevitability of decay—decay civic, architectural, and human.[14]

English Gothic novels were widely translated into French and German. In France, for example, the number of translated English Gothic novels between 1767 and 1828 varied from one to ten a year (with the exception of 1790 and 1804, when no new translations of English Gothic fiction were published in France). All in all, more than a hundred English Gothic novels were translated into French during that period.[15]

In the late eighteenth century, French and German authors began writing their own versions of Gothic tales, which were also immediately translated into other languages. In Germany, the development of Gothic literature culminated in the Romantic works of Friedrich von Schiller (1759–1805) and E.T.A. Hoffmann (1776–1822). Schiller was 'a pioneering author of Gothic literature';[16] his *Schauerroman* ['shudder novel'] *Der Geisterseher* (*The Ghost-Seer*, 1789) was

---

[12]   Anne Williams, *Art of Darkness: A Poetics of Gothic* (Chicago: University of Chicago Press, 1995), p. 1.

[13]   Christina Ceron, 'Manfred, The Brontës, and the Byronic Gothic Hero,' in *The Gothic Byron*, pp. 56, 168.

[14]   Cochran, 'Byron Reads and Rewrites Gothic,' in *The Gothic Byron*, p. 2.

[15]   Terry Hale, 'French and German Gothic: The Beginnings,' in *The Cambridge Companion to Gothic Fiction*, p. 70; 'Translation in Distress: Cultural Misappropriation and the Construction of the Gothic,' in Avril Horner (ed.) *European Gothic: A Spirited Exchange 1760–1960* (Manchester: Manchester University Press, 2002), p. 31.

[16]   Jennifer Driscoll Colosimo, 'Schiller and the Gothic—Reception and Reality,' in Jeffrey L. High, Nicholas Martin, and Norbert Oellers (eds), *Who Is This Schiller Now? Essays on His Reception and Significance* (Rochester, NY: Camden House, 2011), p. 287.

widely read not only in Germany but also, in translation, in France and England (Byron was deeply influenced by *Der Geisterseher*, which he read in a translation, since he could not read German[17]). Hoffmann had an enormous impact on the development of fantastic writing in France as well. His works were translated into French and had countless admirers in France.[18]

In the wake of the craze caused by translated English and German Gothic tales, French authors created their own version of horror fiction in the late eighteenth century, which came to be known as *roman noir* ('black novel'). *Roman noir* flourished until the 1820s. In 1821, Charles Nodier (1780–1844), one of the founding figures of French Romantic movement, published *Smarra ou le demons de la nuit* [*Smarra, or The Demons of the Night*]—a fantastic fable filled with violent imagery and dream sequences. It marked a new development in French Gothic fiction, for which Nodier coined the term *roman frénétique*. According to Nodier, the term *frénétique* refers to writers who, whether in prose or verse, 'flaunt their ... rage and despair over tombstones, exhume the dead in order to terrify the living, or who torment the reader's imagination with such horrifying scenes so as to suggest the deranged dreams of madmen.'[19]

Between 1821 and 1848, more than two hundred novels and collections of short stories, excluding translations, were published in France, which could all be categorized as *frénétique*. One of the most popular *frénétique* novels of the early 1820s was *Le Solitaire* [*The Recluse*] by Charles-Victor Prévot, vicomte d'Arlincourt (1788–1856). Within a few months after its publication in 1821, it was reprinted a dozen times, and translated into ten languages. Many operas, dramatic plays, songs, paintings, and lithographs were based on the novel.

In deliberating the impact of Gothic writers on Lamartine and Chopin, we should consider both their written and their personal contacts. Byron's and Nodier's influences on Lamartine are well documented.[20] Chopin never discussed art and literature in his letters, but we know that he was keenly interested in poetry, long before he moved to Paris. In Dresden, Chopin attended a five-hour performance of Goethe's *Faust* and was deeply impressed by that poetic play. In Warsaw, he spent many days with his friends at the coffeehouse *Dziurka* [The Little Hole], talking for hours about Byron and Schiller.[21]

George Sand, one of Chopin's closest friends at the time, recalls that her mother read d'Arlincourt with passion. Sand herself read, with delight and terror, Ann Radcliffe (in French), felt overwhelmed by Byron's poetry, and read the *frénétique* authors Eugène Sue (1804–57) and Jules Janin (1804–74). Sand enjoyed reading the novel *Fragoletta, ou Naples et Paris en 1799* [*Fragoletta, or Naples and Paris*

---

[17]   Ceron, 'Manfred,' p. 60.
[18]   Reuber, 'Haunted by the Uncanny,' p. 158.
[19]   Hale, 'French and German Gothic,' p. 78; see also Hale, '*Roman noir*' and '*Frénétique* School,' both in *The Handbook to Gothic Literature*, pp. 189–93 and 58–63.
[20]   Lombard, *Lamartine*, pp. 21, 33–4, 94.
[21]   Szulc, *Chopin in Paris*, pp. 44–5.

in 1799], written by another popular *frénétique* writer, Henri de Latouche (1785–1851). He was a close friend of Sand who helped advance her literary career.[22]

We also know that Eugène Sue visited Chopin at the composer's apartment in rue de la Chaussée d'Antin on 13 December 1836, and that Jules Janin was among a small number of invited guests at Chopin's concert at the house of Marquis de Custine on 8 May 1838.[23]

Now we have a much better understanding of Chopin's references to an old clock in a castle, the *eleventh* hour, and the looming terror of midnight. In the interminable list of Gothic fables published across Europe between the 1760s and 1830s, at least six include the word 'midnight' in their title. Dark, crumbling castles and abbeys, with their gloomy mazes of corridors, are traditional Gothic settings in which midnight bells or clocks herald imminent dreadful occurrences. Even the elements—storms on land and at sea—are raging the worst at midnight.[24]

Many aspects of Lamartine's *Les Préludes* are best comprehended within the context of Gothic fiction. Death, a predominant concept in Lamartine's poem, is an overriding notion in graveyard poetry and an omnipresent component in Gothic writings. Another fascinating, mysterious, and entirely misconstrued subject in the poem is the one that is being referred to, alternately, as '*génie*' (Genius) and '*esprit*' (Spirit).

It is mentioned several times by the protagonist: '*ô mon génie!*' ('oh my Genius!' I, 9); '*esprit capricieux*' ('capricious Spirit,' I, 16); '*Esprit consolateur*' ('consoling Spirit,' VI, 2); '*esprit de feu*' ('Spirit of fire,' IX, 1); and '*divin Génie*' ('divine Genius,' XI, 73). Several commentators struggling to explain the genius/spirit reference have proposed that the word meant a poetic muse, or the poet's inspiration, or perhaps 'the poet himself in his different moods,' or even just literary genius.[25]

Anyone familiar with Gothic literature, however, can immediately recognize that the Genius, a guardian spirit, is one of many supernatural beings populating Gothic tales. These fantastic personages appear, for example, in Schiller's play *Warbeck* (1799–1805), in William Beckford's novel *Vathek* (1786), and in Byron's poem *Manfred* (1817). Like the protagonist in *Les Préludes*, the main characters in these Gothic works communicate with their Geniuses.

---

[22] George Sand, *Histoire de ma vie. Œuvres autobiographiques* (Paris: Gallimard, 1971), vol. 1, pp. 171–2, 644–5, 887–8, 1092; vol. 2, pp. 8, 136, 147–8, 150–60.

[23] *Korespondencja Fryderyka Chopina z George Sand i z jej dziećmi*, ed. Krystyna Kobylańska (Warsaw: Państwowy Instytut Wydawniczy, 1981), vol. 1, pp. 34, 39.

[24] Élizabeth Durot-Boucé, 'Midnight Trysts: "Minuit est la plus belle heure du jour,"' *Études anglaises*, 57 (2004/3), pp. 298–303.

[25] Alexander Main, 'Liszt after Lamartine: "Les Preludes,"' *Music & Letters*, 60/2 (April 1979), pp. 141–2; Alphonse de Lamartine, *Méditations*, ed. Fernand Letessier (Paris: Garnier Frères, 1968), p. 786; Lamartine, *Selected Poems from Premières et Nouvelles Méditations*, edited, with biographical sketch and notes, by George O. Curme (Boston: D.C. Heath & Co., 1896), p. 170.

Why, then, have Gothic motifs been overlooked so consistently in both Lamartine and Chopin? The reason, I propose, is that, until about 1970, most critics and commentators considered Gothic fiction a sideshow of Romanticism at best, or an embarrassing and destructive cultural phenomenon at worst. When Gothic was not vilified, it was either politely ignored or offhandedly dismissed as a poor relation to the Romantic movement.[26]

To be sure, Lamartine's poem does not include an entire array of Gothic elements. It depicts no haunted old castles or abbeys, no cemeteries, no exotic locales. These trappings, however, are present, in abundance, in other Gothic writings that were undoubtedly familiar to Chopin.

Unfortunately, we don't know what particular Gothic stories Chopin read or liked. But one point can be stressed with certainty: in Mallorca, as Chopin was working on his Opus 28, he *lived* a Gothic tale.

---

[26] Michael Gamer, *Romanticism and the Gothic: Genre, Reception, and Canon Formation* (Cambridge: Cambridge University Press, 2000), p. 8; Cochran, 'Byron Reads and Rewrites Gothic,' p. 1; Williams, *Art of Darkness*, p. 4.

Chapter 3
The Mallorca Factor

The Wonders and the Tribulations

There were several reasons for Chopin to flee Paris and spend the winter of 1838–39 on the island of Mallorca. Most of them had to do with Baroness Amantine Lucile Aurore Dudevant, née Dupin. Born in 1804, the mother of two was separated from her husband and launched a highly successful literary career. In 1831, she and another young writer, Jules Sandeau, with whom the baroness was romantically involved, together wrote and published a novel under the pseudonym J. Sand. A year later, when she was about to publish her own novel *Indiana*, she refused to sign it with her own name, despite Sandeau's insistence; she wanted to continue using the same *nom de plume* as before. Sandeau suggested that she use the last name Sand, to commemorate their relationship, and the first name George, since their conversation took place on St George's Day. Thus, on 23 April 1832 George Sand emerged into the world, and from that time on the baroness used this name both professionally and personally. Chopin, however, never called her 'George,' always addressing her as 'Aurora' (from the French 'Aurore').[1]

Chopin and Sand became lovers at the end of summer of 1838, and straightaway they met with at least two difficulties (not counting, of course, colossal differences between their personalities, tastes, lifestyles, and viewpoints). One predicament was Chopin's hypersensitive notion of propriety and the desire to protect their reputations in Paris society. The other problem was the young playwright Félicien Mallefille, whom Sand abandoned in order to be with Chopin. Mallefille, however, did not take the rejection sitting down. He armed himself with a pistol and stalked the lovers, reportedly taking a potshot at Sand outside Chopin's Chaussée d'Antin apartment and challenging Chopin to a duel.

Leaving Paris and going to a remote place for a period of time to let the matters cool off seemed like a reasonable solution. Some of their friends suggested the island of Mallorca, off the coast of Spain. For the French, Spain was a southland of palm trees, oranges, and pomegranates, which beckoned as a better alternative than a miserable winter in Paris. Chopin's friends pressured him to spend some time in southern Europe, and his physician, Pierre-Marcel Gaubert, also recommended fresh air, exercise, and a rest in a warmer climate.

---

[1] Tad Szulc, *Chopin in Paris: The Life and Times of the Romantic Composer* (New York: A Lisa Drew Book/Scribner, 1998), pp. 162–3. Incidentally, Lamartine uses the word '*aurore*' four times in his poem: Cantos III/16, III/45, VIII/111, and XI/45.

24 *The Mystery of Chopin's* Préludes

Spain held yet another strong attraction for avid nineteenth-century readers. The country was a popular exotic setting in quite a few Gothic works, such as Matthew Gregory Lewis's *The Monk: A Romance* (1796), Jan Potocki's *Manuscrit trouvé à Saragosse* [*Manuscript Found in Saragossa*] (1804–10), Charles Robert Maturin's *Melmoth the Wanderer* (1820, translated into French in 1821), and Lord Byron's *Childe Harold's Pilgrimage* (1812–18). Prosper Mérimée (1803–70) and Théophile Gautier (1811–72) both 'defined Spain as the romantic country *par excellence.*'[2]

If Chopin's journey to Mallorca is somewhat less documented than other stages in his life, it was because, at that point, he was trying to keep secret his relationship with Sand. Chopin told only his closest friends about his trip to Mallorca, and in his letters to Julian Fontana the composer repeatedly asked him not to tell anyone. To keep the affair concealed, Chopin and Sand (along with her two children, Maurice and Solange) set out on their journey separately before reuniting in Perpignan in southern France.

That clandestineness explains why Chopin dispatched only a few infrequent letters describing his Mallorca sojourn. In his letter to Fontana, written on 15 November 1838, Chopin excitedly shares his first impressions about the city of Palma, the capital of Mallorca. He lists plants that he had never seen outside of greenhouses—palms, cacti, olives, oranges, lemons, figs, pomegranates, and so forth—and describes the turquoise sky, the lapis lazuli sea, the emerald mountains, and the heavenly air. Guitars and songs at night, huge balconies with overhanging vines, and Moorish ramparts complemented the delightfully exotic surroundings. A scant two weeks later, his next letters to Fontana and to Wojciech Grzymala, written on 3 December 1838, are tainted with bitter disappointment and contain a report of his illness and a visit from no fewer than three doctors.

What on earth happened to Chopin in the interim? When he was in Poland, France, or England, other people filled such biographical gaps for us. In Mallorca, though, there were almost no first-hand accounts by others, save for one notable exception: George Sand herself. She, too, posted a handful of letters from Mallorca; moreover, she described their trip in print. Sand's book *Un hiver à Majorque* [*A Winter in Majorca*] was first published in installments in 1841 in *Revue des deux Mondes* before it came out as a book in 1855, six years after Chopin's death. In this book, still keeping up appearances of propriety, Sand does not mention the composer by name, dropping only oblique references, such as 'our invalid.'

The veracity of her chronicle was immediately impugned, and since that time the book has been harshly criticized for 'poetical inventions, distortions, and

---

[2]   Joan Curbet, '"Hallelujah to Your Dying Screams of Torture": Representations of Ritual Violence in English and Spanish Romanticism,' in Avril Horner (ed.), *European Gothic: A Spirited Exchange 1760–1960* (Manchester: Manchester University Press, 2002), p. 163.

exaggerations,'[3] especially in Sand's description of local customs, accommodations, food, and perceived lack of hospitality. When they arrived in Palma, she wrote, they could not find a single inn. They could only rent a couple of semi-furnished rooms in a lodging house, in a questionable neighborhood. Even worse, the rooms were situated right above a barrel-maker's workshop, with incessant hammering that lasted from early morning throughout the day.

The search for a habitable, furnished flat in Palma proved difficult. The reason was that a typical Palma flat for hire, as Sand caustically relates, consisted of roof, floor, and bare walls, without doors or windows. When tenants moved out, they took along not only all the furniture but also the windows, the doors, and even the door hinges. It would take at least six months, Sand marvels, to get the doors, windows, and furnishings made, for there were few carpenters in Palma, and none worked quickly. Moreover, to Sand's utter disbelief, there was no ready-made furniture either to buy or to lease.

After trying in vain to find a suitable place to stay in Palma, Sand and Chopin were about to return to France, when they were offered a house in Establiments, a village north of Palma, into which they moved on 15 November.[4]

Both Chopin and Sand were enamored with the beautiful scenery around Establiments, so wildly different from the landscapes typical of colder latitudes: hills, terrace farming, olives, almonds, oranges, gardens, and peasant cottages. It was strikingly picturesque, not at all like the views of the French countryside. The weather was pleasantly warm, with the lemon trees and myrtles still in bloom.

The house belonged to one Señor Gomez, who named it The House of the Wind (*Son Vent* in Mallorcan, the local variety of the Catalan language). It had simple furnishings, glazed windows in almost every room, but no fireplace, because the house served as a summer villa.[5] When the weather turned foul, wailing winds and hammering rains made the house uninhabitable and its dwellers miserable, particularly Chopin, who grew seriously ill and was coughing grievously.

In her book, Sand rails vociferously at the lack of civilized comforts in Mallorca and at the ineptitude of Spanish medics who could not alleviate the composer's sufferings and who simply declared that Chopin was consumptive and therefore highly contagious. Furthermore, she wrote that the 'boorish' landlord Gomez sent her a letter in which he demanded, 'in Spanish style,' that they should clear out of his house immediately because their company included 'a personage who was harbouring a disease.'[6]

---

[3]   Frederick Niecks, *Frederick Chopin as a Man and Musician* (London: Novello and Company, 1902), vol. 2, p. 26.

[4]   Establiments became part of the city of Palma in 1910.

[5]   The house is still standing in Establiments. Its current owners, however, do not allow sightseers inside the house; one can only view it from the outside.

[6]   George Sand, *Winter in Majorca*, trans. and annotated by Robert Graves, 2nd edn (Chicago: Academy Chicago Publishers, 1992), pp. 46–7.

Sand's rage at almost everything local, except for the island's landscapes, did not remain unanswered. As soon as *Un hiver* came out in *Revue des Deux Mondes*, the Spanish historian and writer José María Quadrado (1819–86) published an indignant refutation, blaming Sand herself for her tribulations.[7] He informed the readers that the literati in Palma were delighted that the famous George Sand was going to honor Mallorca with her visit. They were soon profoundly disillusioned:

> The undistinguished lodging which she chose, her unwillingness to receive visitors, the cold words of disdain that were always on her lips, the rudeness shown the young Marquis ... for whom she carried an introduction, and above all, the equivocal company she brought with her, suggested that she was embarrassed by [Palman] society.[8]

Quadrado deplored Sand's virulent attacks on 'our beloved Balearic island' and wondered what could possibly cause 'the anger which induced such uncivil jokes and absurd reflexions.'[9] He countered Sand's accusations concerning the paucity of decent accommodations in Palma by stating that 'the city boasts four respectable inns,' and that Sand could have stayed in far better living quarters had she not spurned good society and found, as a result, 'every door closed in an island famous for its hospitality.'[10]

Needless to say, Sand's recklessly cruel descriptions of the Mallorcans as barbarians, thieves, monkeys, and savages are unsupported by the reports of other travelers who visited the island at approximately the same time, such as Jean-Joseph Bonaventure Laurens and Barón Karol Dembowski.[11] Moreover, her account of the events prior to the move from Establiments to Valldemossa appears to be not entirely accurate, either factually or chronologically.

To begin with, Sand's timeline, offered in *Un hiver*, is suspect. She wrote that her family and Chopin basked in warm weather for about three weeks after moving to *Son Vent* on 15 November. Then the rains and cold temperatures came (around 6 December, presumably). Consequently, Chopin fell victim to the damp and chill and was declared consumptive, after which Gomez rudely evicted them from his villa, forcing Sand to find a new lodging in a hurry, which happened to be the Carthusian monastery in Valldemossa.

---

[7] Quadrado's article, 'To George Sand: A Refutation,' appeared in *La Palma: A Weekly Journal of History and Literature*, on 5 May 1841. Graves appended the article to his translation of Sand's *Winter in Majorca*.

[8] Sand, *Winter in Majorca*, p. 187.

[9] Ibid., p. 188.

[10] Ibid., p. 191.

[11] J.B. Laurens, *Souvenirs d'un voyage d'art à l'île de Majorque* (Paris: Arthus Bertrand, 1840); Karol Dembowski, *Deux ans en Espagne et en Portugal, pendant la guerre civile 1838–1840* (Paris: Charles Gosselin, 1841).

In fact, Chopin in his letter of 3 December 1838 informs Fontana that he has been sick as a dog for the last two weeks, despite the heat of 18 degrees and despite the roses, orange trees, palms, and fig trees.[12] It is not quite clear which temperature scale Chopin refers to, Reaumur or centigrade. While either reading indicates warm weather, 18 degrees on the Reaumur scale would be closer to the 'heat' mentioned by Chopin (18° R equals 73° F; 18° C equals 64.4° F).

Moreover, in the previous letter of 15 November, Chopin writes that he will probably be living in a wonderful monastery in the most fabulous site in the world. George Sand, too, in a letter written to Carlotta Marliani the day before (14 November), gushes that she is leaving Palma to settle in the country, in a pretty furnished house (*Son Vent*), with a garden and a magnificent view, for fifty francs per month. What's more, she continues, she already has a cell, that is to say, three rooms and a garden full of oranges and lemons, for thirty-five francs *per year* in the large Carthusian monastery in Valldemossa.[13]

Two issues draw attention. In *Un hiver*, Sand claims that Gomez charged them 100 francs a month, which was a high price to ask for a summerhouse that ultimately was unsuitable for cold weather (although she admits that by French standards the rent was modest; by comparison, Chopin charged 20 francs for a 45-minute lesson). In her letter to Marliani quoted above, Sand writes, however, that the rent is 50 francs per month. But that was before she developed an intense loathing for Gomez. In her original and more unrestrained version of *Un hiver*, Sand had described Gomez as 'the most filthily ugly man to be found in the four quarters of the world.'[14] Doubling the actual renting price, in her book, was an attempt to illustrate how the greedy Gomez was robbing the French travelers.

Sand's charge that Gomez evicted them from the house as soon as he heard of Chopin's tuberculosis does not appear to be true, either. It is clear from Sand's and Chopin's letters written on 14 and 15 November, respectively, that the arrangements to move to Valldemossa had been finalized at least by the time they moved into *Son Vent*, if not before.

In mid-November Sand already had an agreement with Ignacio Durán and his wife to take over the rent of the Carthusian cell. Sand's family and Chopin left *Son Vent* at the beginning of December and moved, for the time being, into the house of M. Fleury, the French consul at Palma. Then Sand showed up at Gomez's city home and gave him back the key. Gomez was unpleasantly surprised because he expected that *Son Vent* would be leased for the entire winter. Soon afterward, when the local doctors had diagnosed Chopin with consumption, Gomez demanded money for some damage: he had to have the

---

[12] *Correspondance de Frédéric Chopin*, ed. Bronislas É. Sydow (Paris: Richard-Masse, 1981), vol. 2, p. 274.

[13] Ibid., p. 263.

[14] Sand, *Winter in Majorca*, p. 200.

28 *The Mystery of Chopin's* Préludes

house re-plastered and whitewashed, he claimed, and the furniture replaced in order to get rid of 'contagion.'[15]

When She Is Right, She Is Right

In all fairness, however, it must be said that Sand made several acute observations regarding Chopin and their sojourn in Mallorca that were not only accurate but often revealing, although the validity of some of them was only confirmed much later.

Take, for example, the issue of Chopin's diagnosis of consumption. Chopin famously and humorously described a visit to him by three of the 'most celebrated doctors' in Palma. Upon examination, writes Chopin, one doctor 'said that I had died,[16] the second that I am dying, the third that I shall die.'[17] All three were unanimous that Chopin had tuberculosis.

Sand vehemently rejected this verdict, insisting that 'our invalid' was no more consumptive than she was.[18] Indeed, except for the three Mallorcan doctors, all the physicians who treated Chopin in France (not to mention another local doctor who visited Chopin in Palma before the joint visit by the trio of medics) denied that he had tuberculosis. At the same time, when it came to giving a conclusive diagnosis other than consumption, they were at a loss. Chopin was aware of this medical conundrum. Shortly after his death, the composer's close friend Wojciech Grzymala wrote to Auguste Léo in October 1849 that Chopin 'gave instructions for his body to be opened, being convinced that medical science had never understood his disease.'[19]

Chopin's final wish was granted. Doctor Jean Baptiste Cruveilhier (1791–1874), the leading expert on tuberculosis and pathology in France, was Chopin's last physician. He also performed an autopsy of the composer's body. The full report of the autopsy was lost, and only the death certificate written by Cruveilhier remains. The certificate does give the cause of death as 'tuberculosis of the lungs and larynx,' but nevertheless the mystery remained unsolved. In conversations with Jane Stirling and Chopin's sister Ludwika, Cruveilhier admitted that the

---

[15] Ibid., p. 48. Robert Graves (1895–1985), the English poet, scholar, writer, and translator, not only translated Sand's *Un hiver à Majorque*; he also provided a great deal of detailed and insightful commentaries, informed not only by his meticulous research but also by personal experience. Graves spent most of his life in Deià, a picturesque village near Valldemossa, where Chopin and Sand stayed for almost two months, and he intimately knew local history and customs (Graves's house in Deià is now a museum).

[16] Chopin used a rather crude Polish word that can be translated as 'croaked' or 'kicked the bucket.'

[17] *Chopin's Letters*, collected by Henryk Opieński (New York: Vienna House, 1971), p. 186.

[18] Sand, *Winter in Majorca*, p. 149.

[19] *Correspondance de Frédéric Chopin*, vol. 3, p. 444.

The Mallorca Factor

pathology 'did not disclose pulmonary consumption. ... It is a disease I have never encountered before.'[20]

Why, then, did Cruveilhier not state that on the death certificate? Steven Lagerberg, a doctor and author of today, asserts that Cruveilhier 'was compelled to write something on the death certificate. To write "cause of death unknown" was not acceptable protocol at the time, nor is it today.'[21] As a result of this uncertainty, the stories of Chopin's tuberculosis have persisted into modern times.

Another doctor, John O'Shea, has offered a solution to the confusion surrounding Chopin's illness and put forth a credible alternative to the widespread tuberculosis stories, in his seminal article published in 1987. Considering all the evidence available to him, O'Shea suggested that Chopin most probably suffered from cystic fibrosis.[22]

Cystic fibrosis is a genetic chronic disease that affects the lungs and the digestive system. It typically causes thick mucus to build up in the lungs and pancreas. That makes patients unable to absorb nutrients and prone to frequent and severe lung infections. The symptoms and severity of cystic fibrosis vary; in mild cases, the symptoms may not appear until the teen or even adult years. Today there is still no known cure for the disease.

The cystic fibrosis (CF) hypothesis explains why even such a renowned physician as Dr Cruveilhier, who treated Chopin and conducted his autopsy, could not diagnose the composer's malaise: cystic fibrosis was first described only in the 1930s. Lucyna Majka, Joanna Gozdzik, and Michal Witt all clarify that CF 'was unknown to physicians as a separate clinical entity before that time, although there are historical descriptions of possible CF cases that date back to the Middle Ages.'[23] Majka, Godzik, and Witt continue that although it is still difficult to present a definitive conclusion, CF 'is the only diagnosis that gives the explanation of all Chopin's complaints.'[24] Professor Wojciech Cichy, one of Poland's leading experts on CF, also concurs that Chopin's illness was not tuberculosis.[25]

Dr Lagerberg emphasizes that the CF hypothesis becomes even more credible 'when one learns of the more recent discovery that adult forms of the disease can

---

[20] Steven Lagerberg, *Chopin's Heart: The Quest to Identify the Mysterious Illness of the World's Most Beloved Composer* (CreateSpace, 2011), pp. 81–2.

[21] Ibid., p. 119.

[22] John G. O'Shea, 'Was Frédéric Chopin's Illness Actually Cystic Fibrosis?' *Medical Journal of Australia*, 147 (1987): 586–9. O'Shea then elaborated on this hypothesis in his book *Music and Medicine: Medical Profiles of Great Composers* (London: J.M. Dent, 1990); the second edition of this book was published under the title *Was Mozart Poisoned? Medical Investigations into the Lives of the Great Composers* (New York: St. Martin's Press, 1991).

[23] Lucyna Majka, Joanna Gozdzik, and Michal Witt, 'Cystic Fibrosis – A Probable Cause of Frédéric Chopin's Suffering and Death,' *Journal of Applied Genetics*, 44/1 (2003), p. 77.

[24] Ibid., p. 80.

[25] Lagerberg, *Chopin's Heart*, p. 10.

30   *The Mystery of Chopin's* Préludes

and do exist.' The CF gene was discovered in 1989, and since then 'approximately 1600 mutations of this genetic assemblage of DNA have been uncovered.' These newly observed mutations allow for certain forms of cystic fibrosis that 'may not be nearly as severe as the disease ordinarily seen in children, and their symptoms may not become clinically evident until adulthood.'[26]

Sand's supposed refusal to consider Chopin consumptive, for which she has been rebuked by many Chopin biographers, seems to be correct after all. And we shall soon see that several of her other observations were similarly accurate and enlightening.

The Carthusian Monastery

Chopin's and Sand's letters attest to the reason why they left Palma and Establiments and moved to Valldemossa. It was not because they were evicted from the *Son Vent* villa, nor because they were 'banished' from Palma to 'the remote beauty of an abandoned Carthusian monastery in Valldemosa, perched among mountain crags where the nearest neighbors were the eagles circling overhead.'[27]

The main reason was the irresistible appeal, to both Chopin and Sand, of the uninhabited old monastery, combined additionally with the relative comfort of a furnished, three-room cell that was made available to the travelers. Several questions come to mind. Why were they so strongly attracted, in Chopin's words, to 'a huge, old, ruined monastery of Carthusians'?[28] Why did Chopin and Sand express such excitement about being near the monastery's graveyard, 'the most poetic of cemeteries' as Chopin put it? Why was the monastery deserted? And why did their lowly monastic cell consist of three spacious rooms and a large, fully private garden?

The history of the monastery goes back to 1399, when King Martin el Humano donated his summer residence, the Royal Castle of Valldemossa, to Carthusian monks. The monks adapted the castle to religious purposes and gradually built a large monastery, attached to the former castle. The Royal Carthusian Monastery of Valldemossa differed, in many respects, from the vast majority of Roman Catholic monasteries and abbeys. The Carthusian Order was founded in 1084 by Saint Bruno of Colon, who put much emphasis on hermitic monasticism. He built his first hermitage in the Chartreuse Mountains, in the French Alps; since then, the word *Chartreuse* has denoted a Carthusian monastery in French. In other languages, the names for Carthusian monasteries have derived from the same source, often through the Latin *cartusia*: *charterhouse* in English, *cartuja* in Spanish, and *cartoixa* in Catalan.

---

[26] Lagerberg, *Chopin's Heart*, p. 118.
[27] Benita Eisler, *Chopin's Funeral* (New York: Alfred A. Knopf, 2003), p. 59.
[28] *Chopin's Letters*, p. 186.

The Carthusian Rule requires that the monks, or the hermits, devote themselves to the silence and solitude of their cells. They spend entire days in their cells in prayer, reading, work (both artisan and physical), and meditation. All is done in total silence. Their food is delivered to them though a hatch in the wall of the cell, without any verbal communication except for written notes. Periodically, the hermits attend a Mass at the monastery church and have a communal meal (on a Sunday or a solemn feast), eaten in silence. In the charterhouse of Valldemossa, the hermits would speak to each other for no more than 30 minutes per week.

In accordance with the Rule, only 12 monks and a prior lived in the Royal Charterhouse of Valldemossa, besides several lay brothers who performed menial jobs around the charterhouse: cooking, repairs, laundry, and so forth (although the lay brothers led more-communal lives, they were still bound by the vow of silence). Accordingly, the *cartuja* in Mallorca had 12 cells, one for each hermit. Each cell consisted of three rooms and led into a high-walled garden, completely isolated from the adjoining gardens. In the gardens, the hermits grew plants and meditated. The prior, however, had far better appointed accommodations, including a much larger suite of rooms.

In 1838, when Chopin and Sand arrived on Mallorca, the monks had already been gone from the *cartuja*. Juan Álvares Mendizábal (1790–1853), a good friend to both Chopin and Sand, was appointed Spain's Minister of Treasury and, briefly, Prime Minister; then he became the Spanish Ambassador at Paris. In 1835–37 he issued a set of decrees that resulted in the expropriation and privatization of monastic properties in Spain. These decrees became known as Ecclesiastical Confiscations of Mendizábal [*Desamortización Eclesiástica de Mendizábal*]. The reasons for the confiscations were multifold: many monastic clerics supported the Carlist forces during the civil war of succession; the government also wanted to efficiently develop the underused monastic lands; finally, since the government did not compensate the church for the properties, the expropriations were a source of additional income. The Carthusian monks were expelled from the charterhouse on 15 August 1835, and the monastery was left uninhabited. The government took possession of the premises and leased out some of the cells. One of those tenants, Ignacio Durán, handed over his rented cell, along with its furniture, to Sand and Chopin.

The French travelers were overjoyed. To them, the deserted Carthusian monastery epitomized a perfect Romantic—that is to say, Gothic—getaway. To begin with, the monastery was (and still is) surrounded by breathtakingly gorgeous landscapes. As Élizabeth Durot-Boucé remarks, 'Gothic stories usually open in the daylight in picturesque or sublime surroundings.' While all the important events in Gothic novels take place at night, and especially at midnight, night appears even more mysterious and menacing because it contrasts sharply with the bucolic daylight scenery that surrounds a castle or a monastery.[29]

---

[29] Élizabeth Durot-Boucé, 'Midnight Trysts: "Minuit est la plus belle heure du jour,"' *Études anglaises*, 57 (2004/3), pp. 306–7.

Furthermore, as Fred Botting points out, the Gothic aesthetic was based on feeling and emotion, which made it particularly receptive to the atmosphere of the sublime, associated with grandeur and magnificence. Craggy, mountainous landscapes of Gothic tales aroused powerful emotions of wonder and terror.'[30] Poetic landscapes are an essential component in Alphonse de Lamartine's works in general and in *Les Préludes* in particular. Although that poet depicts no mountains in *Les Préludes*, mountain landscapes figure prominently in his other poems—for example, in *Milly ou la terre natale* from *Harmonies poétiques et religieuses* and in *La solitude* from *Nouvelles méditations poétiques*.[31]

George Sand described such a landscape, as seen from the garden of her cell in the *cartuja*, with remarkable accuracy:

> It is a sublime picture: the foreground framed by dark, fir-covered rocks, the middle distance by bold mountains fringed by stately trees, the near background by rounded hillocks which the setting sun gilds warmly, and on whose crests the eye can make out, though a league away, the outlines of microscopic trees, delicate as a butterfly's antennae, but as sharply black as the stroke of a pen in Indian ink on a field of sparkling gold. … It is one of those overwhelming views that leave nothing to be desired, nothing to the imagination. Whatever poet and painter might dream, Nature has here created: vast general effect, countless detail, inexhaustible variety, blurred shapes, bold outlines, hazy depths—everything![32]

Another part of the monastery that delighted Chopin was the monks' graveyard, surrounded by the walls and windows of the cloisters and, in 1838, already overgrown with grass. The reason why a cemetery would hold so much attraction for the French voyagers is also obvious. In a great many Gothic fables, a decaying, gloomy castle 'was linked to other medieval edifices—abbeys, churches and graveyards especially.'[33]

This cemetery no longer exists; it was paved over and turned into a plaza with outdoor café tables in summer months. But at least one contemporary image of that cemetery remains. Jean-Joseph Bonaventure Laurens (1801–90), a notable French artist, musician, archeologist, and geologist, visited Mallorca soon after Chopin and Sand's stay on the island and immediately published a book containing a detailed account of his journey, more than 50 illustrations, and several local

---

[30]   Fred Botting, *Gothic (The New Critical Idiom)* (London: Routledge, 1996), pp. 2–4.

[31]   See Mary Ellen Birkett, *Lamartine and the Poetics of Landscape* (Lexington, KY: French Forum, 1982), pp. 40, 51–2, and 89.

[32]   Sand, *Winter in Majorca*, pp. 99–100.

[33]   Botting, *Gothic*, pp. 2–3.

Figure 3.1 The cemetery at the Carthusian monastery. Drawing by J.B. Laurens

devotional and folk songs he recorded.[34] In fact, it was this book that prompted Sand to write *Un hiver à Majorque*.

Laurens missed Sand in Valldemossa (Chopin is not named in his book; apparently, the composer's presence there with Sand was still supposed to remain unmentionable). But Laurens seemed quite pleased with the fact that he occupied the same cell as she had just a few months before. He writes wistfully that he saw and touched objects that she could have seen and touched, as well—the same oranges hanging on the trees in the garden; the ripe pomegranates that she had seen blooming only a few months earlier; the simple, rustic lamp as well as her pipe that were still in the cell.

Laurens describes the cemetery, too, and mentions that Sand chose it for her evening meditations—information that he could have gathered only from the locals or directly from the novelist herself, since *Un hiver* had not yet been written. He also includes a drawing of the cemetery with a pensive-looking woman in the foreground. Laurens does not name her in the description of the drawing, but the unnamed woman does bear an uncanny resemblance to George Sand (Figure 3.1). He certainly knew what the famed novelist looked like, and most probably had met her personally: in the book, he refers to her by using the familiar 'George' rather than her surname.

---

[34] J.B. Laurens, *Souvenirs d'un voyage d'art à l'île de Majorque* (Paris: Arthus Bertrand, [1840]).

Figure 3.2   A corridor in the Carthusian monastery. Historical photograph by Charles W. Wood, as found in his book *Letters from Majorca*

In 1838, the *cartuja* was a far different place than it is today. Bartomeu (Bartolomé) Ferrà wrote, in the 1930s, that during the previous century the monastery buildings had lost much of their old, imposing appearance. Not only the cemetery but also the old tower, which once served as a royal falconry, had disappeared. The guesthouse, the cloisters, and the chapels had been modified, he noted, to satisfy the tastes of the private purchasers, whose needs were quite different from those of the Carthusian monks.[35]

Charles William Wood visited Valldemossa almost 50 years later, in 1887. Unlike Laurens, he could not enter the cell in which Chopin and Sand lived; it was locked up. He was deeply impressed, nonetheless, by the 'singularly romantic and picturesque' monastery. Its ancient cloisters with vaulted ceilings struck him by their 'sad, melancholy tone that suggested death and decay, the changing of all things, the passing of generations, the march of time—in short, all that is painful to short-lived mortality.'[36]

On the morning when Wood visited the *cartuja*, the main cloister was gray and gloomy. He did manage, however, to take probably the very first photograph of this historical corridor (Figure 3.2). He commented that 'one ancient dame,' bent with age and supporting herself with a cane, remained in the frame. She, quite possibly, had seen Sand and Chopin and perhaps conversed with them, but Wood could not ask her, being unable to speak Mallorcan.[37]

The three-room cell that Chopin, Sand, and her two children occupied was fairly spacious and led into a private garden with a stunning view over the balustrade. I have always found baffling, though, one particular description that Chopin made of that cell. In his letter to Fontana on 28 December 1838, he wrote that his cell was shaped like a tall coffin. When I visited the cell for the first time several years ago, it did not feel like being in a coffin at all. On the contrary, the room was sunny and rather cheerful. It was only when Concepció Bauçà de Mirabó, the author of the splendid monograph on the history of the *cartuja*, gave me extensive and highly informative tours of the monastery in 2012 that I could finally understand Chopin's comparison.

When we were in the cell, Bauçà de Mirabó pointed up to the ceiling. The sight sent shivers down my spine. The high, vaulted ceiling gently sloped toward a flat rectangle, creating the troubling impression of looking at the lid of a coffin—from the inside (Figure 3.3). Apparently, every time the monks lay down, they would contemplate the *memento mori* molded into the ceiling.[38]

---

[35]   Bartolomé Ferrà, *Chopin and George Sand in Majorca*, trans. James Webb (Palma de Mallorca: Edicions la Cartoixa, 1936), p. 23. A detailed history of the *cartuja* can be found in a superb book by Concepció Bauçà de Mirabò Gralla, *La Real Cartuja de Jesús de Nazaret de Valldemossa* (Salzburg: Institut für Anglistik und Amerikanistik, Universität Salzburg, 2008).

[36]   Charles W. Wood, *Letters from Majorca* (London: Richard Bentley & Son, 1888), p. 368.

[37]   Ibid., pp. 370–72.

[38]   Interestingly enough, the prior's quarters in the *cartuja* have regular ceilings in all the rooms. Evidently, the priors did not need to be continually reminded of the mortality of flesh.

Figure 3.3 The ceiling in Chopin's cell. Photograph by Maria Ezerova

One can only imagine how that architectural design could have affected Chopin's anxious imagination. He always had a peculiar fascination with the morbid; his correspondence, after all, contains many descriptions of coffins and corpses; he had both dread of and fascination for death and was haunted by constant premonitions and fears of his own impending death.[39] In the nineteenth century, of course, this mind-set was not at all unusual. In countless Gothic stories, 'death

---

[39] Jeffrey Kallberg, 'Chopin's March, Chopin's Death,' *19th-Century Music*, 25/1 (Summer 2001), p. 22; Ewelina Boczkowska, 'Chopin's Ghosts,' *19th-Century Music*, 35/3 (Spring 2012), p. 205; Szulc, *Chopin in Paris,* pp. 45, 59.

Figure 3.4   Gothic chair in Chopin's cell. Photograph by Maria Ezerova

proves an omnipresent element, haunting the characters either when, awake, they fear for their lives or, when, asleep, they conjure up nightmarishly gory scenes.'[40]

An added touch to the ambience of the cell was a large Gothic chair of carved oak, which was, as Sand related, being eaten away by worms and rats, found in a disused Carthusian chapel. Sand brought with her a trunk filled with books, and she used the chair as a bookcase. At night, by the gleam of lamplight, the chair's pierced fretwork and tapering spires cast a lacy shadow on the wall, completely

---

[40]   Durot-Boucé, 'Midnight Trysts,' p. 306.

Figure 3.5 A corridor at the Carthusian monastery at night. Photograph by Maria Ezerova

restoring the ancient monastic character of the cell (the chair can still be seen in Chopin's cell at the *cartuja*; Figure 3.4).

After dark, the cloisters outside the cell became much more mysterious and sinister, having an unavoidable effect on the imagination. 'I would challenge the calmest and coolest brain,' Sand writes, 'to preserve sanity here over a long period. ... I confess that I seldom walked through the cloister after dusk without a feeling of mingled distress and pleasure.'[41] I wholeheartedly agree with Sand. Concepció

---

[41] Sand, *Winter in Majorca*, p. 109.

Figure 3.6   The Carthusian monastery in winter. Photograph by Enric Calafell Alemany

Bauçà de Mirabó conducted a night-time tour for me through the monastery, and I must confess that even today the dark cloisters seem shadowy and menacing, in spite of occasional electrical lights (Figure 3.5).

In Gothic fiction, nature and the elements always play a prominent role. During the day, the reader finds beguilingly pastoral, if wild, scenery surrounding a castle or a monastery. At night, especially around midnight, fierce storms and tempests on land and at sea rage with terrifying force. Lamartine's *Les Préludes* comprises both these extremes, and our inhabitants of the *cartuja* experienced them both, as well.

Occasionally, extreme winter elements made the *cartuja* even more secluded and confining. Valldemossa, as Sand observed in *Un hiver*, is one of the coldest parts of the island. On the severest nights, she wrote, they might have two inches of snow, which completely isolated Valldemossa from the outside world. Even today, when snow falls and stays on the ground for a few days, the mountain roads are closed, cutting Valldemossa off from the rest of the island (Figure 3.6).

One more component puts the finishing touches on the Gothic setting at the Valldemossa monastery: frightening ghosts and nightmarish hallucinations. Like protagonists in Gothic tales, Chopin lived through these ordeals, too.

Graves convincingly argues in his 'Historical Summary,' appended to his translation of Sand's *Winter in Majorca*, that Sand's ten-year-old daughter, Solange, played a role in shaping Chopin's belief that monks' ghosts were haunting the cell.

40 *The Mystery of Chopin's* Préludes

She was the only one in the family who could have picked up, as children do, the Mallorcan language, and who was spending much time with the locals, especially while her mother and brother, Maurice (then 16), were in Palma buying food, or perhaps inquiring after the Pleyel piano or fetching it. It was most probably Solange who told Chopin that Maria Antonia, the only other tenant at the *cartuja*, saw the ghostly procession of monks carrying a coffin to the cemetery, and that one of the monks said to her, in Mallorcan, 'Tell him to prepare for this!'

And it was Solange who apparently told Chopin that her playmate saw the ghost of Father Nicolás, the monk who used to live in the same cell, sitting on Chopin's bed. Moreover, in one of her later letters, Solange gleefully described how she and her friend dressed up in monks' robes, which they found in the monastery, and 'frightened Chopin out of his wits by creeping into the cell at dusk.'[42]

Chopin, who almost never ventured for a stroll outdoors, spent his days and nights inside the charterhouse, composing and, occasionally, descending (or ascending, if you will) into hallucinatory states. Sand maintains that for Chopin, 'the monastery cloister was full of terrors and phantoms even when he was well.'[43] She recalls that when she returned with her children from her nocturnal explorations in the ruins, she would find Chopin, 'at ten in the evening, pale at his piano, his eyes haggard, his hair standing almost on end.' It would take Chopin several moments to recognize them.

One day, Sand and Maurice left for Palma to buy some necessities. Solange did not stay in the cell with Chopin, evidently spending time with her companions elsewhere. A storm broke out, with torrential rains that made Sand and Maurice's return nearly impossible. When they eventually arrived, well after nightfall, shoeless and thoroughly wet, Chopin rose from the piano, 'uttered a loud cry, then said with a wild expression and in a strange tone of voice, "Ah, just as I imagined, you have died!"'[44] Moments later, when the composer came back to his senses, he confessed that, while playing the piano, he saw himself dead, drowned in a lake, with heavy drops of cold water falling on his chest.

Altogether, then, the influence of the intensely powerful Gothic ambiance of the Carthusian monastery on the composer and his *Préludes* is difficult to ignore. While the date when Chopin began to compose Opus 28 is uncertain, the date of completion is undeniable. After reiterating in his letters from Mallorca that the *Préludes* were not yet finished, he finally sent them to Paris on 22 January 1838. Jean-Jacques Eigeldinger suggests that Chopin most probably composed in Mallorca Preludes Nos. 2 in A minor, 4 in E minor, 5 in D major, 7 in A major,

---

[42] Graves, 'Historical Summary,' in George Sand, *Winter in Majorca*, pp. 179–82.

[43] George Sand, *Story of My Life: The Autobiography of George Sand* (Albany, NY: State University of New York Press, 1991), group trans., ed. Thelma Jurgrau, p. 1091.

[44] Ibid.

9 in E major, 10 in C♯ minor, 14 in E♭ minor, 16 in B♭ minor, and 18 in F minor; he finished and revised the rest of the set there, as well.[45]

Sand, meanwhile, maintains that Chopin composed the *Préludes* in the Carthusian monastery, which does not actually contradict Eigeldinger's assertion. The process of finishing and revising initial drafts can undoubtedly be defined as 'composition,' and Sand's statements regarding Chopin and the charterhouse have proved to be correct in practically all the other cases—except when she bitterly assailed the islanders and their lifestyle.

Furthermore, in her memoir she offers another intriguing, if cryptic, observation, averring that several preludes bring to mind the visions of dead monks and echoes of funeral chants that besieged the composer.[46] Unfortunately, she does not explain how the *Préludes* reflect Chopin's obsession with dead monks' funeral chants; nor does she clarify what those chants were. This is yet another missing piece in the puzzle of Chopin's *Préludes* that we need to recover.

---

[45]   See Preface to Fryderyk Chopin, *Préludes Op. 28, Op. 45*, ed. Jean-Jacques Eigeldinger. The Complete Chopin: A New Critical Edition (London: Edition Peters, 2003), p. vi.

[46]   Sand, *Story of My Life*, p. 1091.

Chapter 4

Lamartine's *Les Préludes*
and Chopin's *Préludes*

In Pursuit of Programmatic Meanings—or Not

Chopin, as every music lover knows, never wrote a programmatic work. In fact, he expressly disdained the idea of programs being affixed to instrumental compositions, especially to those of his own. In 1831, Chopin wrote to Tytus Wojciechowski that he had almost died from laughter while reading an overly imaginative review of his Variations on *Là ci darem la mano*, Op. 2. The commentator offered a measure-by-measure description of the events that 'occurred' in each variation, declaring, for example, that in the fifth measure of the Adagio, Don Giovanni kissed Zerlina on D♭. In the same letter, Chopin informed Wojciechowski that Count Ludwik Plater, upon reading the review, queried Chopin as to where exactly Zerlina's D♭ was.[1] On another occasion, the composer was irate over the titles 'The Sighs' (Nocturnes, Op. 37), 'The Infernal Banquet' (Scherzo, Op. 20), and 'Murmurs of the Seine' (Nocturnes, Op. 9) given to his published works in England, despite his prohibition.[2]

Yet he did, from time to time, allude to programmatic connotations, at least tête-à-tête with his pupils and, on extremely rare occasions, in his letters. One of these instances, regarding the depiction of 'an old clock in the castle' in the D♭-major Prelude, was discussed earlier in Chapter 2. There were at least two more allusions to Gothic horrors in Chopin's conversations with his students. He stressed the narrative character of his Mazurka in B minor, Op. 33, No. 4, when he explained that in the last eight measures a strong bell toll (G-C-G-C) and the subsequent arrival of the final chords 'sweeps away the cohorts of ghosts.'[3] In the B♭-minor Scherzo, Op. 31, Chopin insisted that the opening (and persistently recurring) motif with ascending triplets in parallel octaves must be delivered with utter softness, a questioning inflection, and, at the same time, a portentous

---

[1] *Chopin's Letters*, collected by Henryk Opienski (New York: Vienna House, 1971), p. 155.

[2] *Selected Correspondence of Fryderyk Chopin*, trans. and ed. Arthur Hedley (New York: McGraw-Hill, 1963), pp. 208–9.

[3] Jean-Jacques Eigeldinger, *Chopin: Pianist and Teacher as Seen by His Pupils* (Cambridge: Cambridge University Press, 1990), p. 75.

significance. The resulting atmosphere, he once said, should be that of 'a house of the dead.'[4]

Explaining to a student the character of his Etude, Op. 25, No. 1, Chopin suggested imagining 'a little shepherd who takes refuge in a peaceful grotto from an approaching storm. In the distance rushes the wind and the rain, while the shepherd gently plays a melody on his flute.'[5] We should feel lucky that this Etude, often referred to as 'Aeolian Harp,' has not acquired the moniker 'A Little Shepherd.'

When Chopin taught Nocturne in F♯ minor, Op. 48, No. 2, to Adolf Gutmann, the composer told Gutmann that the middle section of the Nocturne should be played as a recitative: Chopin said that each set of two forte chords (with a crescendo into the second chord) was to be played as 'a tyrant commands,' while in the following soft passage 'the other asks for mercy.'[6]

Once, Chopin even entertained the idea, apparently, of adding a programmatic subtitle to his work: he initially considered naming Nocturne in G minor, Op. 15, No. 3, 'After a representation of the tragedy of Hamlet.' Eventually Chopin abandoned this notion, saying: 'Let them guess for themselves.' On a different occasion, according to Wilhelm von Lenz, Chopin declared, 'I indicate; it's up to the listener to complete the picture.'[7]

Such indications, however unspecific, are still tangible in Chopin's Ballades. Jonathan Bellman convincingly analyzes Ballades Op. 23 and Op. 38 from a programmatic perspective. Bellman views poems of Adam Mickiewicz as points of inspiration for Chopin, tracing connections between Mickiewicz's *Konrad Wallenrod* and Chopin's Ballade, Op. 23 and relating Ballade, Op. 38 to Mickiewicz's other works.[8]

Similarly, it is quite possible to interpret Chopin's *Préludes* as a series of tone-painting reflections of Lamartine's poem *Les Préludes.* One can hear in the preludes many of the poem's images (albeit not in the same order), expressed through established means of musical expression.

The murmuring wave, limpid stream, water ripples, plaintive waves of the muted flood of tears, and flowing river, which are described in Cantos III, IV, VI, and IX, may be reflected in the incessantly running sixteenth notes in Preludes 3 (G major) and 23 (F major), which mirror easily recognizable textural patterns that depict the babbling brook in some of Schubert's songs, such as 'Das Wandern,' 'Wohin?,' 'Am Feierabend,' and 'Eifershucht und Stolz' from the ever-popular *Die Schöne Müllerin* (the Schubert–Chopin connections will be discussed in more detail later). The 'whisper of a fragrant breeze' that passes over the protagonist's

---

[4] Ibid., pp. 84–5.

[5] Ibid., p. 69.

[6] Ibid., p. 81.

[7] Ibid., p. 278.

[8] Jonathan D. Bellman, *Chopin's Polish Ballade: Op. 38 as Narrative of National Martyrdom* (Oxford: Oxford University Press, 2010), pp. 19–34, 55–85, and 145–70.

soul in Canto IX may be heard in the gossamer wisps of rapidly descending passages in Prelude 10 (C♯ minor).

The harp-like arpeggios of Prelude 19 (E♭ major) portray, conceivably, 'la harpe obéissante / A frémi mollement sous son vol cadencé / Et de la cord frémissante / Le souffle harmonieux dans mon âme a passé' (Canto II).[9] The heaving sound waves in Prelude 24 (D minor) evoke the image of a stormy seascape, with the ship plunging down in the end of the piece and, indeed, at the end of the entire opus (Canto V).

Prelude 16 (B♭ minor) may represent a battle scene, preceded by an opening trumpet call (Canto VIII). But so may Preludes 12 (G♯ minor) and 22 (G minor), sans the initial trumpet. And hereby lies the problem with attempts to attach a programmatic meaning to music. Some of such attempts may be helpful, a few useless, and others downright misleading.

A case in point is the wretched history of the finale of Chopin's Sonata in B♭ minor, Op. 35. Ever since Anton Rubinstein reportedly likened it to the wind howling over graves after the funeral march, most pianists play it as fast as possible, often with a great deal of pedal blur added for good measure. As it happens, Chopin *did* leave a well-documented description of the finale, and it had nothing to do with winds of any kind, over graves or not. In his letter to Julian Fontana, the composer tersely mentioned that in the short finale 'the left hand and the right hand gossip in unison after the March.'[10]

Chopin's statement drastically changes the widely established concept of the finale. Instead of a teary-eyed image of the wind blowing over the graves of the departed, Chopin offers an acerbic scene of malicious gossip after the protagonist's demise. This programmatic meaning calls for a slower tempo than the all-too-familiar prestissimo (in place of the presto indicated in the score). Consequently, the finale gains back its original structural and expressive complexity, blending sharply edged speech-like inflections with the texture of Bach's Suites for cello solo (which Chopin knew well) and infusing its richly idiosyncratic thematic contents with elements of sonata form.[11]

I hope the programmatic inferences that I attached earlier to some of the preludes are not so off the mark as the 'wind over graves' construal of the finale of the B♭-minor Sonata. In any case, it does not really matter, since I do not insist on my programmatic readings of the préludes. Nor do I intend to pursue much further this line of inquiry, and not because such pursuits are often unproductive. In fact, they might be fruitful, given a suitable approach.

Thus, the poem's wildly chaotic hodgepodge of images, emotions, and ideas may explain Schumann's portrayal of Chopin's Opus 28 as 'strange pieces,'

---

[9]   'The obedient harp / Trembled indolently under its cadenced flight, / And from the vibrating string / Harmonious inspiration has entered my soul.'

[10]   *Selected Correspondence of Fryderyk Chopin*, p. 181.

[11]   See Anatole Leikin, 'The Sonatas,' in Jim Samson (ed.), *The Cambridge Companion to Chopin* (Cambridge: Cambridge University Press, 1992), pp. 174–5.

'sketches' and 'ruins,' 'a wild motley' containing 'the morbid, the feverish, the repellent.' While Schumann does not publicly mention the Lamartine–Chopin connection, his description fits both works perfectly. Furthermore, the stark proportional incongruities between the cantos of the poem (from four to 116 lines) correspond to similar proportional discrepancies within Opus 28.

Yet, despite possible benefits, I am still reluctant to attach programmatic content to every prelude. My reservations are twofold. First, such illustrative readings are more applicable to other nineteenth-century composers, rather than Chopin. Indeed, Liszt's programmatic tone poem *Les Préludes*, overtly inspired by Lamartine, exhibits precisely this kind of pictographic approach. Second, however programmatic correspondences between the poem and Opus 28 may play out, they are subjective, widely open to individual considerations, and therefore inconclusive.

In the meantime, substantive bonds between Lamartine's *Les Préludes* and Chopin's *Préludes* can indeed be identified as much more factual and consequential. Exploring these bonds reveals a trove of valuable information. And if it can be proven that Chopin's *Préludes* collectively reflect a single poetic work, this attribute alone would both unify Opus 28 and turn these supposedly supplemental introductory pieces into a full-fledged, independent artistic work whose individual components require no consequents.[12]

The Binary Subsets

One of the more important bonds between Lamartine's poem and Opus 28 is structural. The symmetrical layout of alternating pairs and singles works admirably well in this poem of 11 cantos. Chopin's set consists of 24 rather than 11 preludes. The reason for this is obvious: having a collection of preludes in all the keys conveys, at least ostensibly, a traditional sense of completeness.

Many composers, as well as music theorists and teachers, published collections containing 24 piano preludes prior to Chopin's Opus 28: Clementi, Hummel, Würfel, Kalkbrenner, and Czerny, to mention only the most prominent. Yet, as Jean-Jacques Eigeldinger avers, Chopin 'was only in the slightest degree' dependent on his immediate predecessors.'[13] Even Hummel's 24 preludes, which anticipate the same arrangement of keys as the one used in Opus 28, did not influence the music of Chopin's *Préludes*. A quick comparison of the C-major and A-minor Preludes

---

[12] The poetic nature of Chopin's *Préludes* is discussed by James William Sobaskie in his essay 'Precursive Prolongation in the *Préludes* of Chopin,' *Journal of the Society for Musicology in Ireland*, 3 (2007–2008), pp. 26–7. Sobaskie, however, draws no parallels between Opus 28 and Lamartine's poem.

[13] Jean-Jacques Eigeldinger, 'Twenty-Four Preludes Op. 28: Genre, Structure, Significance,' in Jim Samson (ed.), *Chopin Studies* (Cambridge: Cambridge University Press, 1988), p. 173.

from Hummel's Opus 67 and Chopin's Opus 28 (compare Examples 1.1 and 1.2 with Examples 5.4a, b, c and 5.6) makes it abundantly clear that Opus 28 does not emulate Hummel's collection. If anything, it rather masquerades as Hummel's set of preludes in the same keys.

Bach's *Well-Tempered Clavier*, on the other hand, did serve as a model for Opus 28, despite the difference in the order of keys. Moreover, an analysis of Chopin's *Préludes*, presented in Chapter 5, will show that Chopin's pieces are influenced not merely by the Preludes in the *Clavier* but rather by both the Preludes *and* the Fugues.

One apparent impediment is that Lamartine's idiosyncratic succession of diptychs separated by interludes cannot be extended in such a way that it would fit the requisite number of 24. The structure employed in the poem can be expanded from 11 up to 14, 17, 20, 23, or even 26 components, making infeasible a series of 24 preludes with the same 2 + 1 arrangement. It is possible, nonetheless, to at least partially reproduce the symmetry of the poem by coupling preludes into 12 pairs (with no interludes in between). The most logical way to implement this construction, of course, is to begin with the opening C major/A minor pair and then link together the remaining major and minor preludes with identical key signatures.

A strong rationale can be adduced for bringing together two preludes in relative keys. The affinity between the relative major and minor keys has a special significance in Chopin's oeuvre: in Slavic music, both folk and professional, relative major and minor keys often intertwine. In Russian music theory this modal pattern is known as the 'параллельно-переменный лад,' which can be translated as the 'relative major–minor fluctuating mode.' This fluctuating mode has not one but two relative tonal centers that alternate without actual modulation.[14]

Several of Chopin's mazurkas exhibit this modal pattern. For example, in Chopin's Mazurka in C major, Op. 24, No. 2, the mode in mm. 5–12 oscillates between C major and A minor; in mm. 1–16 of Mazurka in A minor ('Notre temps,' No. 2), the configuration is reversed, commencing in A minor. Furthermore, some of Chopin's compositions are, in fact, written in two alternating relative keys: Waltz, Op. 70, No. 2 (F minor/A♭ major); Scherzo, Op. 31 (B♭ minor/D♭ major); *Fantaisie*, Op. 49 (F minor/A♭ major).

The problem is that in Lamartine's poem the connections within each diptych are demonstratively specific, while the modal ties between two relative keys constitute merely a precondition for putting two preludes together rather than a strong bond within a pair. There must be a musical analogue to poetic links, one imagines. Conveniently enough, such an analogue had already existed at the time,

---

[14] Igor Sposobin, *Elementarnaya teoriya muzyki* [*Foundations of Music Theory*] (Moscow: Gosmuzizdat, 1959), pp. 145–7; Igor Sposobin, *Lektsii po kursu garmonii* [*Lectures on Harmony*], ed. Y. Kholopov (Moscow: Muzyka, 1969), pp. 198–9; Andrei Myasoedov, *O garmonii russkoy muzyki* [*On Harmony in Russian Music*] (Moscow: Prest, 1998), p. 49.

48 *The Mystery of Chopin's* Préludes

and it was intrinsic to the genre of prelude: namely, a prelude was supposed to introduce not only the key but also some of the thematic material of the main piece. Several didactic prelude collections, including those by Czerny and Hummel, mention this important attribute of the prelude. Still, the most splendid examples of motivic anticipation can be found in Bach's *Well-Tempered Clavier*.

Eigeldinger argues that 'Bach's influence on the Preludes, as well as on Chopin's music in general, is infinitely more powerful and subtle than that of any of the post-classical composers.'[15] Ever since Chopin was introduced to—nay, brought up on—Bach's music by his first teacher, Adalbert Zywny, the Baroque master remained an indispensable part of Chopin's creative world. One of Chopin's students, Wilhelm von Lenz, recalls that when Chopin played for himself, he would play nothing but Bach. When Chopin was preparing for a concert, he, according to Lenz, did not practice his own compositions that he was supposed to play at the concert but rather played Bach for several weeks prior to the concert. Another student, Friederike Müller, mentioned that during one of her lessons Chopin played to her from memory 14 of Bach's preludes and fugues in a row.[16] And, as far as we know, Bach's *Well-Tempered Clavier* was the only musical score Chopin took with him to Mallorca, where he completed the Preludes.

In *The Well-Tempered Clavier,* every prelude introduces not merely the key but also the thematic material of the following fugue. Surprisingly, very few attempts have been made to analyze motivic connections between the preludes and the subsequent fugues in *The Well-Tempered Clavier.* The most notable endeavors to examine such connections were undertaken by Wilhelm Werker and Johann Nepomuk David.[17] Hermann Keller later remarked, however, that although both Werker and David drew attention to and clarified some previously neglected thematic relationships, their conclusions were frequently unpersuasive.[18]

Keller proceeded to expand on the issue of thematic links in *The Well-Tempered Clavier*, but he, too, was not always successful at discerning significant thematic connections. Neither he nor his predecessors realized that, while similarity of intervallic patterns is important, the bonds between similar motifs strengthen considerably when these motifs are positioned on exactly the same notes. Identical pitches noticeably facilitate aural recognition of thematic links.

---

[15]   Eigeldinger, 'Twenty-Four Preludes,' p. 173.

[16]   Jean-Jacques Eigeldinger, 'Placing Chopin: Reflections on a Compositional Aesthetics,' in John Rink and Jim Samson (eds), *Chopin Studies 2* (Cambridge: Cambridge University Press, 1994), p. 120.

[17]   Wilhelm Werker, *Studien über die Symmetrie im Bau der Fugen und die motivische Zusammengehörigkeit der Präludien und Fugen des "Wohltemperierten Klaviers" von Johann Sebastian Bach* (Leipzig: Breitkopf und Härtel, 1922); Johann Nepomuk David, *Das Wohltemperierte Klavier: Der Versuch einer Synopsis* (Göttingen: Vandenhoeck & Ruprecht, 1962).

[18]   Hermann Keller, *The Well-Tempered Clavier by Johann Sebastian Bach*, trans. Leigh Gerdine (London: George Allen & Unwin Ltd, 1976), p. 29.

Thus, while listing and, occasionally, analyzing most of the preludes and fugues with strong thematic connections, Keller mentions a few pairs in Book I in which motivic relationships presumably cannot be demonstrated.[19] The links between preludes and fugues, he continues, are 'even more difficult to prove in Book II than in Book I.'[20] If, however, we listen carefully to pitch identities, the presumably negligible or even absent motivic connections come to the fore and instantly become apparent.

When Keller does find thematic correlations between preludes and fugues, he usually compares the beginning of a prelude with the fugue opening. For example, Keller correctly points out that in Prelude and Fugue in G♯ minor from Book II 'the beginning notes of the prelude are also those of the fugue subject.'[21] Even more meaningful, however, as well as more easily perceptible, are the thematic links that join the conclusion of a prelude with the beginning of the ensuing fugue. This is exactly what happens in the G♯-minor Prelude and Fugue from Book II (see the corresponding braces and square brackets in Examples 4.1a, b).

Example 4.1 Bach, *The Well-Tempered Clavier*, Book II, Prelude and Fugue in G♯ minor, (a) Prelude, m. 50, (b) Fugue, mm. 1–2

Keller establishes motivic relationships between many preludes and fugues in Book I, but contends that there are none between the preludes and fugues in E♭ major, E major, A major, A minor, and B♭ major.[22] Had he looked for pitch identity, however, he would have had no difficulty finding motivic relationships in these preludes and fugues, too. Thus, the E♭-major Prelude from Book I intermittently includes, in augmentation and on the same pitches, some sections of the Fugue's subject and answer. In the last eight measures of the Prelude, all the notes of the

---

[19] Ibid., pp. 28–9.
[20] Ibid., p. 135.
[21] Ibid., p. 182.
[22] Ibid., pp. 28–9.

50   *The Mystery of Chopin's* Préludes

Example 4.2   Bach, *The Well-Tempered Clavier*, Book I, Prelude and Fugue in E♭ major, (a) Prelude, mm. 63–70, (b) Fugue, mm. 1–2

Example 4.3   Bach, *The Well-Tempered Clavier*, Book I, Fugue in E♭ major, m. 37

Fugue's subject do surface—mostly in augmentation, divided among several voices, and, once again, on identical pitches (with occasional passing tones). The common notes are numbered 1 through 16 in Examples 4.2a, b. Additionally, the chromatically embellished descent from notes 14 to 16 in the last three measures of the Prelude (E♭-[D]-D♭-C-C♭-B♭) rhymes with the ending of the Fugue (compare mm. 68–70 in Example 4.2a with Example 4.3). Similar motivic relationships can be identified in the other preludes and fugues that Keller pegged as lacking in thematic connections.

To be sure, obvious differences may readily be noted between *The Well-Tempered Clavier* and Chopin's Opus 28. Every prelude in *The Well-Tempered Clavier*, for example, introduces a fugue in an identical key, while Opus 28 contains neither fugues nor two pieces in the same key. Nevertheless, in Opus 28 the commonality of key is substituted, to an extent, with the closeness of the relative major/minor modal linkage. Furthermore, the relative major and minor tonic triads partially coincide, having two common notes between them. A few writers have noticed that some pairs of the preludes in Opus 28 are linked by single pitches common to the two relative tonic triads, when the last note of one prelude serves, reharmonized, as the opening note of the following piece. Kresky writes that Nos. 11–12 are connected by D♯, which belongs to both B-major and G♯-minor tonic triads, Nos. 17–18 by C (A♭ major/F minor), Nos. 19–20 by G (E♭ major/C minor), and Nos. 21–22 by B♭ in the bass (B♭ major/G minor).[23]

Both Kresky and Eigeldinger agree that Nos. 3–4 are linked by the octave B-B (common to G major/E minor). Charles J. Smith notes, as well, that the concluding bass A in No. 7 (A major) becomes the first bass note in No. 8 (F♯ minor). Smith also tries to establish common-pitch ties between the even-numbered and the odd-numbered preludes, too, but concludes that in six cases such interconnections are non-existent (Nos. 4–5, 6–7, 8–9, 10–11, 18–19, 20–21). His attempts to identify pitch connections between the other five pairs of even- to odd-numbered preludes remain unconvincing because, when Smith cannot find direct pitch links between the endings and the beginnings of two adjoining preludes, he picks and chooses random pitches within these pairs.[24]

Common pitches between two relative tonic triads cannot, however, always explain the common-pitch connectors within the prelude pairs. Eigeldinger remarks that E in the treble concludes the C-major Prelude 1 and opens Prelude in A minor.[25] The A-minor Prelude, though, does not commence with the A-minor tonic—it begins with an E-minor chord instead. Furthermore, Preludes 16 (B♭ minor) and 18 (F minor) start on the dominant rather than the tonic; and yet they still share common pitch links with the preceding major-key preludes.

Evidently, the common pitch links within prelude pairs are important enough to be introduced even when no relative tonic triads are involved. The significance of these pitch connectors is that they in fact replace the missing common tonic triads that would otherwise unite prelude and fugues written in the same key.

Furthermore, there is always more than a single common pitch that binds together every pair of odd- and even-numbered preludes. If Chopin was inspired

---

[23] Jeffrey Kresky, *A Reader's Guide to the Chopin Preludes* (Westport, CT: Greenwood Press, 1994), p. xvi.

[24] Charles J. Smith, 'On Hearing the Chopin Preludes as a Coherent Set: A Survey of Some Possible Structural Models for Op. 28,' *In Theory Only*, 1/4 (1975), pp. 8–9, 12.

[25] Eigeldinger, 'Twenty-Four Preludes,' p. 180.

by Lamartine—and guided by Bach—the prelude pairs would have to be integrated more thoroughly than merely being in two relative keys and sharing a single common pitch. Are they truly more thoroughly integrated, and is *every* odd-numbered prelude in Opus 28 tied to the following even-numbered prelude?

Yet another harmonic feature must also be considered, the one that Bach's preludes and fugues lack. As Jeffrey Kallberg notes, many preludes in Opus 28 are open-ended. Specifically, 11 of them end with imperfect cadences. In addition, an accented E♭ is added to the concluding tonic triad in the F-major Prelude, divesting the piece of a full closure. Such uncertain endings, adds Kallberg, are consistent with the nature of a prelude.[26]

Kallberg's observation can be qualified further: some of the pieces in Opus 28 are more 'preluding' than others. In fact, most of the major-mode preludes have inconclusive endings except for Nos. 7 (A major) and 9 (E major). In No. 7, though, the leading thematic voice in the last two measures, as I shall discuss in the next chapter, ends on the third scale degree in the alto (C♯), which leaves only the E-major Prelude, No. 9, as having a truly conclusive ending.

On the contrary, all but two of the minor-mode preludes close with a perfect cadence. The two open-ended minor endings are brought about by special circumstances. In the B-minor Prelude, the bass carries the melody. After a perfect cadence in mm. 21–22, the bass outlines the tonic triad for the last time and comes to rest on the first scale degree in the final two measures. The ending of the F-minor Prelude on C in the upper voice is part of a larger symmetrical design: both this and the preceding A♭-major Prelude open and close with C in the top voice, which becomes one of the links bonding Preludes 17 and 18.

Only one out of the 48 preludes in *The Well-Tempered Clavier* has an 'uncertain ending' (to use Kallberg's expression): the C-minor from Book I. And even then, if one plays the concluding descending figure in RH, C-G-F-D-E, with a typical Baroque over-legato, the upper C, as well as the following lower G, will be held down so that a full C-major chord emerges in the end, with the tonic note on top.

As far as the early nineteenth-century preludes are concerned, Hummel's 24 are closer to Chopin's 24 than the other collections because of an identical tonal plan. Unlike the Chopin preludes, however, all but three of Hummel's short preambles end with perfect cadences, and out of the three 'uncertain endings' only one is in a minor-key prelude (F♯ minor).

The two types of prelude endings (open and closed) certainly help unite the preludes into binary subsets, similarly to the couplings of cantos in Lamartine's poem. Are these prelude parings strengthened by motivic links, as well, as in Bach's preludes and fugues? We'll settle this question in the next chapter, when we'll delve into the matter of motivic links within prelude pairs.

---

[26] Jeffrey Kallberg, *Chopin at the Boundaries: Sex, History, and Musical Genre* (Cambridge, MA: Harvard University Press, 1996), pp. 152–7.

Right now, though, let me pose another question: why does every open-ended major prelude function as a preamble to the subsequent minor prelude? Or, in other words, why did the minor preludes become the main pieces?

The Eschatological Aspect

To proceed further, we have to step back and ask yet another question: why is Lamartine's poem titled *Les Préludes* in the first place? The word *prelude* does not appear in the text of the poem except as a verb in Canto I, when the protagonist implores the Genius, 'Come, prelude as you like!' In fact, the initial title of the poem was the noncommittal *Les Chants*.[27] The second and final title, *Les Préludes,* is rather puzzling. One cannot help but wonder, in André Gide's words, 'Preludes to what?'

The most insightful answer to this question was put forward by Liszt. His tone poem *Les Préludes (d'après Lamartine)* was premiered in 1854 and published two years later. There is a modern view, formulated in 1931 by Peter Raabe, that the title and the subtitle of Liszt's tone poem are both misleading. Raabe maintains that Liszt's symphonic poem is in fact his unpublished overture to *Les Quatre Élémens*, a set of four choruses with texts by Joseph Autran.[28] Raabe's position is supported by Émile Haraszti, as well, who insists that Liszt's *Les Préludes* has nothing in common with Lamartine's poem.[29]

The Raabe–Haraszti revisionist assumption is compellingly debunked by Alexander Main, who proves that Liszt merely recycled the music of the earlier overture, incorporating parts of it into a completely new work—a common enough practice among composers.[30] One of Main's arguments is that Liszt maintained a close friendship with Lamartine and admired his poetry (in 1853 Liszt published a set of piano pieces titled after Lamartine's set of poems *Harmonies poétiques et religieuses*). Andrew Bonner, while contesting some of Main's statements, eventually agrees with him that Liszt's decision to name his orchestral work after Lamartine's poem was 'neither hasty nor arbitrary'; rather, the composer's programmatic intent 'should be understood as well-considered and sincere.'[31]

Alexander Main draws detailed parallels between the poem and Liszt's *Les Préludes*, but for our purposes these analogies are irrelevant, since Chopin's

---

[27] Alphonse de Lamartine, *Méditations*, ed. Fernand Letessier (Paris: Garnier Frères, 1968), p. 786.

[28] Peter Raabe, *Franz Liszt*, 2nd edn (Tutzing: Hans Schneider, 1968), vol. 2, p. 96.

[29] Émile Haraszti, 'Genèse des préludes de Liszt qui n'ont aucun rapport avec Lamartine,' *Revue de Musicologie*, vol. 35, no. 107/108 (December 1953), p. 112.

[30] Alexander Main, 'Liszt after Lamartine: "Les Preludes,"' *Music & Letters*, 60/2 (April 1979), pp. 133–48.

[31] Andrew Bonner, 'Liszt's *Les Préludes* and *Les Quatre Élémens*: A Reinvestigation,' *19th-Century Music*, 10/2 (Autumn 1986), p. 107.

54   *The Mystery of Chopin's* Préludes

Préludes and Liszt's symphonic poem are too dissimilar, both musically and conceptually. What matters more is Liszt's program—or, rather, programs—attached to the music. He wrote three different versions of the program, every time giving a slightly different précis of the long, 375-line poem.

The first version of the program, probably dated 1854, was quite extensive, with several quotations from Lamartine. The second, much shorter, account was prepared for the concert that Liszt conducted in Berlin in 1855. The well-familiar variant, the shortest of the three, was printed as a preface to the score published in 1856.[32] Despite the differences, all three versions include the portrayal of life as 'a series of preludes to that unknown hymn, the first and solemn note of which is intoned by Death.'[33]

This phrase is found nowhere in the poem. Where does it come from, then? Was Liszt's construal of Lamartine's poem a precipitous revelation? This seems highly unlikely, simply because when Liszt's synopsis of the poem was published, no one was surprised. No critic praised the program as an eye-opener or criticized it as a fallacy. More important, Lamartine never objected to the program, either. Which leads to the only possible logical assumption: Liszt's interpretation of the poem was not news; he merely expressed a long-standing notion that must have already been familiar to readers.

It is entirely possible, first, that Lamartine himself was the source of Liszt's understanding of the poem and of its title, and, second, that it did not suddenly surface 30 years after the poem had been published. Lamartine could have been queried by his friends (a circle that included Liszt, Chopin, and Sand) about the poem's enigmatic title, after which he might have provided an explanation.

If the poem, in accordance with the title and Liszt's reading, indeed relates a series of preludes to death, the arrangement of the pieces in Chopin's Opus 28 into groups of two makes perfect sense. The notion of life as a prelude to death is introduced already in the opening mini-set, Preludes 1 and 2. The C-major Prelude is one of Chopin's most exuberant, joyful affairs—an epitome of life. The bleak A-minor Prelude, on the contrary, is one of his most despondent creations.

The remaining major/minor pairs of preludes likewise generate striking contrasts in emotional content, with the second piece supplying either a mournful or a dramatically tragic closure. The second prelude of a diptych can be a doleful

---

[32]   There was also a fourth version, which Hans von Bülow wrote for his concert in Prague in 1860. This version was not approved by Liszt. All four versions are published in Theodor Müller-Reuter, *Lexikon der Deutschen Konzertliteratur* (New York: Da Capo Press, 1972); first published in Leipzig (C.F. Kahnt, 1909), pp. 297–301.

[33]   Here are the original French and German texts: 'Notre vie est-elle autre chose qu'une série de Préludes à ce chant inconnu dont la mort entonne la première et solennelle note?'; 'Was andres is unser Leben, als eine Reihenfolge von Präludien zu einem unbekannten Gesang, dessen ersten und feierliche Note der Tod anstimmt?'

Lamartine's Les Préludes *and Chopin's* Préludes

elegy, as in the B-minor Prelude; or a funeral march (the C-minor Prelude); or, as Eigeldinger notes, a paraphrase on Bach's 'Crucifixus' (the E-minor Prelude).[34]

Prelude 2 (A minor) holds the most definitive clue. That Prelude contains several references—motivic, genre, and structural—that collectively and unequivocally suggest the symbolic meaning of this prelude: death. The most tangible among these references are quotations from the medieval chant from the Requiem Mass, the *Dies irae.*

Thomas Higgins points out that the LH opening of Prelude 2 contains 'a melodic fragment which resembles the Gregorian sequence *Dies irae.*' He also adds that the fragment reads B-A♯-B-G, while the exact quotation from the *Dies irae* should have sounded B-A♯-B-G♯.'[35] The change of quality of melodic intervals in the A-minor Prelude, however, is immaterial. Chopin simply employs a common fugal technique in which the qualities of melodic intervals can be altered when a recurrent theme is moved to another mode or to a different set of scale degrees—a developmental procedure that became common in later, homophonic styles as well.

Elsewhere, I proposed that the *Dies irae* quote in Prelude 2 extended beyond the initial four pitches and also included the RH part.[36] At that time, however, I did not realize that, as far as references to the *Dies irae* were concerned, the A-minor Prelude was not at all unique in Opus 28. A detailed thematic analysis, contained in the next chapter, will show that not only the A-minor Prelude but rather *all* the preludes include copious quotations from the *Dies irae* plainchant. Evidently, Chopin moved further in the eschatological direction than Lamartine, and certainly much further than Liszt.

In the nineteenth century, this chant became one of the more powerful and quite familiar musical symbols of death. Two notable secular compositions that precede Chopin's Opus 28 are Hector Berlioz's *Symphonie fantastique* (1830) and Charles-Valentin Alkan's *Trois Morceaux dans le Genre Pathétique*, Op. 15 (1837). The *Symphonie fantastique* is clearly the more celebrated of the two, but it is difficult to assess how it influenced the *Préludes*. To begin with, in the finale of the symphony, '*Songe d'une nuit du sabbat*' [Dream of a Witches' Sabbath], the quote from the plainchant is an ironic reference to Roman liturgy,

---

[34]   Eigeldinger, 'Twenty-Four Preludes,' p. 176.

[35]   Thomas Higgins, 'Chopin Interpretation: A Study of Performance Directions in Selected Autographs and Other Sources' (PhD Dissertation, University of Iowa, 1966), p. 161.

[36]   I described the *Dies irae* quote in the A-minor Prelude in the paper 'Genre Analysis in the Music of Chopin,' presented at the Joint Meeting of the Pacific Southwest and Northern California Chapters of the American Musicological Society, Santa Barbara, California, 28 April 1985, as well as in my dissertation 'The Dissolution of Sonata Structure in Romantic Piano Music (1820–1850)' (PhD dissertation, University of California, Los Angeles, 1986), pp. 21–7. A more detailed analysis of the *Dies irae* in the Prelude can be found in my article 'Chopin's A-minor Prelude and Its Symbolic Language,' *International Journal of Musicology*, 6 (1997), pp. 149–62.

56   *The Mystery of Chopin's* Préludes

an exuberant depiction of a Black Mass. Berlioz's approach is far removed from the moods that prevail in Opus 28; besides, Chopin was certainly not fond of Berlioz's music in general.

Alkan's treatment of the chant differs from the one used by Berlioz. In his three-movement piano suite, the first two pieces are titled '*Aime-moi*' [Love Me] and '*Le vent*' [The Wind]. The *Dies irae* is quoted in the third piece, '*Morte*' [Death]. Here the chant is indeed a signifier of death. It is neither a church prayer nor a mocking caricature of it (and, in any case, Alkan was Jewish).[37]

The macabre atmosphere of '*Morte*' apparently did not sit well with Robert Schumann, who vilified the piece for being depressingly 'black on black' and having 'a considerable flavour of [Eugène] Sue and [George] Sand.' Eugène Sue was, as mentioned before, a friend of George Sand's and a prominent representative of French Gothic, *école frénétique*. We do not have a record of Chopin's reaction to Alkan's suite, but Liszt, to whom the suite was dedicated, definitely liked the music. He read and reread the score many times, and found it 'distinguished' and 'likely to excite the deep interest of musicians.'[38]

Robin Gregory and Malcolm Boyd have separately described the secular use of this plainchant in the nineteenth and twentieth centuries, from Berlioz onward, and give numerous examples of various secular works containing the *Dies irae*.[39] Boyd's citation of the *Dies irae*, though, is limited to the opening two stanzas of the chant. Indeed, this initial portion of the chant was used in Liszt's *Totentanz (Paraphrase über 'Dies irae')*, composed in 1849, and in numerous works by others afterward.

If anything unites Berlioz's '*Songe d'une nuit du sabbat*' and Alkan's '*Morte*,' it is the fact that both composers quote four stanzas of the *Dies irae,* rather than the two stanzas examined by Gregory and Boyd. Although twice as long, the four-stanza segment is still a relatively small part of the entire chant, which, all in all, consists of 19 stanzas. Yet these opening four stanzas lay the musical foundation of the chant. They are the most iterated part of the entire melody, since the music to which stanzas 1–4 are set is repeated, refrain-like, in stanzas 7–10 and 13–16 (Example 4.4).

The inevitable question is whether Chopin was, in principle, receptive to the very idea of embedding evocative musical quotations in his *Préludes*, thus generating an implied program. For quite some time Chopin was not suspected of 'borrowing' from other people's music. He was apparently considered to be above committing even an occasional musical appropriation. One notable exception was his B-minor Scherzo, Op. 20: the traditional Polish Christmas carol *Lulajze Jezuniu* can be immediately recognized in the middle (B-major) section.

---

[37]   At the time Alkan wrote *Morte* in 1837, he and Chopin were not only good personal friends but also neighbors in the Square d'Orléans in Paris.

[38]   William Alexander Eddie, *Charles-Valentin Alkan: His Life and His Music* (Aldershot: Ashgate Publishing, 2007), p. 43.

[39]   Robin Gregory, 'Dies Irae,' *Music & Letters*, 34/2 (1953), pp. 133–9; Malcolm Boyd, 'Dies Irae: Some Recent Manifestations,' *Music & Letters*, 49/4 (1968), pp. 347–56.

Example 4.4 *Dies irae*, stanzas 1–4, with an English translation

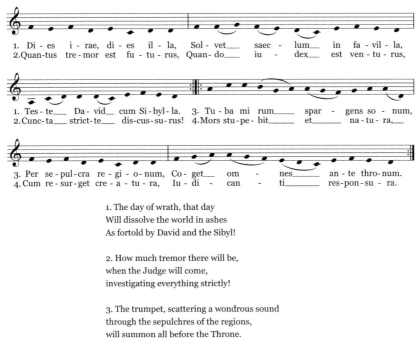

1. The day of wrath, that day
Will dissolve the world in ashes
As fortold by David and the Sibyl!

2. How much tremor there will be,
when the Judge will come,
investigating everything strictly!

3. The trumpet, scattering a wondrous sound
through the sepulchres of the regions,
will summon all before the Throne.

4. Death and nature will marvel,
when the creature arises,
to respond to the Judge.

Later, however, musical borrowings from Field, Hummel, and Moscheles have been spotted in many of Chopin's works.[40] The establishment of these links breaches the somewhat romanticized—and unrealistic—myth that Chopin would never stoop to musical borrowings.

Other Romantic composers frequently used evocative quotations that not merely referred to other pieces of music but even conveyed coded symbolic messages. Among such examples are Schumann's famous self-quotation from *Papillons* in *Carnaval,* as well as his references to Beethoven's *An die ferne Geliebte* in *Fantasie*, Op. 17, and Tchaikovsky's insertion of the liturgical funeral chant *So sviatymi upokoy* [*Rest in Peace with the Saints*] into the first movement of his Sixth Symphony.

---

[40] Richard Davis, 'The Music of J.N. Hummel: Its Derivations and Development,' *The Music Review*, 26 (1965), pp. 169–91; David Branson, *John Field and Chopin* (New York: St. Martin's Press, 1972), Chapters 4–9; Jim Samson, *The Music of Chopin* (London: Routledge & Kegan Paul, 1985), p. 61.

Example 4.5 *Dies irae* motifs written separately

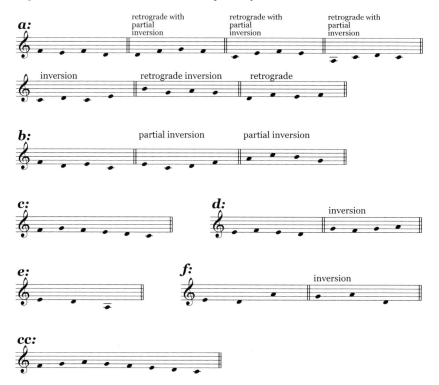

Chopin also indulged, albeit rarely, in using covert symbolic codes. When he sent his Waltz in D♭ major (published posthumously as Op. 70, No. 3) to Titus Woyciechowski, he marked one passage with an 'X,' saying that 'no one will know its meaning except yourself.'[41] And to this day no one does—for Woyciechowski kept the secret well. Normally, however, Chopin never divulged his intentions, and the only way now to infer possible ciphered messages, and thus to enrich the understanding and interpretation of his music, is through analyzing Chopin's compositions and finding references to music with distinct semantic contents. For instance, the first movement of his Cello Sonata, Op. 65, composed during the difficult period of his breakup with George Sand, reveals strong musical ties with Schubert's *Winterreise*. Evidently, the main theme of the *Winterreise*—a despairing lover forced to leave his beloved—paralleled the circumstances of Chopin's life at that time.[42]

---

[41] Alfred Cortot, *In Search of Chopin*, trans. Cyril and Rena Clarke (New York: Abelard Press, 1952), p. 50.

[42] Anatole Leikin, 'The Sonatas,' in Jim Samson (ed.), *The Cambridge Companion to Chopin* (Cambridge: Cambridge University Press, 1992), pp. 185–7.

Lamartine's Les Préludes *and Chopin's* Préludes   59

Still, Chopin's handling of the plainchant in Opus 28 is so subtle and ingenious that the presence of the *Dies irae* in the *Préludes* went undetected for more than a century and a half, despite George Sand's testimonial that Chopin at the time was besieged by visions of dead monks and the sounds of their funeral chants.[43] Her recollection seemed to have spurred no inquiries into what the dead monks' funeral chants could actually mean—perhaps because this statement was thought to be one of her frequent flights of fancy. Besides, Chopin's treatment of the *Dies irae* differs from that of other contemporary composers. Both Berlioz and Alkan (and, a few years later, Liszt) introduce the *Dies irae* clearly and conspicuously. Yet in the *Préludes* the plainchant never sounds as an undivided whole, from the beginning to the end, although its opening and the most recognizable four-note motif appear repeatedly. As mentioned earlier, Chopin truly preferred to 'indicate' rather than declare.

Malcolm Boyd states that the melody of *Dies irae* does not 'lend itself readily to intellectual processes of composition. Few composers have attempted canons, inversions, retrogrades and so on, though many have presented the melody in varied rhythms.'[44] That is not so. We will soon see that Chopin incorporated the *Dies irae*, applying a wide variety of thematic developments typical of older polyphonic styles—inversions, retrogrades, and inversions in retrograde—as well as some less-common motivic permutations.

In another comment, Boyd remarks that the melody of the *Dies irae* is

> … clearly not likely to appeal to a composer on its purely musical merit. The low *tessitura* and the restricted range (all the notes of the first two lines are contained within the interval of a perfect fourth) combine to suggest a mood of dark foreboding, perhaps, but as a tune the "Dies irae" is far less attractive than other sequence melodies, such as the well-known "Victimae paschali laudes" and "Veni sancte spiritus."[45]

The *Dies irae* chant may perhaps lack an irresistible melodic allure. It does, however, possess an astonishing intricacy of structural design. The *Dies irae* is a marvelously crafted melody. It can be divided into approximately seven motifs, shown in Example 4.5. Several motifs are related to each other: *d* is an abbreviated *c*, while *cc* is an embellished *c*, with an added upper neighbor; motifs *e* and *f* differ only by an octave transposition of the last note. Motifs *a*, *b*, and *d* are symmetrically varied through inversions and retrogrades. Example 4.6 illustrates how all the motifs interlock in the chant, both within the 12 phrases (indicated by the bar lines in Examples 4.4 and 4.6) and across the boundaries, connecting the ending of a previous phrase with the beginning of the next one. Consequently,

---

[43]   George Sand, *Histoire de ma vie. Œuvres autobiographiques* (Paris: Gallimard, 1971), vol. 2, p. 410.

[44]   Boyd, 'Dies Irae,' pp. 347–8.

[45]   Ibid.

Example 4.6 *Dies irae*, inner motivic structure

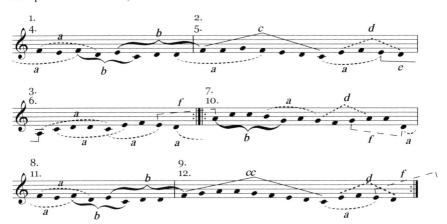

depending on how we view the melody, first one motif and then another may come to the fore, as in a turning crystal prism (Example 4.6).

Thus, motif *a*, marked by a dotted curve in Example 4.6, commences the chant; its inversion, retrograde, retrograde inversion, and retrograde with a partial inversion interlock with each other as well as with other motifs later in the melody. The last note in phrases 3, 7, and 10 and the first four notes in the ensuing phrases (4, 8, and 11) form a clever palindrome involving *a* and its retrograde that precedes *a* by one note, D-F-E-F-D (Example 4.6). This particular palindrome will feature prominently in the B-minor and G♯-minor Preludes.

While Chopin does not quote the *Dies irae* as a complete, undivided whole, he does closely follow permutational treatments of short motivic segments found in the chant: all the motifs listed in Examples 4.5 and 4.6 find their way into the *Préludes*.[46]

The use of symmetric permutations of the chant in Opus 28 involves two principles: first, a long melody is broken into shorter motifs, which are then developed through inversions and retrogrades; and second, the quality of melodic intervals is sometimes retained (that is, major intervals remain major, minor intervals stay minor) and sometimes altered. These methods of motivic development in Chopin's *Préludes* are in perfect agreement with the composer's prior counterpoint studies.

At the Warsaw Conservatory, the young Chopin spent six hours every week learning strict counterpoint with Joseph Elsner (the conservatory curriculum mandated three years' study of counterpoint and composition). In his teaching

---

[46] Intriguingly, in Dan Hofstadter's translation of Sand's *Histoire* (New York: Harper & Row, 1979, p. 231), we read about 'snatches of funeral plainsong' (singular) rather than '*chants funèbres*' (plural), which are mentioned in Sand's book. Did Hofstadter know something no one else knew at the time? His translation describes what takes place in the *Préludes* even more accurately than the French original: there are indeed 'snatches of funeral plainsong,' rather than 'funeral chants.'

Example 4.7 (a) Kirnberger, *Die Kunst des reinen Satzes in der Musik*,
(b) Cherubini, *Cours de contrepoint et de fugue*

Elsner followed the tradition of Johann Philipp Kirnberger and Johann Georg Albrechtsberger, most probably using as textbooks the former's *Die Kunst des reinen Satzes in der Musik* (1774–79) and the latter's *Gründliche Anweisung zur Komposition* (1790).[47] Luigi Cherubini's textbook *Cours de contrepoint et de fugue* (1835) became available to Chopin later, in Paris.

These textbooks teach melodic permutations on the basis of relatively short melodic segments. In addition, both Kirnberger and Cherubini include an interesting retrograde procedure in their textbooks. They present initial melodies of two to three measures, and then continue on to retrograde and retrograde inversions of these melodies, but not in the usual manner, beginning with the last note of the entire melodic line and ending with the first one. Instead, their retrograde examples move forward from the beginning to the end of the melody, yet every single measure is given in retrograde or retrograde inversion (see Examples 4.7a, b).[48] The implication is that shorter melodic units facilitate the aural recognition of retrogrades and retrograde inversions.

The textbooks also divide all the imitations, including those in inversion and retrograde, into two categories. In a strict (also called regular or exact) imitation, the quality of melodic intervals does not change. In a simple (or free, or irregular) imitation, the quality of the melodic intervals need not be preserved.[49]

Chopin does not merely replicate the short motifs and their permutational developments contained in the *Dies irae* chant—instead, he vastly expands those,

---

[47] Halina Goldberg, *Music in Chopin's Warsaw* (Oxford: Oxford University Press, 2008), pp. 114–18.

[48] Johann Philipp Kirnberger, *Die Kunst des reinen Satzes in der Musik* (facsimile of the original edition of 1771–79) (Hildesheim: Georg Olms Verlagsbuchhandlung, 1968), part 1, p. 203; Luigi Cherubini, *A Course of Counterpoint and Fugue*, trans. J.A. Hamilton (London: R. Cocks & Co., 1841, originally published in 1835), vol. 1, pp. 164–5.

[49] Johann Georg Albrechtsberger, *Methods of Harmony, Figured Base, and Composition*, trans. Arnold Merrick (London: R. Cocks & Co., 1834), vol. 1, pp. 197, 217–18; vol. 2, pp. 243, 392; Cherubini, *A Course of Counterpoint and Fugue*, pp. 151–2.

Example 4.8 *Dies irae*, a complete chart of all the motifs

Lamartine's Les Préludes *and Chopin's* Préludes   63

employing various combinations of inversions and retrogrades. All the motivic permutations used in the *Préludes* are listed in Example 4.8.

Inversions always involve a fixed pitch between the original theme and its inverted form, the so-called axis of inversion, or the axis pitch. In tonal music, the axis of inversion is frequently the third scale degree, which divides the tonic triad. This way, the notes of the tonic triad always invert within this triad: the tonic third remains in place, the tonic root inverts into the tonic fifth, and vice versa (see, for instance, the inversions of the subject in Book 1 from *The Well-Tempered Clavier*, in Fugues in D minor, F♯ minor, G major, A minor, and B major).

In modal music, and especially in exact inversions, more often than not the axis of inversion is the note that divides the tritone (or, specifically, the diminished triad) in half, that is, D in 'the modes on white keys.' This axis pitch ensures, first of all, that there will be no unpleasant surprises due to the unexpected occurrence of a tritone, since one note of a tritone will invert into the other; and if a tritone is avoided in the original, it will not occur in the inversion. Second, the progression of tones (T) and semitones (S) proceeds symmetrically from D in either direction: T-S-T-T-S-T. Consequently, all melodic intervals in an inversion will be exactly the same as in the original, except for the direction.[50] Since the *Dies irae* is in the Hypodorian mode, the motivic chart in Example 4.8 holds D as the axis of inversion in most cases. One notable exception involves motif f and its inversion f^1: I simply copied this inversion from the chant (Example 4.6), where the axis pitch in this particular case is F.[51]

Did other contemporary composers employ a similar approach to thematic development of the *Dies irae*? Berlioz did not; the chant in his *Symphonie fantastique* only undergoes diminution. Alkan (two years before Opus 28) and Liszt (ten years after it), however, both employed the same devices, although not as extensively as Chopin, which is understandable: 'Morte' and *Totentanz* are much shorter works than the *Préludes*. Alkan used motifs a^1, a^2, a^3, b^1, c, c^1, c^3, d, d^1, d^2, d^3, e^1, e^2, e^3, e^4, e^6, and e^7; Liszt motifs a, a^1, a^2, a^6, b, b^5, b^6, c, c^1, c^2, d, e, and e^4. Even though Liszt did not quote stanzas 3 and 4 of the chant, he nevertheless introduced motifs f^1 and cc into the variations.

A few more issues need to be considered before we proceed to analyses of the *Préludes*. Several motifs included in Example 4.8 undergo partial inversions. Although this developmental procedure is normally not found in textbooks, composers by no means shy away from it in their music (see Example 4.9).

The motivic components of the *Dies irae*, as well as their derivatives, are not particularly distinguishable, especially the shorter ones. Melodically, they consist mainly of ascending and descending steps interspersed with occasional leaps;

---

[50]   Cherubini, *A Course of Counterpoint and Fugue*, pp. 160–63.

[51]   Incidentally, I seriously doubt that Chopin ever put down on paper either a motivic analysis of the *Dies irae* comparable to Example 4.6 or a chart of symmetrical permutations similar to Example 4.8. He probably heard all these details in his head without having the need to write them down.

Example 4.9 Beethoven, Piano Sonata, Op. 7, No. 3, movement 4, (a) mm. 87–89, (b) mm. 106–108

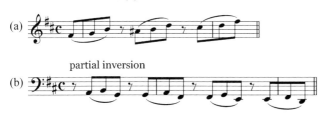

motif *b* is a brief sequence of broken thirds; motifs *e* and *f* are a perfect fourth and a perfect fifth, respectively, with a second attached to either end. In and of themselves, these motifs may not even be recognizable as segments of the *Dies irae* (save for the chant's four-note signature incipit) and can be found in many compositions that are not related to the somber medieval chant.

For example, Haydn's Sonata in E♭ major (Hob. XVI:49) opens with ascending broken thirds, G-B♭-A♭-C. Although this melodic gesture matches motif b^1, the likeness is purely coincidental. No other *Dies irae* motifs are present in the Sonata; consequently, there is no appropriate context for declaring this gesture to be part of the *Dies irae*. Even within Opus 28, had an entire prelude contained, say, only a single statement of motif *d* and nothing else, there would be no reason to attribute this gesture, E-F-E-D (or its transposition), to the *Dies irae*. What allows us to identify these thematic kernels as ingredients of the *Dies irae* is their context: in every prelude, these motifs always appear not as an isolated event but as a large group. For example, motif *d* does not appear alone in Prelude 15 (D♭ major); far from it. The piece also includes motifs *a*, a^4, *b*, b^2, *c*, cc^2, d^2, e^2, e^4, and f^4 (see pp. 113–15).

Moreover, when the *Dies irae* motifs are quoted in a prelude, they are usually repeated multiple times, which underscores their purposeful rather than incidental inclusion. Thus, motifs *d* and cc^3 are not individualized and may coincidentally occur in many musical works that have no connections to the *Dies irae*. If, however, they are repeated in the LH part of Prelude 3 (G major) persistently, in 29 out of 33 measures total, the chance that this occurrence is a coincidence is very low indeed (see pp. 79–80).

Shorter melodic gestures, such as *e*, *f*, and their derivatives, are even more generic than the *d* and *cc* motifs. In thematic analyses of the *Préludes* in the next chapter, these motifs will only be indicated if they occupy prominent positions: at the very beginning or very end of phrases, at climactic points, or in the course of multiple reiterations.

The nondescript nature of the *Dies irae* motifs and their permutations, as applied by Alkan, Chopin, and Liszt, closely corresponds to the equally unremarkable quality of thematic samples that demonstrate inversions and retrogrades in the textbooks of Kirnberger, Albrechtsberger, and Cherubini. The melodic motifs and their permutations, presented in these textbooks, lack any distinguishable individual features. These motifs are thematically neutral: they can undergo various symmetrical rearrangements without any perceivable distortion or loss of thematic integrity.

The inversion and retrograde examples from these textbooks are based on melodic patterns that are effectively modal (and therefore comparable to those in the *Dies irae*). Modal melodic structures are inherently more neutral than tonal ones. A modal melody contains only one stable note, the *tonus finalis*. The remaining modal scale degrees are all more or less equally unstable, without clear differentiation between them. The same is true for modal harmony, where any chord can generally follow any other chord within the same mode. As a result, melodic notes in pretonal music do not generate strong gravitational directions, which means that the listener does not have well-defined expectations after every melodic note or chord.

Tonal music, conversely, is based on clear differentiations between the stable (1st), relatively stable (3rd and 5th), and unstable scale degrees. Furthermore, the unstable scale degrees assume various levels of instability, depending on their harmonic function at any given moment. This interaction between melody and harmony largely determines melodic individuality and, consequently, expressivity.

For example, the intensity of a melodic note C changes dramatically when harmonized by the following chords and functions: chord A♭-C-E♭ (in A♭ major); G-B♭-C-E (in F minor); G♭-B♭-C-E (in B♭ minor); F-A-C-E♭ (in B♭ minor); B♭-D-F-A♭-C (in E♭ major); or E♭-G-D♭ (in A♭ major). I did not make up this chord series on a whim; rather, it is an actual chord progression that accompanies a melodic line that, despite being relatively static (mostly a reiterated C), is nonetheless one of the more beguiling and beloved tunes in Romantic music: Liszt's *Notturno III* from *Liebesträume*. Various functional harmonies impart different gravitational energies to the same note, C, and create certain expectations for continuation—which, of course, may or may not be realized.

Such gravitational energies, generated by tonal harmonic functions, are chiefly responsible for melodic individuality and expressiveness. That is why tonal music encompasses an immeasurable number of distinct, emotionally charged, instantly recognizable, and memorable melodies.

In one respect, though, modal melodies hold an advantage over the more individualized tonal melodies. Unlike the latter, modal melodies, due to their thematic neutrality, can undergo intervallic permutations with no perceivable distortion or loss of character. It is hard to imagine, for instance, the opening theme of Chopin's C♯-minor Waltz, Op. 64, No. 2, as being in inversion or retrograde. Conversely, a modal melody, including the *Dies irae*, neither loses nor gains its appeal after any symmetric permutation.

Even though the chant itself is modal (and medieval), we will see that Chopin's treatment of the *Dies irae* motifs is noticeably influenced by fugal techniques. Chant motifs find their place in all textural voices, and often in imitation. When the motifs are transposed to different keys, rather than staying in the original Hypodorian mode, the qualities of melodic intervals, as in a fugue subject, change accordingly (perfect intervals to diminished ones, major to minor, and so forth).

In fugues, abridged statements of the subject are common, especially in episodes; likewise, partial statements of the *Dies irae* motifs can often be heard in the *Préludes*.

Despite the fact that the *Dies irae* motifs are treated contrapuntally in Opus 28, they are embedded into homophonic rather than clearly defined polyphonic textures. The placement of the chant motifs crosses typical hierarchical boundaries between the melody and accompaniment; these motifs may appear in the melodic line, in the bass, or in the middle voices. Understandably (though, perhaps, regrettably), Chopin did not mark the voices of varied importance by indicating the *Hauptstimme* and *Nebenstimme*, as Schoenberg later did in his own compositions. But it is vital to know, for both the performance and the perception of the *Préludes*, where precisely in musical texture these motifs are located, just as it is critical to be aware of all the subject entries in a fugue. Furthermore, it is often up to the pianist to highlight and project these motifs as meaningful events.

The primary objective of the next chapter, therefore, is twofold: first, to pinpoint the motivic links that bond pairs of preludes together, and, second, to trace the most essential thematic material on which the *Préludes* are based—the *Dies irae* motifs—throughout the set.

Chapter 5
Deciphering the *Préludes*

Preludes 1 (C major) & 2 (A minor)

Prelude 1 (C major)

The opening prelude has been often compared to Bach's C-major Prelude from the first book of the *Well-Tempered Clavier*, since both C-major pieces consist of arpeggiated chords. Chopin's much shorter prelude is written in the form of a period, with the second phrase extended to almost three times the length of the first phrase (8 and 21 measures, respectively). The main melodic voice is carried by the RH thumb until m. 29, when a higher middle voice in RH takes over. The broadly molded, undulating melody is placed in the sensuous-sounding middle range and is reverberated in upper octaves. The continuous offbeats (except in mm. 18–20 and 25–26) infuse the melody with almost hyperventilating excitement.[1]

The *Dies irae* motifs are so well concealed in Prelude 1, which serves as an ebullient 'prelude' to No. 2, that without knowing in advance what to look for, they would be nearly impossible to find. In reality, the C-major Prelude includes as many as ten *Dies irae* motifs: a^2, a^3, a^4, b, c^1, d^2, d^3, f^1, f^2, and f^4. They are seamlessly woven into the melody and the bass. The bass line commences with motif a^2 in mm. 1–4; after a^2 returns in mm. 9–12, it is followed by motif d^2 in mm. 13–16. The last two notes of d^2 in the bass overlap with the beginning of c^1 in mm. 15–20 (Example 5.1).

The oscillating, trill-like melodic figure, heard in mm. 1–3, 5–7, and 9–11 (see Example 5.1), is ubiquitous in Opus 28.[2] At its first entrance, in mm. 1–3, the origin of this gesture is unclear, but not for long. When the same oscillating figure comes back two measures later, its provenance becomes obvious. The first three notes of this gesture, E-D-E in mm. 5–6, belong to a^4, while the next three notes

---

[1] Some pianists emphasize the last two treble notes in every measure instead of the melodic line an octave lower. In my view, this approach seems less successful. First, it eliminates the subtle but nevertheless expressive shifts between the times when the melodic notes appear *after* the downbeats or *on* the downbeats, as in mm. 18–20 and 25–26. Second, consigning the melody to the second half of every measure turns refined exhilaration into unstoppable hiccups.

[2] See Jim Samson, *The Music of Chopin* (London: Routledge & Kegan Paul, 1985), p. 79; and see Andreas Boelcke's DMA dissertation 'Chopin's 24 *Préludes*, Opus 28: A Cycle Unified by Motion between the Fifth and Sixth Scale Degrees' (University of Cincinnati, 2008).

68 *The Mystery of Chopin's* Préludes

begin *a³*, so that *a⁴* and *a³* are linked as symmetrical reflections of each other—forming the oscillating figure in question (Example 5.1).

Looking back from this vantage point, the similar but inverted oscillating gesture in the opening three measures of the Prelude can reasonably be construed as abbreviated motifs *a*, or, as the case may be, *a¹* and later, in mm. 8–10, *a* (without the last note). At the end of m. 2, the abridged *a¹* interlocks with *c¹*, also shortened by one note. A complete and almost identical statement of *c¹* returns in mm. 10–13 and is then imitated an octave lower in the bass in mm. 15–20. Simultaneously with the beginning of *c¹* in the bass, motif *b²* is stated in the melody (see Example 5.1; shortened motifs are enclosed in parentheses in music examples).

The *f* motifs are introduced in mm. 22–28, when *f¹* occurs in the bass. Before *f¹* is over, *f³* and *f⁴* interlock with each other in the melodic line in quick succession (see Example 5.1).[3]

Finally, mm. 29–32 contain a persistently repeated *b* (A-F-G-E). In a rushed, breathless excitement, the last two notes of motif *b* (G and E) are fused and sound simultaneously rather than consecutively (Example 5.1).

The conversion of melodic thirds into harmonic ones is not at all unusual. In fact, this transformation is described in Johann Philipp Kirnberger's textbook, which illustrates how melodies consisting of broken thirds can be reconsidered in a vertical alignment (Example 5.2).[4]

The Links

The opening diptych of Preludes is joined together by both shared single pitches and common short motifs. One shared melodic pitch, like a linchpin, connects the concluding E in RH of the C-major Prelude with the opening E in RH of the A-minor Prelude. But there is more than a single shared pitch between the preludes. A look beyond modern editions reveals yet another common pitch.

In the last two measures of Chopin's autograph, three LH ties connect three bass notes, C-G-C (mm. 33–34). The last measure, however, includes a discernible E in LH just above the bass C, with no additional tie leading to it (see Figure 5.1). Two early impressions of the French first edition, based on Chopin's manuscript, as well as the English first edition (which derives from the second impression of the French first edition), also contain this additional E in LH. Moreover, a personal copy of the second impression of the French edition, belonging to Chopin's pupil Marie Scherbatoff, includes the composer's markings and corrections; the low E is not crossed out in Scherbatoff's score

---

[3]   Other partitions into motifs *f* are also possible—for instance, E-D-G (*f²*), starting with the downbeat in m. 24. Having various interpretational possibilities at the performer's disposal should be considered a positive rather than negative circumstance.

[4]   Kirnberger, *Die Kunst des reinen Satzes in der Musik*, Part 1, p. 209.

Example 5.1   Chopin, Prelude 1 from Opus 28

Example 5.2 Kirnberger, *Die Kunst des reinen Satzes in der Musik*

(Example 5.3a). Only in the German first edition, based on Fontana's copy of Chopin's manuscript, is the low E absent.[5]

This note is also missing, unfortunately, in all the later editions of Opus 28. Furthermore, the Paderewski and the Ekier editions categorically declare the low E erroneous.[6] Indeed, it is difficult to justify the sudden and seemingly inexplicable appearance of the low E in the last measure of the Prelude, unless we fully realize that Prelude 1 introduces Prelude 2, and that the LH E in the last measure of Prelude 1 serves as a connector between the two preludes—the same E reappears as the opening bass note in Prelude 2. This pitch plays yet another role: it generates a disquieting shift from the tranquil C-major arpeggio to a foreboding chord with the touch of E minor that portends the gloom of Prelude 2 (see Examples 5.3a, b). This shift can become even more conspicuous if a pianist plays the last two measures of Prelude 1 ritardando and diminuendo, and especially if the performer slightly desynchronizes the bass and the treble Es in a typical nineteenth-century manner.

Figure 5.1 Chopin's manuscript, Prelude 1, mm. 29–34

In addition to the shared pitches, Preludes 1 and 2 are linked by two common motifs. They are introduced consecutively: E-D (mm. 5–7, marked by circles in Example 5.4a) and B-A-G (mm. 8–9, indicated by triangles in Example 5.4a). Then, in mm. 22–24, they come back in reverse order, B-A-G and E-D (Example 5.4b). In mm. 25–32, until the concluding C-major chord, these two motifs are repeated multiple times (motif B-A-G is retrograded and effectively truncated,

---

[5] See Fryderyk Chopin, *Préludes Op. 28, Op. 45*, ed. Jean-Jacques Eigeldinger. The Complete Chopin: A New Critical Edition (London: Edition Peters, 2003), p. 63.

[6] Chopin, *Preludes*, ed. Ignacy J. Paderewski, 30th edn (Cracow: PWM, 2001), p. 64; Chopin, *Preludes Opp. 28, 45*, ed. Jan Ekier (Warsaw: PWM, 2000), Source Commentary, p. 6.

Example 5.3 (a) Chopin, Prelude 1, mm. 28–34, (b) Prelude 2, mm. 1–4

since B is first placed in the middle voice and practically dissolves in the surrounding harmony and then disappears altogether; Example 5.4b). Prelude 2 opens with motif E-D doubled in the bass and the treble, while the tenor carries motif B-A-G in mm. 1–6 (see the notes in circles and triangles in Example 5.4c).

Prelude 2 (A minor)

Of all Chopin's œuvre, no piece was so objectionable to listeners and critics as his Prelude in A minor. Some earlier criticisms contended that the prelude was 'ugly, forlorn, despairing, almost grotesque, and discordant,' and that it 'ought not to be played, as it is bizarre.'[7] André Gide declared that this Prelude was 'not a concert piece,' and that he could not imagine 'any audience liking it.'[8] Even today pianists rarely, if ever, include it in their programs unless the entire set is performed.

Indeed, Prelude 2 is anything but appealing. Its melody is not at all Chopinesque: it is rigid and monotonous, rather than pliant and expressive. The LH accompaniment consists of bizarre alternations between hollow and sharply dissonant intervals. The LH part becomes even more dissonant in mm. 18–19, where the pedal prescribed by Chopin blurs together the minor second C-B with the minor ninth E-F.

The Prelude lacks the clarity of form. Harmonically, it meanders about for a long time until the main key, A minor, materializes toward the end (in m. 15 out of 23 measures total). The final two and a half measures unexpectedly and

---

[7] James Huneker, *Chopin: The Man and His Music* (New York: C. Scribner's Sons, 1900; rpt. 1923), p. 221; George Charles Ashton Jonson, *A Handbook to Chopin's Works*, 2nd edn (London: W. Reeves, 1908), p. 173.

[8] André Gide, *Notes on Chopin*, trans. Bernard Frechtman (New York: Philosophical Library, 1949), p. 46.

72 *The Mystery of Chopin's* Préludes

Example 5.4 (a) Chopin, Prelude 1, mm. 1–9

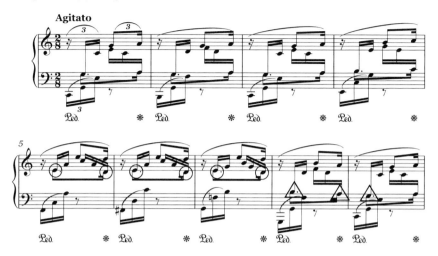

Example 5.4 (b) Prelude 1, mm. 21–34,

Example 5.4 continued (c) Prelude 2, mm. 1–7

without any obvious justification introduce a passage that Jeffrey Kresky finds 'oddly church-like.'[9]

Many critics have attempted to explain the oddities of the A-minor Prelude, with varied degrees of success.[10] The largely unappreciated value of Prelude 2 is that it provides, as the very first minor-mode prelude in the cycle, the key to the understanding of the entire cycle; consequently, it sets the tone for all the following pieces and, retroactively, casts a somber shadow on Prelude 1, as well.

To begin with, the presence of the *Dies irae* in Prelude 2 is much more conspicuous than in the other preludes. The plainchant spawns both the melody and the accompaniment of the piece. An outline of the chant's beginning can be heard initially in LH, which plays motif *a* of the *Dies irae*. On a first glance at the score, neither of the two accompanying voices seems to contain a coherent melody (see Example 5.4c).

---

[9] Jeffrey Kresky, *A Reader's Guide to the Chopin Preludes* (Westport, CT: Greenwood Press, 1994), p. 12.

[10] See, for example, Leonard B. Meyer, *Emotion and Meaning in Music* (Chicago: Chicago University Press, 1956), pp. 93–7; Heinrich Schenker, *Free Composition*, trans. and ed. Ernst Oster (New York: Longman, 1979), Example 110 No. a3; Rose Rosengard Subotnik, 'Romantic Music as Post-Kantian Critique: Classicism, Romanticism, and the Concept of the Semiotic Universe,' in Kingsley Price (ed.), *On Criticizing Music: Five Philosophical Perspectives* (Baltimore, MD: Johns Hopkins University Press, 1981), pp. 88–95; Jean-Jacques Eigeldinger, 'Twenty-Four Preludes, Op. 28: Genre, Structure, Significance,' in Jim Samson (ed.), *Chopin Studies* (Cambridge: Cambridge University Press, 1988), pp. 175–6; Lawrence Kramer, *Music as Cultural Practice, 1800–1900* (Berkeley: University of California Press, 1990), pp. 72–101; Jeffrey Kresky, *A Reader's Guide to the Chopin Preludes*, pp. 9–13. An extensive review of analytical writings on the A-minor Prelude is presented by Jim Samson in his *The Music of Chopin* (London: Routledge & Kegan Paul, 1985), pp. 143–58.

In actual sound, however, the upper note of every odd interval and the lower note of every even interval form motif *a*. This motif emerges because we tend to perceive adjacent pitches as an unbroken melodic line, even if they ostensibly belong to different voices. Moreover, Chopin himself conceived this melody entirely within one part rather than dividing it between the middle voice and the bass. The composer's original notation of the first two measures proves that, beyond any doubt. Although this notation, in which the motif B-A♯-B-G is united by upward stems and a single beam, is not reproduced in most publications, it is retained in several Urtext editions (Example 5.3b).[11]

It may be somewhat painful for a pianist with smaller hands to play the widely spaced LH intervals legato and without the sustaining pedal (one must always respect Chopin's painstaking pedal markings—or, in this particular case, in mm. 1–17, the lack thereof). Another notational variant, found in George Sand's handwritten copy of Prelude 2 and most probably suggested or, at least, approved by Chopin, facilitates performance. In this little-known version, the top notes in mm. 1–5, 8–16, and 18–19 are played by the RH thumb, while LH carries motif *a* legato with ease (Example 5.5).[12]

Example 5.5   Chopin, Prelude 2, mm. 1–8 in George Sand's copy

---

[11]   See, for example, the Norton Critical Score: Fryderyk Chopin, *Preludes, Opus 28*, ed. Thomas Higgins (New York: W.W. Norton, 1973), p. 12; Fryderyk Chopin, *Preludes Opp. 28, 45*, ed. Jan Ekier (Warsaw: PWM, 2000); Fryderyk Chopin, *Préludes Op. 28, Op. 45*, ed. Jean-Jacques Eigeldinger. The Complete Chopin: A New Critical Edition (London: Edition Peters, 2003), p. 3.

[12]   *Korespondencja Fryderyka Chopina z George Sand I z jej dziećmi*, ed. Krystyna Kobylańska (Warsaw: Państwowy Instytut Wydawniczy, 1981), vol. I, plate 27. This version is also referred to in Fryderyk Chopin, *Préludes Op. 28, Op. 45*, ed. Jean-Jacques Eigeldinger, p. 63.

Example 5.6   Prelude 2

The origin of the uncharacteristically austere melody in Prelude 2 can also be traced back to the *Dies irae*. The treble consists almost exclusively of motifs a^6, e, and e^4, often interlocked. The last motif a in m. 19 (C-B-C-A in LH) is then imitated in the treble in an abridged form (B-C-A) in mm. 21–23 (see Example 5.6).

Each of the first three melodic phrases in the Prelude ends on a dotted-rhythm repetition of one pitch; in mm. 20–23 the dotted-rhythm figure is placed in the middle of the phrase. This particular gesture is rhythmically and melodically identical to the opening of Chopin's funeral march from Piano Sonata, Op. 35;

76   *The Mystery of Chopin's* Préludes

the similarly swaying accompaniment in the left hand of the march underscores the correlation.

Doleful references to funeral marches are no strangers to Chopin's music. Even though he wrote only one piece titled as such—the early C-minor *Marche funèbre* (ca. 1826)—he injected elements of funeral march into many of his other compositions. From the French revolutionary composers to Beethoven, Tchaikovsky, and Mahler, the nineteenth-century funeral march was consistently characterized by: (1) the minor mode, (2) duple meter, (3) regular stride in a slow tempo, and (4) melodic line of a limited range, frequently with dotted rhythms and repeated notes. Under these criteria, the slow introduction of Chopin's F-minor *Fantaisie*, Op. 49, for example, is a straightforward, though undesignated, funeral march. Four out of Chopin's six duple-meter nocturnes in the minor mode (Op. 27, No. 1—in RH part; Op. 37, No. 1; Op. 48, No. 1; and Op. 55, No. 1) are also marked by funeral-march traits.

The last two and a half measures of the A-minor Prelude introduce yet another ecclesiastic allusion, in addition to the *Dies irae*: a chorale. Chopin wrote only two works for the church, both of them for the wedding of his former pupil Sofia Rosengardt to Bohdan Zaleski in 1846. One of them was a *Veni creator* (the unpublished autograph might still exist in a private collection); the other piece remains unidentified. The composer also took organ lessons in his teenage years and after 1825 regularly played for church services in Warsaw on the organ, the *aeolomelodikon*, and the *choraleon* (the last two were newly invented instruments related to the organ). Subsequently, stylized chorales appeared within some of Chopin's works, although only one such chorale was marked *religioso* (Nocturne, Op. 15, No. 3).[13]

The interchangeability of melodic and harmonic thirds, which Chopin introduced into Opus 28 in Prelude 1, and which Kirnberger had brought up, sheds a new light at the chorale ending of Prelude 2. In mm. 21–22, there is a perfectly unremarkable progression, V-V/V-V (see Example 5.6). This progression features three parallel thirds in the middle voices in RH, from the top notes down: G♯-E, F♯-D♯, and G♯-E (see the square brackets in Example 5.6, mm. 21–22). The first two thirds, when viewed melodically instead of harmonically, spell motif *b*. The upper line, in combination with the last harmonic third, can also be heard as motif *a*: G♯-F♯-G♯-E (Example 5.6). A fusion of these two motifs is logical: they converge in the chant, as well, since the last two notes of *a* serve as the first two pitches of *b*.

It is, however, ultimately up to the performer whether to play these three chords as an ordinary chord progression or to project the thirds as a meaningful thematic event. One performing possibility is to highlight these parallel thirds rather than the

---

[13]   In its most manifest form, chorale can be heard in Nocturne, Op. 37, No. 1 (the middle section), in *Fantaisie*, Op. 49 (*Lento sostenuto*), and in *Polonaise-Fantaisie*, Op. 61 (mm. 148–52). In addition, Chopin occasionally combined chorale with other genres: march (Nocturne, Op. 48, No. 1, midsection), funeral march (the C-minor Prelude), and even mazurka (the A-major Prelude from Op. 28, see pp. 92–3).

Deciphering the Préludes 77

repeated B in the upper voice, playing them legato (without the sustaining pedal, of course) while the other voices move along in a slightly disconnected manner. After the parallel thirds, the emphasis may shift to the upper voice, which imitates the last three notes of *a*, B-C-A, from mm. 18–19 (LH part in Example 5.6).

The chorale fragment in the Prelude is not tragic per se. Its sorrowful connotation is contextually induced: immersed in a milieu dominated by the *Dies irae* and funeral march, this otherwise ordinary chorale becomes part of the pervading mournful discourse. Similarly, the hermeneutic meaning of the swaying accompanimental figures in the reverberating lower register is contextually induced: within the given milieu, this accompanimental pattern evokes the funereal tolling of church bells.[14]

Unlike the *Dies irae* quotations, the references to funeral march, chorale, and funereal knell can be considered nonquotational allusions.[15] None of these references is highly conspicuous: Chopin dissembles each of them in his typically understated manner, staying away from the programmatic proclamations of mainstream Romanticism. But all four of these allusions aim toward one focal point, collectively helping us open 'a hermeneutic window' on this music (using Lawrence Kramer's expression[16]) and to perceive its symbolic meaning: death.

This hermeneutic reading of the A-minor Prelude may well account for its unorthodox tonal structure. As many commentators have noted, the Prelude has an unusually ambiguous tonal construction. The opening E-minor chord can be construed as the minor dominant of the main key, but only retrospectively.[17] After the E-minor chord, the highly dissonant harmonies drift through G major and D major in mm. 4–10. Any traditional functional analysis of the following few measures, until the preparation of the final cadence at the end of m. 14, simply proves inadequate. Only the final three measures—by the time both the *Dies irae* and the funeral march are over and the concluding chorale replaces them—contribute consonant harmonies and functional clarity.

The unique (for the 1830s) disintegration of tonal structure parallels the symbolic meaning of the Prelude. The singularly desolate character of the Prelude evokes the most terrifying, entropic aspect of death: 'destruction, ruin, and decay.'[18]

The image of death as disintegration is contained in the text of the *Dies irae* ('the world will dissolve in ashes'), and is one of the leading threads in Gothic fiction in particular and Romantic literature in general. Lamartine describes a slow

---

[14] A similar swaying, bell-ringing pattern is heard in the accompaniment of Chopin's march from Opus 35.

[15] V.A. Howard defines the 'nonquotational allusion' as referring to 'the more global, ubiquitous features of a musical genre or style rather than denoting specific passages' ('On Musical Quotation,' *The Monist*, 58/2 [1974], p. 309).

[16] Kramer, *Music as Cultural Practice*, pp. 9–10.

[17] Samson, *The Music of Chopin*, p. 144.

[18] William Shakespeare, *Richard II*, Act III, Scene 2.

78 *The Mystery of Chopin's* Préludes

corrosion 'under the rust of fate.'[19] In Shelley's words, 'Life, like a dome of many-coloured glass, / Stains the white radiance of Eternity, / Until Death tramples it to fragments.'[20] Adam Mickiewicz, Chopin's favorite poet, later used a similar allegory in his folkloristic verse drama *Forefathers' Eve*: 'Death has cracked the house of clay.'[21] Likewise, the invocation of death in Prelude 2 crumbles the foundations of tonality.

The above analysis of the A-minor Prelude is important not only because it ascertains the Prelude's symbolic meaning. Many musicians have recognized that meaning intuitively, without delving into analytical depths. James Huneker declared that, in this Prelude, 'there is aversion to life.'[22] One nineteenth-century poetic description, attributed to Hans von Bülow and titled 'Presentiment of Death,' described the mood of the Prelude through such metaphors as 'the melancholy tolling of a funeral knell' and 'the inexorable voice of death.'[23]

The detailed analysis of the A-minor Prelude is helpful in two respects—for an exploration of the piece itself and for its role in decoding the entire cycle. Diagnostic medicine uses a concept called the index of suspicion. Put in simple terms, it means that if a clinician does not think of a certain possibility, he or she will never find it.[24] The identification of topics in Prelude 2, particularly the *Dies irae*, supplies strong impetuses for further investigation. I played Opus 28 for many years but never recognized the presence of the *Dies irae* in the preludes. Only after analyzing the A-minor Prelude, and after my index of suspicion was sufficiently raised to include the *Dies irae*, was I able to hear its motifs in all the other preludes, which, in turn, led to other findings: connections to Lamartine's *Les Préludes*, cyclic links between the preludes, and so forth.

Preludes 3 (G major) & 4 (E minor)

Prelude 3 (G major)

The serene *perpetuum mobile* of Prelude 3 is written as a period consisting of two phrases. In late eighteenth- and early nineteenth-century piano music, fast perpetual motion in the accompaniment did not necessarily carry any allusive significance—until Franz Schubert's *Die Schöne Müllerin*. In that hugely popular and influential song cycle, the brook is the most faithful companion of the young journeyman: his best and, in fact, only friend. Throughout the cycle the brook

---

[19]   Alphonse de Lamartine, *Les Préludes*, Canto V, l. 28.
[20]   Percy Bysshe Shelley, *Adonais: An Elegy on the Death of John Keats*, 52.
[21]   Adam Mickiewicz, *Forefathers' Eve*, Part II.
[22]   Huneker, *Chopin*, p. 221.
[23]   Rosengard Subotnik, 'Romantic Music as Post-Kantian Critique,' pp. 94–5.
[24]   Richard W.O. Beebe and Deborah L. Funk, *Fundamentals of Emergency Care* (Albany, NY: Delmar, 2001), vol. 1, p. 294.

is portrayed by an incessant flow of fast notes in the accompaniment. The LH part in the G-major Prelude continues this tradition, quite possibly alluding to Lamartine's depictions of running streams.

The question may be raised, of course, whether attempts to draw parallels between Schubert and Chopin are justified. Interestingly, in Chopin's day these parallels were widely accepted. According to one review of a recital the latter composer gave in 1841, 'in Chopin's works one finds the same delightful perfection of harmony and melody' as in the music of Schubert. Another critic begins his review with a discussion of Schubert 'because there is no one else so similar to Chopin. The one has done for the piano what the other has done for the voice. Both have drawn their many-splendored, tender, sad, and passionate inspirations from the same well.' The reviewer comes to the conclusion that Chopin's compositions featured in that concert are 'destined to become as popular as the most beautiful of Schubert's melodies.'[25] Needless to say, Chopin frequently heard Schubert's songs in concerts and even performed them on occasion.[26]

The rippling accompaniment is meaningful in other respects beyond its illustrative role. This accompaniment participates in a polyphonic interplay with the RH melody, as Kresky points out.[27] Example 5.7 shows, in a somewhat more extended and detailed way than Kresky's example, how the treble mirrors, in augmentation and with a vertical rearrangement, some salient points of the accompaniment.

Example 5.7   Chopin, Prelude 3, imitation between LH and RH, (a) LH, m. 1, (b) RH, mm. 3–6

As for the *Dies irae* motifs, the accompaniment part is brimming with continually reiterated motifs d and cc^3 (Example 5.8a). The RH melody also consists almost entirely of *Dies irae* motifs. At the beginning of No. 3, the RH part contains a fusion of motifs e^5 (B-E-D) and a^3 (in parallel and overcrossing thirds and sixths; B-C-B-G and D-E-D-B), followed by a repeated motif e^3 (see Example 5.8a). Example 5.8b illustrates how motif d^3 shapes the melody in mm. 16–18; the

---

[25] William G. Atwood, *Fryderyk Chopin: Pianist from Warsaw* (New York: Columbia University Press, 1987), pp. 234–6.
[26] Ibid., pp. 48, 99, 101, 124, 150, 218, and 226.
[27] Kresky, *A Reader's Guide*, p. 16.

Example 5.8 (a) Chopin, Prelude 3, mm. 1–10

last three notes of this motif coincide with the beginning of motif *a* (mm. 17–20). Immediately afterward, the RH melody concludes with overlapping motifs *a* and a^7 (mm. 21–26; Example 5.8b).

The Links

Preludes 3 and 4 are joined together through common pitches as well as shared motifs. One of the common pitches is G, the top note in the concluding chords in LH (Example 5.9); the same G is repeated in the bass of m. 1 in No. 4 (Example 5.10a). The other link is the result of Chopin's later addition: as Eigeldinger

Example 5.8 (b) Prelude 3, mm. 16–26

affirms, the sketch for No. 4 clearly shows that the ascending octave B-B in the pickup of No. 4 was inserted afterward (Example 5.10a).[28] This is the same octave that frames the repeated G-major chord in RH in the last two measures of No. 3.

To find common motifs that unite the Preludes, it is helpful to look for a clue in mm. 28–31 in Prelude 3. This segment of the Prelude may appear to be excessively repetitive and therefore superfluous. One can easily imagine skipping from m. 27 directly to m. 32, playing G rather than D on the downbeat of m. 32, and then finishing the Prelude with the last two chords.

---

[28] Jean-Jacques Eigeldinger, 'Twenty-Four Preludes Op. 28: Genre, Structure, Significance,' in Jim Samson (ed.), *Chopin Studies* (Cambridge: Cambridge University Press, 1988), p. 180.

Reiteration, however, as is often the case, demonstrates the composer's intention. The running sixteenths at the end of No. 3 include two melodic gestures: the first is E-D-C-B-A (sixteenth notes marked by '+' in mm. 26–29, Example 5.7), and the other is B-A-G and its inversion G-A-B (asterisked sixteenth notes in mm. 26–31, Example 5.9).

Example 5.9   Chopin, Prelude 3, mm. 26–33

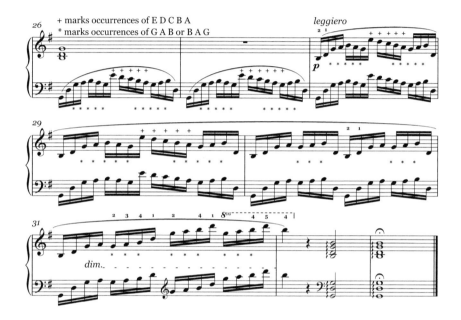

In Prelude 4, the upper voice in LH in mm. 1–12 repeats the first gesture, E-D-C-B-A, with a couple of chromatic fill-ins. At the same time, the melody in mm. 4–8 presents the second gesture, also in a chromatically modified form: B-B♭-A-G♯ (Example 5.10a). The motif B-A-G comes back in the upper voice of LH, in mm. 20–23 of Prelude 4, first in its original diatonic form, B-A-G, and then chromatically varied, B♭-A-G♯-G (Example 5.10b).

Prelude 4

In an insightful analysis of Prelude 4, Carl Schachter states the following:

> The 5-6-5 and 6-5 neighbor-tone figures in minor have a long association with the affect of grief (inherited from Phrygian compositions of the Renaissance); and minor-mode basses descending chromatically to 5 (also embodying Phrygian characteristics) have been lament figures since the seventeenth century. Semitonal

Example 5.10 (a) Chopin, Prelude 4, mm. 1–12, (b) Prelude 4, mm. 20–23

intensity combined with downward motion seems an appropriate musical analogue to actions and feelings associated with loss, sadness, and death.[29]

Schachter concludes that the E-minor Prelude's motivic design and other stylistic aspects render it as 'a vision of death' and relate 'to countless explicitly death-oriented pieces—funeral marches, threnodies, operatic scenes, and the like.'[30] In an earlier article, Eigeldinger finds a referential angle that strengthens Schachter's assertion. According to Eigeldinger, in the E-minor Prelude 'the layout of the left hand, with its chords in close position, cloaks the descending, chromatic movement of three independent lines'; this motion 'represents Chopin's response to the harmonic polyphony of the "Crucifixus" from the B-minor Mass.'[31]

---

[29] Carl Schachter, 'The Triad as Place and Action,' *Music Theory Spectrum*, 17/2 (Fall 1995), p. 152.

[30] Ibid.

[31] Eigeldinger, 'Twenty-Four Preludes,' p. 176.

Example 5.11   Bach, Crucifixus, mm. 1–4

Example 5.12   Chopin, Prelude 4, mm. 1–10 (LH)

Example 5.13   Bach, Crucifixus, mm. 5–14 (chorus reduction)

Deciphering the Préludes

Eigeldinger's observation can be expanded further. The E-minor Prelude, obviously, is written in the same key as the 'Crucifixus.' The ostinato figure in the bass of the 'Crucifixus,' a chromatic descent from E to B (the so-called *passus duriusculus*, Example 5.11), finds its way into the Prelude, as well. It first appears in the upper line of the LH part (mm. 1–8); then it is imitated, in a *stretto* fashion, in the bass (mm. 6–10; see Example 5.12). During the second half of the Prelude, this chromatic descending gesture gradually disintegrates.

The staggered choral parts in the 'Crucifixus' (immediately following the orchestral introduction) outline the melodic contour of four pairs of pitches: B-C; F♮-E; A-F♯; F♯-E in mm. 5–13 (Example 5.13). Prelude 4 includes identical pairs of pitches, usually reiterated. These notes are marked by '+' signs in Example 5.14: B-C in the melody (mm. 1/2, 2/3, 3/4, 13/14, 14/15, 15/16; F♮-E in the bass (mm. 3–4); A-F♯ in the melody (mm. 9–11). The melodic closure of the Prelude, except for the final three chords, unites the last two pairs of pitches, A-F♯ and F♯-E (mm. 18–23). This ending, in fact, imitates the same gesture that first appears in the LH top voice in m. 17 (Example 5.14).

In the 'Crucifixus' the top melodic line in mm. 13–14 is formed by F♯-E in the altos and G-A♯-B-C-B in the sopranos (Example 5.13). A retrograde of the latter motif, B-C-B-A♯-G, surfaces in mm. 15–16 of the Prelude, followed by the first of these two gestures, F♯-E, at the end of m. 16; see pitches indicated by 'x' in Example 5.14. The first four notes in the Prelude's melody in m. 12 (G-F♯-C-B) may be a reflection of the choral incipit in the 'Crucifixus' (C-B-F♮-E): two descending semitones separated by an augmented fourth, with one semitone (C-B) identical in both cases.

In the last three measures, the 'Crucifixus' modulates to G major, with the concluding G-major tonic featuring B in the top voice. Similarly, but in reverse, the E-minor Prelude is preceded by a G-major Prelude in which the concluding tonic has B in the melody. The key reversal actually renders the E-minor Prelude more desolate than the 'Crucifixus.' While the chorus leads from E minor to G major, from death to revival—and to the 'Et resurrexit' as the next movement in the Mass—the Prelude's path proceeds in the opposite direction.

The *Dies irae* references in Prelude 4 are quite intermittent and far less noticeable than in the previous minor prelude, No. 2, most probably because Bach's 'Crucifixus' and the *Dies irae* chant have so little in common thematically. Nevertheless, the two works share one element. As I have already mentioned, the melodic commencement of Prelude 4 reflects the choral incipit of the 'Crucifixus.' In the Prelude, however, the semitone B-C turns into an obsessively persistent oscillation between pitches B and C: it is reiterated in the melody (mm. 1–4 and 13–16) and then restated multiple times in the bass in mm. 9–12 and 18–22 (Example 5.14).

Once again, repetition suggests intention. Continual trill-like oscillations were first heard in Prelude 1, where they were the outcome of the symmetrically conjoined motifs a^4 and a^3. At the same time, the alternating pitches B and C in Prelude 4 hark back to the end of Prelude 2. When A-minor was finally established

Example 5.14   Chopin, Prelude 4, mm. 1–23 (Crucifixus motifs)

+ marks occurrences of C-B; F♮-E; A-F♯; F♯-E
× marks occurrences of B-C-B-A♯-G

in No. 2, these pitches were part of motif *a* (C-B-C-A in LH in mm. 15–16 and 18–19; see Example 5.6). The same pitches also appeared in Prelude 2 in the abridged imitation of *a* in RH in m. 22 (Example 5.6).

Abridged statements of fugue subjects are common in a fugue's episodes; likewise, thematic fragmentation is a normal developmental procedure in homophonic music. Chopin uses this compositional technique in the *Préludes*, as well, regardless whether its origin is polyphonic or homophonic. In Prelude 2, an abbreviated motif *a* is missing its first note. In Prelude 4, on the contrary, the first three pitches of *a* are present and the last note is omitted. And it is hardly a coincidence that this partial statement of *a* in No. 4 consists of exactly the same notes (B and C) as motif *a* at the conclusion of Prelude 2.

The ending of the shortened *a* in the top voice of No. 4 (mm. 1–5) overlaps with *d* in mm. 3–5, with an added chromatic passing tone: B-C-B-(B♭)-A. In mm. 7–9, motifs d^3 (B-A-G♯-A) and d^1 (A-G♯-A B) are interlocked symmetrically in a palindrome (Example 5.15a). In the second half of the Prelude, in mm. 15–16, motif *d* appears as a chromatic version in RH (B-C-B-A♯; see Example 5.15b). At the climactic point in m. 17, the melody outlines—save for the wide leap to the top C—motif a^2; this is followed by b^1 in mm. 17–18 (Example 5.15b). The Prelude concludes with motif a^7 in RH in mm. 19–21, supplemented by a chromatic variant of *d* in the bass in mm. 20–23 (B-C-B-B♭; Example 5.15b).

Example 5.15 (a) Chopin, Prelude 4, mm. 7–9 (RH), (b) Prelude 4, mm. 17–23

Example 5.16   Chopin, Prelude 5

Preludes 5 (D major) & 6 (B minor)

Prelude 5 (D major)

A current of fast sixteenths, set in motion by the previous two major-mode pieces (in C major and G major), resumes in the D-major Prelude. The prelude also evokes another parallel with Schubert. The alternating major and minor seconds in the melodic line of Prelude 5 (eighth notes B-A, B♭-A), as well as other major-minor fluctuations (compare m. 7 with m. 8, m. 15 with m. 16, and mm. 6–7 with mm. 22–23 in Example 5.16), are all reminiscent of Schubert's characteristic chiaroscuro effects.

Prelude 5 opens with an obsessively repeated trill-like figure (mm. 1–4). This oscillating figure—as a whole step—was introduced in Prelude 1, primarily in a combination of motifs a^4 and a^3. In the E-minor Prelude, the same oscillating figure—as a half step—breaks away from a and acquires a life of its own as a relatively independent thematic event. In Prelude 5, this oscillating gesture, repeated in mm. 17–20 as well, alternates between whole steps and half steps. In mm. 12–16, this two-note theme shifts to LH and consists of only half steps (alternating C♯ and D), while in mm. 29–32 the same thematic element is transposed down a third, consisting of B♭ and A. All in all, this trill-like theme appears in mm. 1–4, 12–20, and 29–32—in 17 measures out of 39 measures total.

Another partial statement of a *Dies irae* motif originates in the ending of Prelude 2, where the first note of motif a is cut off and the other three notes, B-C-A, remain. A retrograde of this partial motif, A-C(♯)-B, is molded by the last three sixteenths in RH in m. 6 of the D-major Prelude (Example 5.16). Then it comes back, either at the same pitch level or transposed, at the end of every measure in mm. 8–11 and 22–27 (Example 5.16).

Besides these two persistently reiterated partial motifs, few complete *Dies irae* motifs can be found in Prelude 5. I could point out motifs e, e^3, e^4, f, f^2, and f^4, but they are rather inconspicuous, buried in continuous runs of sixteenths in RH (Example 5.16). A more discernible motif is a^3 in mm. 16–17; and the most prominent motif here is b^1, which is used repeatedly in the last four sixteenth notes of every measure in mm. 6, 9–11, 22–23, and 25–27 (Example 5.16).

The Links

The pairing of Preludes 5 and 6 is not immediately evident, until we consider the role of the LH part in No. 6. This cello-like melody carries a double function: the harmonic bass (often adorned with an arpeggio), and the melodic line. It is only logical to presume that a common motif can be found in the LH part of Prelude 5, as well.

One of these common melodic gestures is D-C♯-D, which is heard in LH of No. 6 in m. 1 (Example 5.17). To locate this gesture in Prelude 5, all we have to do is look at the LH part in its last three measures. The single D in the bass of m. 37 of

Prelude 5 is an extension of the repeated D's in the bass of mm. 30–36, with four measures (mm. 34–37) being played on one continuous pedal (Example 5.16).

This D is two octaves lower than the D that appears on the second beat of m. 1 in Prelude 6, yet the remaining two notes of the motif, C♯-D, sound in exactly the same register as in Prelude 6. In Prelude 5, these two notes are played by LH thumb—the strongest finger, according to Chopin's views on piano technique (see the circled notes in Example 5.16, mm. 38–39).[32] Other multiple entries of the same two-note motif in No. 5 can also be heard if the pianist chooses to emphasize them in performance (Example 5.16, circled notes in mm. 12–16).

The treble in Prelude 6 consists mainly of repeated pitches, rhythmically organized in groups of two. Prelude 6 contains only two instances when the repeated eighths in the top voice morph into melodic formations. The first time, it happens in mm. 6–8, where the melody joins the bass in a duet. This melody is bookended by D-C♯-D in m. 6 and D-C♯ in m. 8 (Example 5.17).

The second melodic event in the upper voice of Prelude 6 takes place in mm. 22–23, while the bass is standing still. This melodic turn is unusual: the first scale degree of B minor moves down to the natural seventh (A), which, against expectations, does not move down stepwise but instead skips to F♯ (Example 5.17). Furthermore, the unresolved natural seventh scale degree is underscored by an accent. This motif, B-A-F♯, is anticipated in Prelude 5, where it occurs twice, on RH offbeats in mm. 4 and 20 (see notes marked by '+' in Example 5.16).

Prelude 6 (B minor)

This soulful elegy (constructed as a period consisting of two phrases) brims with *Dies irae* motifs. The lower voice, except for the arpeggios, is made almost entirely of various *Dies irae* motifs. When the treble shifts from repeated pitches to more independent melodic developments in mm. 6–8 and 21–23, these melodic lines also consist of the chant's motifs. Even the brief melodic segment of the middle voice in m. 7 quotes from the chant.

To begin with, the last LH note of the ascending arpeggio in m. 1 and the following three pitches form a^1 (B-D-C♯-D). The last three notes of this a^1 motif, however, overlap with the next motif and serve as the beginning of *a* (D-C♯-D-B, Example 5.17), thus creating a palindromic combination of a^1 and *a*—just as in the *Dies irae* chant itself, in which three pairs of phrases are conjoined likewise: 3/4, 7/8, and 10/11. In each pair, the last note of the preceding phrase and the opening four pitches of the subsequent phrase form a palindrome of intertwined a^1 and *a* (see Example 4.6). In Prelude 6, these dovetailed motifs are sequentially repeated in mm. 3–4 and then, again in B minor, in mm. 9–10 and 23–24. Each time, Chopin highlights these motifs with crescendo-diminuendo hairpins (Example 5.17).

---

[32] In several preludes, the main melodic line is carried either by the right or the left thumb.

Example 5.17   Chopin, Prélude 6

In mm. 5–8, the use of chant motives gathers steam. Motif e^5 in LH of m. 5 is immediately followed in the same part by c^3 (mm. 6–7), while, at the same time, d^1 is placed in the treble. The next measure is even more polyphonically elaborate, with a simultaneous arrangement of three motifs. In LH in m. 7, the last two notes of c^3 (C♯-D) become the first two pitches of a^3 (C♯-D-C♯-A♯). Simultaneously, a^1 (A♯-B-A♯-C♯) emerges in middle voice, while c appears in the treble (see Example 5.17). This profusion of *Dies irae* motifs tapers off in mm. 8–9, when the last note of c (the last sixteenth note in RH of m. 7) initiates a^2 (B-A♯-B-D).

Measures 11–12 contain overlying motifs d^2 (D-E-F♮-E) and a^3 (E-F♮-E-C♮), with three shared notes between them. Motif c then reappears in mm. 15–16, this time in LH; earlier, in m. 7, it was stated in RH. The four sixteenths in m. 17 are a symmetric amalgamation of e and e^4 around the interval of a fourth (A-G-D-E; Example 5.17). When the same three-measure melodic phrase comes back in in mm. 19–21, it is preceded by an anacrusis at the end of m. 18. This pickup note immediately adds an additional motif into the mix, a^5 (Example 5.17).

In the meantime, the treble in mm. 14–22 consists of yet another oscillating figure, B-A♯. It is reminiscent of the oscillating lines from the C-major, E-minor, and D-major Preludes, but it is certainly closer to the latter. In the D-major Prelude, the trill-like pattern consisted of B-A-B♭-A; in the B-minor Prelude, only the top two pitches of that pattern, B and B♭/A♯, are involved in the oscillation. The end of this oscillating figure in Prelude 6 eventually develops into a^3 in mm. 21–22 (see Example 5.17).

Preludes 7 (A major) & 8 (F♯ minor)

Prelude 7 (A major)

The A-major Prelude is often described as 'mazurka-like.'[33] In fact, the Prelude blends two genres. One is indeed a mazurka. Yet if this piece were an actual mazurka, it would have sounded quite differently, as shown in Example 5.18.

This prelude, however, is more hesitant and contemplative than a bona fide dance. Each of the two-measure motifs opens with a typical mazurka 'hop,' but as soon as a chord appears on the second beat of every odd measure, the mazurka fades and another genre surfaces. The chords are then repeated in measured fashion, typical of an entirely different type of music: the chorale. The back-and-

Example 5.18   Chopin, Prelude 7 (modified)

---

[33]   Higgins, 'Chopin Interpretation: A Study of Performance Directions in Selected Autographs and Other Sources' (PhD dissertation, University of Iowa, 1966), p. 187; Samson, *Chopin* (New York: Schirmer Books, 1997), p. 158.

forth shifts between two seemingly incompatible genres become more apparent if the pianist plays the repeated chords not with a bouncy, mazurka lilt but rather as a gently reflective chorale (Example 5.20).

Furthermore, the relationship between the two genres in Prelude 7 is far from static. Block chords of a chorale always incorporate harmonic changes. In the first ten measures of the Prelude, though, the block chords are merely repeated. Consequently, in mm. 1–10 the chorale remains an understated backdrop for a much more prominent mazurka.

This state of affairs changes in mm. 11–14. The harmonic movement within the block-chord component of the Prelude elevates the chorale into a more prominent position. In performance, although not indicated in the score, the two-measure phrases in mm. 1–10 call for a slight diminuendo toward the end of each phrase. Chopin's only dynamic marking after the initial *piano* is a crescendo wedge in mm. 11–12, which underscores the chorale ingredient. Then, in the last two measures, the chorale recedes into the background again, accompanied by an unmarked but implied diminuendo (Example 5.20).

Another interesting structural feature of the A-major Prelude is its static rhythmic configuration: all the two-measure phrases are rhythmically identical. Moreover, one can hear that these phrases are quite similar thematically, as well: every phrase is built on the same underlying sequential pattern. This pattern undergoes subtle variations in the course of the Prelude: some of its notes are moved to another register (mm. 0/1, 8/9, and 11), or moved to the middle voice (mm. 3 and 15), or inverted (mm. 5 and 14–15). Example 5.19 shows this underlying pattern for each of the eight two-measure phrases of the Prelude; the square brackets in Example 5.19 indicate the omitted (but implied) notes.

Example 5.19   Chopin, Prelude 7, eight sequential patterns

The sequential motifs listed in Example 5.19 derive from the *Dies irae*. These are motifs *b*, *b³*, and *b¹*. In addition, the middle voice in mm. 13–14 includes motif *d* (A♯-B-A♮-G♯). The last *Dies irae* motif in the Prelude is *b¹* in mm. 14–16. It begins in the treble, but its last pitch, C♯, ends up in the middle voice, since an extra A is added above it. Nonetheless, this C♯ is more important thematically and should be emphasized accordingly in performance, far more so than A at the top (the parentheses in Example 5.20 indicate underlying or implied motifs).

Example 5.20   Chopin, Prelude 7

The Links

The last note of motif b^1 in the A-major Prelude and the repeated C♯ in the RH middle voice (mm. 15–16), along with the concluding A in the bass, all link Prelude 7 with Prelude 8, which opens with the thirds A-C♯ on beats 1 and 2 of m. 1 (Example 5.21).

Another connector between the two preludes is first presented in Prelude 7 on the downbeats of mm. 1 and 9 (C♯-D); the pickup to m. 15 and the following downbeat in the middle voice contain the same melodic pitches in reverse, D-C♯ (Example 5.20). The C♯-D-C♯ connector commences the main melody in Prelude 8 and is repeated in the next measure; D-C♯ is instantly imitated in the tenor, in augmentation, in the second half of measures 1 and 2 (Example 5.21).

Finally, the most thematically important melodic line in the middle voice of Prelude 7, A♯-B-A♮-G♯-D-C♯ in mm. 13–15 (Example 5.20), is mirrored in the melody in m. 4 of Prelude 8, with two additional passing notes (indicated in brackets): A-B-A-G♯-[F♯-E♯]-D-C♯ (Example 5.21).

Prelude 8 (F♯ minor)

The first prelude in Opus 28 thus far that is more expansive than a period is Prelude 8, which is in a ternary form with a coda. Considering the etude-like virtuosic quality of this piece, the melodic richness of every textural layer is astounding. To begin with, the leading melodic line in Prelude 8, as in Prelude 1, is carried by the RH thumb and reverberates in upper octaves. At the same time, the LH thumb plays a slower-moving countermelody, while the bass line, at the bottom of arpeggiated chords, proceeds in a syncopated fashion on offbeats.

Example 5.21 Chopin, Prélude 8, mm. 1–4

The thirty-second notes in RH fulfill two functions: doubling the melody in octaves and filling in the chords. The chordal figurations, however, are thematically significant; a great many of them spell motif b^2.

The leading melody of the Prelude also contains *Dies irae* motifs. Arguably, most of these motifs are relatively neutral and less individualized; in fact, they

Example 5.22   Chopin, Prelude 8, mm. 9–19 (RH)

Example 5.23   Chopin, Prelude 8, mm. 22–24 (RH)

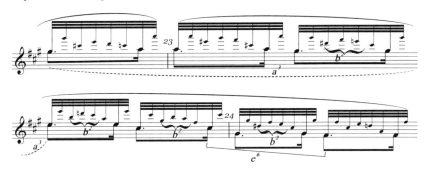

Example 5.24   Chopin, Prelude 8, mm. 27–34

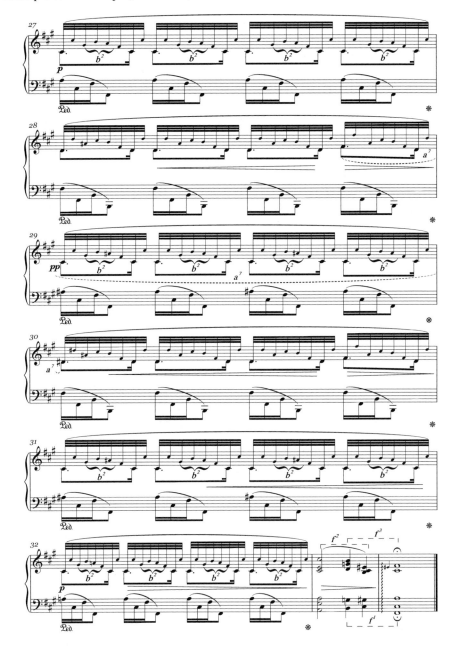

98   *The Mystery of Chopin's* Préludes

can be attributed to the *Dies irae* only within the entire context of Opus 28. The melody begins with a chain of *e* motifs (*e³, e³, e⁵*) and *f⁵* in mm. 1–2 (Example 5.21). The first phrase of the first period continues in mm. 3–4 with motifs *d, d,* and *c*, which is a longer version of *d* (Example 5.21). The same motifs feature in the second phrase, too.

In the middle section of the piece, besides previously sounding motifs *e³, e⁵,* and *d*, we find *cc³* in mm. 11–12, *a⁴* and *c¹* in mm. 13–14, and *d¹, e¹,* and *a⁵* in mm. 15–19 (Example 5.22).

Yet more versions of *a* and *e* motifs, *a³* and *e⁶*, join the host of the chant motifs in mm. 22–24 (Example 5.23).

The coda adds to this mix *a⁷* in mm. 28–30, as well as symmetrically dovetailed *f²* and *f³* in mm. 33–34 (Example 5.24).

Finally, Schubertian minor-major fluctuations, prominent in Prelude 5, come to the fore again at the end of Prelude 8 in mm. 27–32 (Example 5.24).

Preludes 9 (E major) & 10 (C# minor)

Prelude 9 (E major)

The most persuasively assertive prelude in the entire cycle is Prelude 9. First of all, the composer blends two genres that help create the piece's character: the hymn and the march. Then he adds an accompaniment in triplets, which, in this context, helps create the atmosphere of exaltation, similar, for example, to the apotheosis at the end of Chopin's Nocturne in C minor, Op. 48, No. 1.

All of that is combined with what is often referred to as pavane rhythm: ♩ ♫ ♩ ♩ or ♩ ♫ ♩ ♫, in a relatively slow duple time. The most notable nineteenth-century examples of this solemn genre before Chopin include the slow movement of Beethoven's Seventh Symphony and Schubert's songs 'Der Tod und das Mädchen' ('Death and the Maiden,' later used by the composer in his String Quartet in D minor, D. 810) and 'Das Wirtshaus' from *Winterreise*.

Finally, Prelude 9 is one of the two major-mode preludes in the set that have stable endings, with the tonic note in the melody. Prelude 9 attains the final tonic in the top voice somewhat laboriously. In the first phrase (mm. 1–4, Example 5.25), the melody rises from B to E, but when E is reached and repeated in m. 3, there is no tonic in the harmony, and the melody rolls down back to B. In the second phrase (mm. 5–8), the melody also climbs from B to a reiterated E, but the E-major tonic is again sidestepped. The melodic line rises past E to a remote A♭ and then falls down to B once more.

The third phrase (mm. 9–12) begins with a similar ascent from B, and this time the goal is finally attained; the concluding E is fully supported by the tonic. The triumphant ending is bolstered by two circumstances. One is a wide dynamic range: the last phrase begins *p* and, in the short span of four measures, arrives

Example 5.25   Chopin, Prelude 9

at *ff*. The second one is rhythm. The third phrase introduces energetic, double-dotted rhythms into the melody for the first time in this Prelude, imparting prodigious vitality and determination (Example 5.25).[34]

---

[34]   I am grateful to Marina Ritzarev for sharing with me some of her observations regarding the E-major Prelude.

100   *The Mystery of Chopin's* Préludes

Rhythm in the first two phrases of Prelude 9 is subject to controversy. Chopin notated the subdivided beats as triplets in the middle part, set against dotted eighths and sixteenths in the melody. In many other cases, including the first movement of Beethoven's 'Moonlight' Sonata and Chopin's Nocturne in C♯ minor, Op. 27, No. 1, the sixteenth notes are expected be played after the last notes in the triplets.

Here, however, conditions are different. Both Higgins and Eigeldinger insist that performance ought to follow the Baroque practice (which Chopin knew well) by timing the sixteenths with the last notes of the triplets.[35] One rationale for this approach is the presence of double-dotted eighth notes in the Prelude. Double-dotted rhythms became widely used after Leopold Mozart. Dissatisfied with the vagueness of earlier usage of dotted rhythms, which ranged from triplets to dotted to overdotted patterns, he introduced double-dotting in the second edition of his *Violinschule*.[36]

If Chopin did not entirely eliminate the ambiguity of dotted rhythms in Prelude 9, he at least reduced it by indicating which short notes ought to be played after the triplets. In the first two phrases of this period (mm. 1–4 and 5–8), only the bass line contains double dots. The single-dot rhythms in the melody are supposed to be played not only ahead of the thirty-second-notes in the bass but also, according to Baroque practice, at the same time as the last triplet note. In the third phrase, however, the rhythms in the melody sharpen due to double-dotting, with the exception of the fourth beat of m. 10, in which the last melodic note is again played before the thirty-second in the bass.

An even stronger argument in support of timing the sixteenth notes in the melody with the last eighths in the triplets can be found in Chopin's manuscript. There the composer aligned the dotted rhythms with the triplets; furthermore, he connected most of the melodic notes and the accompanimental triplets with single stems.[37]

The opening three chords in the E-major Prelude are an exact repeat (save for the triplets) of the three chords in the chorale conclusion of Prelude 2 (Example 5.6, mm. 21–22). As in No. 2, the parallel thirds in the middle voice in m. 1 (G♯-E, F♯-D♯, G♯-E) are thematically noteworthy, definitely more so than the static B in the melody. The device of compressing melodic thirds into harmonic ones, employed at the end of Prelude 1 (see pp. 68–9) and continued in the chorale

---

[35]   Higgins, 'Chopin Interpretation,' pp. 194–6; Fryderyk Chopin, *Préludes Op. 28, Op. 45*, ed. Jean-Jacques Eigeldinger, pp. vii, 12.

[36]   Leopold Mozart, *Versuch einer gründlichen Violinschule* (Augsburg: Johann Jacob Lotter, 1756), p. 40.

[37]   Few later editions replicate Chopin's original notation. Those include Jan Ekier's *Preludes Opp. 28, 45* (Warsaw: Polskie Wydawnictwo Muzyczne, 2000) and Jean-Jacques Eigeldinger's *Préludes Op. 28, Op. 45*, in The Complete Chopin: A New Critical Edition (London: Edition Peters, 2003).

Deciphering the Préludes   101

segment of Prelude 2, resumes in Prelude 9. The first two thirds, G♯-E and F♯-D♯, are a harmonic compression of motif *b*. At the same time, the upper line, in combination with the last harmonic third, is a semi-harmonic version of motif *a*: G♯-F♯-G♯/E (see the bracketed thirds in Example 5.25, m. 1).

Only the first two of these thirds return at the beginning of the second phrase of the period in m. 5 due to the sudden shift to G major on beat 3 of this measure. The third phrase, however, restores the original progression of thirds (and, consequently, restores motifs *b* and *a*)—and in addition these thirds are emphasized through sequential repeats in F major and G minor/major (Example 5.25, mm. 9–11).

The melodic line develops mainly stepwise, with a single leap occurring in m. 8. Considering, however, the importance of climactic points in mm. 3, 8, and 12, they can be heard as the focal points of symmetrically interlocked motifs c^2–*c*, shortened by one note, in the first phrase; e^7–e^6 in the second phrase; and c^1 in the third phrase (see Example 5.25).

The Links

The persistent melodic E at the end of Prelude 9, struck five times in a row, immediately reappears on the first downbeat of Prelude 10, where it is played by the LH thumb and reharmonized as the third of C♯ minor.

Prelude 9 includes three melodic ascents from B to E, both in diatonic and chromatic forms: B-C♯-D♯-E in mm. 1–3, B-C♮-D♮-E in mm. 5–6, and B-C♮-D♮-D♯-E in mm. 9–12 (Ex 5.25). An octatonic version of these ascending figures, B♯-C♯-D♯-E, emerges four times in Prelude 10, in mm. 4, 12, 15–16, and 17–18 (Examples 5.26a, b).

Prelude 10

The four phrases in the C♯-minor Prelude feature a dialogue between gossamer cascades of rapid sixteenths and somber mazurka responses, with characteristic accents on weak beats. The first halves of the dialogue are really quite static: harmonized by alternating chords i and iv, they are identical in the first, second, and fourth phrases. Only the third phrase diverges from this pattern; it is transposed to F♯ minor, and the rhythm of harmonic changes speeds up slightly.

The two segments of the dialogue are sharply contrasting, even confrontational; and yet they both are built on *Dies irae* motifs. The runs of sixteenths are constructed almost entirely on motifs a^3 and *c* (Example 5.26a). The first mazurka reply in mm. 3–4 draws on motif c^1; in the next retort in mm. 7–8, c^1 is shortened by one note and supplemented with e^1 (Example 5.26a). The conclusion of the Prelude, D♯-E-C♯ in mm. 16 and 18, rhymes with the melodic endings of Preludes 2 (B-C-A) and 6 (C♯-D-B), which all represent the last three pitches of motif *a* (Example 5.26b).

102   *The Mystery of Chopin's* Préludes

Example 5.26   (a) Chopin, Prelude 10, mm. 1–8, (b) Prelude 10, mm. 15–18

Preludes 11 (B major) & 12 (G♯ minor)

Prelude 11 (B major)

The B-major Prelude, as Eigeldinger suggests, resembles the beginning of an impromptu.[38] And indeed, Chopin's Impromptu, Op. 29, printed just two years before the publication of the *Préludes*, has a similar, gracefully gentle flow of triplets that occasionally give way to duple division (compare mm. 5 and 9–10 in Prelude 11 with mm. 23–24 in Op. 29).

---

[38]   Fryderyk Chopin, *Préludes Op. 28, Op. 45*, ed. Jean-Jacques Eigeldinger, p. vi.

Example 5.27 (a) Chopin, Prelude 11, mm. 1–5 (b) Prelude 11, mm. 10–15
(c) Prelude 11, mm. 20–27

The treble consists, for the most part, of two voices, in either concurrent or consecutive motion, even though only in mm. 13–14 are the two voices notated with independent stems and rhythms. These two measures, with longer upper notes, provide a clue for the performance of the two RH melodic lines in the rest of the Prelude. Similarly to mm. 13–14, the upper notes of RH harmonic intervals in mm. 3–5, 7–12, 15–17, and 19–20, can be played, and most probably *should* be played, in a Baroque overlegato fashion, that is, held down longer than their notated values.

Both melodic voices are constructed of *Dies irae* motifs. The opening presents a highly intricate chain of intertwined motifs *c*, d^2, *d*, and *a*, of which the first motif *d* (F♯-G♯-F♯-E in mm. 3–4) is an abbreviated imitation of *c* from mm. 2–3 in the upper voice (Example 5.27a). In mm. 4–5, the chant motifs are stated simultaneously in both melodic voices: *d* in the upper part (C♯-D♯-C♯-B) and d^2, *d*, and *a* in the lower RH voice (Example 5.27a).

The middle section introduces motif b^2 in the top voice (G♯-B-A♯-F♯; the latter third is played harmonically rather than melodically), accompanied by e^5 (B-E-D♯)

and e^4 (D♯-A♯-B) in the lower RH part (Example 5.27b). The next two measures of the middle section feature f^3 in the treble and a palindromic conjunction of a^5 and a^1 (G♯-E-F♯-E-G♯, in which the first four pitches form a^5 and the last four pitches a^1; Example 5.27b).

In a short bridge to the reprise, the bass acquires thematic significance, connecting the midsection to the reprise with motif b; actually, this b is a *stretto* imitation, just one eighth later, of b^4 in the RH part (Example 5.27b). Another moment of thematic prominence for the bass line occurs in mm. 18–19, when it doubles motif c in the treble in parallel tenths (Example 5.28).

The final entries of motif a^3 can be found in the middle voices, with an imitation from the (implied) alto to the tenor in mm. 20–21 and 23–25 (Example 5.27c).

The Links

As is most frequently the case, the last melodic note in Prelude 11, D♯, is the first RH note in Prelude 12, reharmonized from B major to G♯ minor. The abovementioned doubling of the treble in the bass line in m. 18 (Example 5.28) turns out to be more significant than a mere amplification of the melody. The same thematic gesture, C𝄪-D♯-E-D♯-C♯-B (Example 5.28, LH), reappears in the melody in mm. 23–24 of Prelude 11 (Example 5.27.c), and then in the treble of Prelude 12, in mm. 4–6 (Example 5.29).

Example 5.28 Chopin, Prelude 11, mm. 18–19

Prelude 12 (G♯ minor)

The turbulent G♯-minor Prelude is usually described as an etude. Indeed, fast repetitions in RH of single, double, and triple notes, as well as widely spaced leaps in LH, are sufficiently demanding to deserve such a definition. What is usually missing in the assessment of this Prelude is its contrapuntal complexity.

In the first section of the Prelude (mm. 1–16), the leading melodic line is situated not in the top voice, as commonly performed, but in the tenor, played by the LH thumb (the treble, however, contrapuntally contains the aforementioned connecting thematic link between Preludes 11 and 12 in mm. 4–7; see Example 5.29). The tenor line begins with an interlocking palindrome of motifs a^4 and a— identical to the motivic palindrome both in the chant and in the B-minor Prelude

Example 5.29 Chopin, Prelude 12, mm. 1–16

(see mm. 1–4, 9–10, and 23–24 in Example 5.17). Motif *a* then dovetails with *a⁷*, which, in turn, intertwines with *a¹* (mm. 1–12; Example 5.29). In mm. 14–16 of Example 5.29, the tenor articulates motif *a*, E-D♯-E-C♯.

In the middle section (mm. 17–40), the tenor fades into the background and the treble and alto parts in RH come to the fore. The alto, played by the RH thumb, takes over the oscillating portion of *a* (E-D♯-E-D♯-E-D♯-E-D♮-E), while the treble introduces a quadruple statement of *e³* (mm. 18–20, Example 5.30). The continuation of the midsection consists of an alternation between motifs *d³* and *a* in mm. 21–28 (Example 5.30).

Then motif *c²* appears in the soprano (mm. 29–30); this entry of *c²* is extended by one note, which moves it closer to *cc²*. After intense contrapuntal juxtapositions of the oscillating, trill-like gesture in different rhythms and between different voices, in both RH and LH, the middle section concludes with *d¹*, followed by a

Example 5.30 Chopin, Prelude 12, mm. 18–40

Example 5.31 Chopin, Prelude 12, mm. 47–81

sequential declaration of d^3 and d against the octave pedal point A♯ in RH, and, finally, e^4 (mm. 36–40, Example 5.30).

The reprise brings back the familiar intertwined string of motifs a^4, a, and a^7 in the tenor (mm. 41–49). At this point, the tenor continues with motif a^2, and the bass introduces a descending Phrygian tetrachord, G♯-F♯-E-D♯, in mm. 49–52—a traditional lament gesture (Example 5.31).

As soon as the Phrygian tetrachord ends in m. 52, motif c emerges in the soprano (mm. 52–53), immediately followed by d^1 in the bass (mm. 54–57). The persistently reiterated trill-like figure in the soprano spins out into motif a, while at the same time a downward scale in LH concludes with motif c^3 (mm. 57–65; Example 5.31).

At the beginning of the coda, the leading thematic part shifts to the middle voice again, carried here by the RH thumb. This thematic line commences with a partial motif a (C♯-B-C♯-B) in mm. 64–65, which seamlessly flows into motifs a^1, c, and d^3 (mm. 64–73; Example 5.31). These motifs, buried in the middle of busy texture, are in fact not difficult to project in performance. They are presented in longer notes than the staccato bass and the scampering treble. Even without additional accentuation, the longer quarter notes stand out.

In the concluding measures, in the soprano, the composer gradually builds the same Phrygian tetrachord from the bottom up: first just a single D♯ in mm. 74–75, then E-D♯, then F♯-E-D♯, and, finally, G♯-F♯-E-D♯ (mm. 74–80; Example 5.31).

The polyphonic sophistication of Prelude 12 contrasts with the much more common homophonic approach to the piece. As various voices are highlighted, bringing out a multitude of *Dies irae* motifs, the Prelude acquires textural richness and compelling interpretational depth.

Preludes 13 (F♯ major) & 14 (E♭ minor)

Prelude 13 (F♯ major)

The F♯-major Prelude is a nocturne, but one with an atypically busy and thematically saturated accompaniment. The importance of the LH part was originally emphasized in the manuscript with the marking 'espress[ivo]'; Chopin later deleted that indication and replaced it with the unassuming 'legato.' The faster-moving lower voices and the overall polyphonic intensity explain why the sustain pedal is used so sparingly in this piece.

The prevalent *Dies irae* motif in the first and last sections of this ternary form is b^1. It is repeated persistently in the LH part (mm. 1–5, 7, 9–17, 19, 28–33, and 35). In places where the steady pattern with b^1 breaks, motif e^3 comes to the fore (mm. 6, 16, 18, 20, 31–32, 34, and 36). In addition, the hidden melody in upper eighth notes in LH in mm. 7–8 outlines motif c, shortened by one note (Example 5.32). The absence of the last note in motif c, as well as the seemingly unnecessary long, ascending RH appoggiatura in m. 9 (RH could easily play the

Example 5.32 Chopin, Prelude 13, mm. 1–20

Example 5.33 Chopin, Prelude 13, mm. 22–28

entire downbeat chord in m. 9 without breaking it), can be explained by the entry of another motif. The last two LH notes of m. 8 (A♯-G♯) and the first two RH notes in the middle voice of m. 9 (A♯-C♯) imitate the identical motif a^2 that surfaced earlier in the treble of m. 4 (Example 5.32). The same motif, consisting of identical pitches, reappears in the melodic line in m. 12.

Other *Dies irae* motifs in the first section in the RH part include b^3 in mm. 4–5; c^2 in mm. 12–15 (G♯-A♯-B-C♯-D♯-C♯); and a in mm. 15–17 (B-A♯-B-G♯; the RH sixteenth in m. 15, D♯, belongs in a middle voice and moves to E♯ on the downbeat of m. 16). As in the original plainchant, the last two notes of a, B-G♯, serve as the beginning of b. Motif b is then immediately repeated in RH in mm. 18–20 (Example 5.32).

Simultaneously with this second statement of b in the melody, LH plays b^1 in m. 19, while the middle voice of the RH part states motif d in mm. 19–20, B-C♯-B-A♯ (Example 5.32).

In the middle section, a persistently repetitive bass line in m. 22 brings to prominence symmetrically arranged motifs e^2, e, e^2, e^3, and e^5 (Example 5.33); a similar chain of motifs, only consisting of alternating e^2 and e, is heard in the bass in m. 24 (Example 5.33).

Motif a^2 comes back in RH, stated three times in a row in mm. 25–26 on precisely the same pitches as in the first section: A♯-G♯-A♯-C♯. At the end of m. 24,

Example 5.34   Chopin, Prelude 13, mm. 36–38

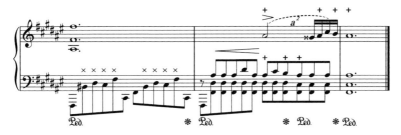

while the treble repeats motif a^2, the alto and the bass join in, beginning an intricate contrapuntal web that consists of d^2, d^3, d^1, d, and a^6. Motif b^1 in the bass in m. 28 leads into the reprise (Example 5.33).

The abbreviated reprise of the ABA form brings back the motivic contents of the first section and yet another statement of a^2, with almost identical pitches as before, in the concluding two measures, A♯-G𝄪-A♯-C♯ (Example 5.34).

The Links

The connecting pitch between the two pieces is A♯/B♭. It is doubled in octave in the last two measures of No. 13 (Example 5.34), but the actual identical pitch is the lower A♯, played by RH thumb, since it comes back in the same register (as B♭) in the first measure of No. 14.

Preludes 13 and 14 are also linked by two identical melodic figures. One of them is a slightly embellished oscillating gesture, A♯-B-A♯. It commences melodic phrases in Prelude 13 (mm. 1–4 and 9–12) and returns at the close of the Prelude 13 in mm. 37–38, where it is doubled in the RH middle voice (see notes marked with '+' in Example 5.34). Prelude 14 opens with the same motif in mm. 1–2, notated as B♭-C♭-B♭ (indicated with '+' in Example 5.35a).

In m. 36 of the LH part of Prelude 13, there is a repeated motif B♯-D♯-C♯-F♯. It comes back in mm. 3–4 of Prelude 14, notated as C♮-E♭-D♭-G♭ (both motifs are marked with 'x' in Examples 5.34 and 5.35a).

Prelude 14 (E♭ minor)

Besides the finale of the B♭-minor Sonata, Op. 35, Prelude 14 is the only other example in Chopin's music that is written entirely in parallel octaves played by both hands. Just as in the later sonata movement, the tessitura of the Prelude corresponds to the cello range and exhibits a wealth of hidden melodic lines, typical in Bach's monophonic works.[39] The single melodic line in Prelude 14 is perhaps

---

[39] For connections between the finale of Chopin's Sonata, Op. 35 and Bach's works for cello solo, see Anatole Leikin, 'The Sonatas,' in Jim Samson (ed.), *The Cambridge Companion to Chopin* (Cambridge: Cambridge University Press, 1992), pp. 174–5.

Example 5.35 (a) Chopin, Prelude 14, mm. 1–5 (b) Prelude 14, mm. 9–19

Deciphering the Préludes   113

less polyphonically developed than the one in the finale of Opus 35. There are two mostly hidden melodic lines, each doubled in octaves and frequently syncopated; these lines can be highlighted in performance by overlegato.

Chopin makes extensive use of thematic fragmentation in the Prelude. One of the motifs that connect Preludes 13 and 14, B♭-C♭-B♭, in the upper voice, is a partial a^1 motif. This oscillating gesture, ever-present in Opus 28, is mirrored in inversion in the lower voice as a partial a motif, E♭-D♮-E♭ (Example 5.35a). Many short sequential phrases are capped with another fragmented motif, a^4 in mm. 3, 4, and 7–9. A shortened (by one note) motif c^3 appears in the lower voice in mm. 9–11 (Examples 5.35a, b).

The middle voice becomes thematically active in mm. 12–13, initiating a palindromic grouping of motifs c and c^3 (G♭-G♮-G♭-F-E♭-F). In mm. 14–15, a similar palindromic combination of c and c^3 comes back in the lower voice. The Prelude concludes with yet another palindrome of c and c^3 (mm. 17–18; Example 5.35b).

Preludes 15 (D♭ major) & 16 (B♭ minor)

Prelude 15 (D♭ major)

George Sand left a famous account in her autobiography, *Histoire de ma vie*, of how she and her son, Maurice, returned from Palma to the monastery, late at night, under pouring rain, only to find Chopin, weeping and hallucinating, playing the piano. Sand did not specify which prelude he was playing, but many have guessed since then. The D♭-major Prelude, Prelude 15, is now widely regarded as the 'Raindrop' because of the ostinato patter of the reiterated A♭/G♯ throughout the piece. But at least two other likely candidates have been suggested. Frederick Niecks proffers that 'it is generally and reasonably believed' that the prelude referred to by Sand was Prelude 6 in B minor. Niecks also remarks that Liszt considered the Prelude in question to be No. 8 in F♯ minor.[40]

Yet, in the end, it does not matter which Prelude might be called the 'Raindrop,' especially since Chopin strenuously objected to programmatic titles. What is far more important for the performance and perception of the piece is locating *Dies irae* motifs in different polyphonic voices of the Prelude's texture—and then displaying them in performance.

To begin with, the oscillating melodic patterns, which represent the abridged a motif and its inversion, figure prominently in this Prelude, in various voices. But quite a few complete motifs are heard as well, embedded into the melodic lines, beginning with e^4 in m. 1 (D♭-A♭-B♭). The treble then continues with cc^2 (B♭ up to G♭ and down to E♭), doubled in parallel sixths (Example 5.36a).

---

[40]   Frederick Niecks, *Frederick Chopin as a Man and Musician* (London: Novello and Company, 1902), vol. 2, p. 45.

Example 5.36 (a) Chopin, Prelude 15, mm. 1–4, (b) Prelude 15, mm. 8–13, (c) Prelude 15, mm. 16–20 (RH)

The new thematic developments in the first section stressing motifs c and d, as well as their transmutations, anticipate a heavy emphasis on these motifs in the middle section of the Prelude. These motifs mesh both contrapuntally and linearly; within one line, symmetrical palindromes abound (Examples 5.36b, c). Occasionally, other motifs emerge, as well: b^2 in mm. 10–11 and 16–17; a^4 in mm. 12–13; a in mm. 19–20; and f^4 in mm. 12 and 16; and e^2 in 18 (Examples 5.36b, c).

In the lugubrious middle section, the ostinato becomes even more relentless, without so much as a momentary interruption. Motifs d^2 and d are particularly prominent here, but other chant motifs play a role, too, often with palindromic symmetries and contrapuntal interplay (Examples 37a, b). Motif b in the bass connects the midsection with the reprise (Example 5.37c).

Example 5.37 (a) Chopin, Prelude 15, mm. 28–35, (b) Prelude 15, mm. 60–64, (c) Prelude 15, mm. 75–76

The Links

Prelude 16, in B♭ minor, is the only one in the set that begins with a contrasting introduction, whose main purpose seems to be to better connect Preludes 15 and 16. Without the introduction, the links between the two pieces would be less pronounced. The connecting pitch, F, is underscored well in the melody in the last two measures in No. 15 (Example 5.38). But the opening F in the treble of *Presto con fuoco* (m. 2) is very short, only a sixteenth note in a fast tempo, and the ear has scarcely enough time to register this F as a connector.

Example 5.38 Chopin, Prelude 15, mm. 84–89

A slightly more tangible tie is that between the brief alto solo in m. 85 of Prelude 15, D♭-E♭-D♭ (Example 5.38), and Prelude 16, even though this solo occurs in measures 85–86 of No. 15 rather than immediately before No. 16. The leading middle voice in Prelude 16, played by LH thumb (the role of this voice will be discussed shortly), also follows D♭-E♭-D♭ in mm. 2–9 of the B♭-minor Prelude (Example 5.39b).

The introduction to Prelude 16 strengthens the ties considerably. The last two melodic pitches in No. 15 are G♭-F, introduced in mm. 84–85 and repeated in mm. 86–89 (see notes marked by '+' in Examples 5.38 and 5.39b). The introduction to No. 16 begins with the same pitches. Furthermore, after the first descending second G♭-F in mm. 84–85 of Prelude 15, the descent continues in the middle voice in mm. 85–86, reaching C (this descent is indicated by an 'x' in Examples 5.38 and 5.39b). The introduction to No. 16 consists entirely of a similar melodic descent from G♭ to C. Finally, the lower note of the descending gesture in No. 15, C in RH, resolves into D♭ in m. 88. In Prelude 16, the exactly same C in the LH part (m. 1) moves to D♭ in m. 2 (see arrows in Examples 5.38 and 5.39b).

Prelude 16 (B♭ minor)

One of the most misconstrued pieces in Opus 28—perhaps the most—is Prelude 16. Like Prelude 12 (G♯ minor), the B♭-minor Prelude is usually rendered with a dizzyingly rapid passagework over a light-footed accompaniment. Kresky's view of the Prelude is symptomatic:

> For all its surface bravura, this raucous piece may well disappoint. The relentless treble business, superimposed on a stubbornly unchanging bass gesture that outlines an unadventurous harmonic life, ultimately makes for a noisy assertion of fairly feeble ideas. Rather like an etude in its insistence on a single technical challenge, the piece makes none of the poetic discoveries offered throughout the companion preludes, and is one of the low points of the group.[41]

---

[41] Kresky, *A Reader's Guide*, p. 83.

Example 5.39(a) Chopin, Prelude 16, mm. 1–6 (Paderewski edition)

This perception of Prelude 16 is reinforced by the pedal indications found in many modern publications, including the highly influential Paderewski edition, in which the pedal changes every half measure (Example 5.39a).

In Chopin's autograph, however, the initial instructions to change the pedal twice per measure are crossed out, and the new indications direct the pianist to sustain the pedal much longer, for up to three measures at a time (Example 5.39b). The amended pedal markings seem inexplicable, and most pianists do not abide by Chopin's corrected pedaling—either because they are unaware of it or because the longer pedal, in their opinion, may sound too blurry, if not amateurish. I have heard only one pianist in concert who tried to intermittently follow Chopin's finalized pedaling directions, yet that halfhearted attempt was not entirely successful. In that pianist's performance, the running sixteenths in RH were treated as the main melody and stressed accordingly. As a result, the treble, performed as the most prominent textural layer, came out as overly 'busy' and muddy, and no viable thematic alternative was offered.

Some pianists argue that the extended sustain pedal in the Prelude sounded quite acceptable once upon a time on the pianos of the 1820s and 1830s, which of course cannot be replicated on the modern grand pianos of today. Actually, Chopin's revised pedaling in Prelude 16 sounds blurry on all the early Erard and Pleyel instruments that I have played. While there is indeed a noticeable difference in the pedal resonance between the earlier and the modern pianos, the distinction can be easily minimized by a more-shallow application of the pedal on modern grand pianos.

Nonetheless, an explanation of Chopin's unusual pedaling can be given that casts the Prelude in an entirely different light. In this view, the RH runs are *not* the main melody, and therefore they must be downplayed to remain in the background.

118 The Mystery of Chopin's Préludes

Example 5.39(b) Prelude 16, mm. 1–30

120 *The Mystery of Chopin's* Préludes

Example 5.39(b) Prelude 16, mm. 1–30 (continued)

Example 5.39 (c) Prelude 16, mm. 35–36

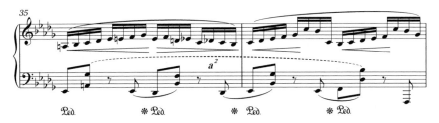

The most important thematic line is, in fact, placed in the middle voice, played by the LH thumb and occasionally doubled in the bass. This line is filled, almost entirely, with *Dies irae* motifs, in which some of the motivic notes (reiterated, of course) last as long as three measures. Chopin's 'inexplicable' pedal markings carefully follow the individual notes of these motifs: a^1 (mm. 2–9, 10–12), c (mm. 14–16), a^2 (mm. 17–24, 26–28, and 35–36), b^2 (mm. 23–25), and a^7 (mm. 25–26). In addition, a descending chromatic lament in the bass occurs in mm. 18–30 (B♭-B♭♭-A♭-G♮-F♯-F♮-E♭-F; Example 5.39b).

Performed in this manner, with the *Dies irae* motifs trumpeted in LH against the flurries of pedaled sixteenths in the treble, the Prelude's character changes dramatically. Instead of a lighthearted, dancelike affair, it becomes a terrifying vision.

Preludes 17 (A♭ major) & 18 (F minor)

Prelude 17 (A♭ major)

Eigeldinger dubbed the A♭-major Prelude a stylized 'romance' *alla serenata*.[42] The luscious cantabile melody, in conjunction with the gracefully slithering chromatic motion in the inner voices, made it a favorite among many musicians, including Mendelssohn and Clara Schumann.

The most remarkable feature of Prelude 17, however, materializes in the last statement of the refrain (the entire piece is shaped as a rondo; see Examples 5.40 and 5.43). Forzando bass, struck periodically against *pp* and sotto voce in the melody and harmony, seems puzzling, until we read Paderewski's recollection of his conversation with Camille Dubois, Chopin's former pupil, which I briefly cited earlier and which is now quoted in full:

---

[42] Fryderyk Chopin, *Préludes Op. 28, Op. 45*, ed. Jean-Jacques Eigeldinger. The Complete Chopin: A New Critical Edition (London: Edition Peters, 2003), p. vi.

Example 5.40 Chopin, Prelude 17, mm. 65–67

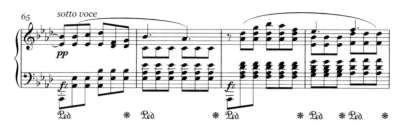

Example 5.41 (a) Chopin, Prelude 17, mm. 1–10 (RH)

Example 5.41 (b) Prelude 17, mm. 24–31

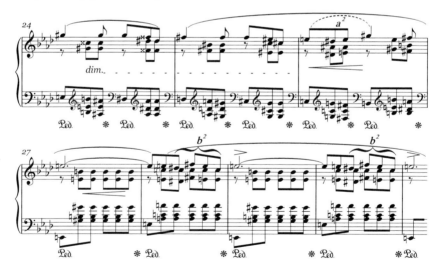

Example 5.42 (a) Chopin, Prelude 17, mm. 43–50, (b) Prelude 17, mm. 51–61

Chopin himself used to play that bass note with great force throughout, in spite of playing everything else in these bars diminuendo. "He always *struck* that note in the same way and with the *same* strength, because of the meaning he attached to it. He accentuated that bass note—he proclaimed it, because the idea of that Prelude is based on the sound of an old clock in the castle which strikes the *eleventh* hour." Madame Dubois told me that I should *not* make that diminuendo as I intended, in accordance with the right hand which plays diminuendo continually, but said that Chopin always insisted the bass note should be struck with the *same* strength—no diminuendo, because the clock knows no diminuendo. That bass note was the clock speaking.[43]

As I mentioned in Chapter 2, Chopin's remark about the castle and the *eleventh* hour evoked Gothic references and triggered a new line of inquiry in this study. Interestingly, an earlier version of the Prelude, reproduced in Eigeldinger's

---

[43] Eigeldinger, *Chopin: Pianist and Teacher as Seen by His Pupils* (Cambridge: Cambridge University Press, 1990), p. 83.

edition of the *Préludes*, has only ten strikes of the clock, which does not generate the presentiment of sinister events that are about to take place at midnight in a castle.

The *Dies irae* motifs here are woven primarily into the melodic line, except for the second episode and the coda. The first phrase of the refrain (mm. 3–10) commences with e^2, followed by three entries of b^2, of which the first two are interlocked with a^7 (Example 5.41a). The second phrase is similar to the first, except for the ending.

The first episode includes a^2 and b^2 in mm. 26–30. In addition, the bass in mm. 24–26 outlines the lament pattern, *passus duriusculus*, which comprises the same pitches as the one in the E-minor Prelude (E-D♯-D♮-C♯-C♮-B; Example 5.41b).

In the second episode we find dovetailed d^1 and d^2, trailed by cc^1 (which is shortened by one note). Simultaneously, the middle voices in LH carry motifs d and d^1; in the latter (D♯-C♯-D♯-E), the last note is moved to the bass (mm. 43–6). When the same phrase is repeated sequentially in mm. 47–50, the last d^1 in the middle voice is replaced in m. 49 by e^4 (Example 5.42a). The melody then continues with two interlocked motifs b in mm. 51–53. Next come intertwined d^3 and d^1, followed by e^4 in mm. 56–57 (Example 5.42b).

The second episode ends with the same concluding phrase as the first episode, with a repeated b^2, but transposed from E major to E♭ major (Example 5.42b).

Finally, the coda contains an iterated motif f and a series of oscillating parallel thirds (C-A♭, B♭-G), mirroring similar parallel thirds from Preludes 1, 2, and 9 formed by conflated motifs a and b (see Example 5.43).

Example 5.43   Chopin, Prelude 17, mm. 80–90

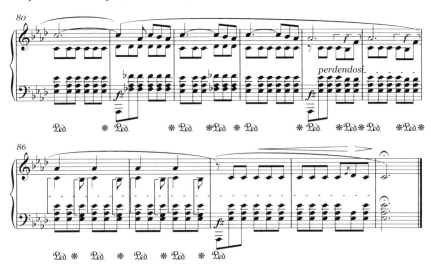

Deciphering the Préludes 125

The Links

The connecting pitch between Nos. 17 and 18 is C—the first and the last top notes in both Preludes 17 and 18 (Examples 5.41a, 5.43, 5.44a, and 5.44c). There is also a truly conspicuous short motif in Prelude 17, C-D♭. It appears in the RH part in the concluding measures, framing the Prelude symmetrically (see mm. 1–3 and 88–89). It also features in the middle voice in mm. 80–82 (Example 5.43).

The identical motif, C-D♭, opens Prelude 18 both melodically and harmonically, as a minor ninth in LH (mm. 1–2, Example 5.44a).

Prelude 18 (F minor)

This is yet another largely misconstrued Prelude. As Kresky puts it,

> There can be little doubt that this is the weakest of the preludes. It barely comes across as a composition, in that its elements—themselves ill-formed—do not seem "composed" into an arrangement of any satisfaction. The piece presents a short list of items clumped into locally cohering successions that relate to each other in only the starkest ways, without true forward motion. By the time the piece is over, nothing seems to have happened; the cadence just puts a stop to the noise.
>
> The individual gestures are actually ugly. The unapologetic minor dominant ninth in m. 1 seems spat at us, and it is made even more unappealing by the interference of the stressed passing F above it.[44]

The role of the minor dominant ninth as a connector between Nos. 17 and 18 has already been explained. The F-minor Prelude in its entirety can be best understood in conjunction with its 'prelude,' No. 17. The A♭-major Prelude sets up a Gothic scene in a castle, shortly before midnight, and the F-minor Prelude carries it on.

The recitative outbursts in the Prelude may indeed appear unhinged, even 'ugly.' And, if performed metrically precise, they most probably comes across as meaningless, because 'nothing seems to have happened' in the course of the piece.

In a Gothic context, however, this incoherent monologue makes perfect sense. One fundamental source of Gothic terror was a fear of insanity. Mad characters inhabit Horace Walpole's *The Castle of Otranto* (1764), Charles Maturin's *Melmoth the Wanderer* (1820), and numerous other popular Gothic tales of horror. Moreover, rumors abounded that some writers of Gothic fiction, including Ann Radcliffe, were actually driven insane.[45]

---

[44] Kresky, *A Reader's Guide*, p. 95.

[45] Helen Small, 'Madness,' in Marie Mulvey-Roberts (ed.), *The Handbook to Gothic Literature* (New York: New York University Press, 1998), pp. 152–6.

Example 5.44 (a) Chopin, Prelude 18, mm. 1–4, (b) Prelude 18, mm. 9–13, (c) Prelude 18, mm. 14–21

Deciphering the Préludes   127

Chopin himself experienced terrifying hallucinations at the monastery in Mallorca, seeing frightening phantoms in the cloister and even being convinced during one of those delusional moments that he was already dead.[46]

The raving soliloquy in Prelude 18 is entirely in line with Gothic speech: 'multifarious, duplicitous, and paradoxical.'[47] Like the 'speaker' in the F-minor Prelude, speakers in Gothic literature 'may become "incoherent," the "nonsense" they utter derived not only from violations of the linguistic rules but also from the speaker's own breakdown in madness.'[48]

The *Dies irae* motifs in Prelude 18 are often part of both the recitative utterances and the accompanimental chords. In the rambling recitative, the motifs may be almost indistinguishable because of the precipitous tempo, but they are present nevertheless. In mm. 3–4, there is a succession of motifs f^4, f^5, and e^5 (Example 5.44a). The recitative exclamation in mm. 9–10 begins with f^3, and the one in mm. 11–12 includes f^3 and b^2. The next recitative phrase opens with f^3 and b^2 in m. 12 and concludes with a symmetrical fusion of e^1 and e^5 in m. 13 (Example 5.44b).

The latter combination of motifs (e^1 and e^5) is repeated in m. 14, as well. In m. 15, the intertwined motifs involve f^5 and f^4. The top line of the accompanimental chords forms motif a^2 in mm. 9–12 and, in octaves, dovetailed motifs f^5 and f^4 in m. 16 (Examples 5.44b, c).

Although the *Dies irae* motifs are not conspicuous in this piece, the pianist should still be aware of where they are in the text of the Prelude. Another performing issue concerns the work's overall countenance. Given its peculiar nature, the Prelude becomes more effective when its recitative portions are performed not in a perfectly measured and smooth delivery but instead more impulsively, with recitative phrases separated from each other by small, erratically implemented time intervals. Then the Prelude will sound both profoundly unsettling and riveting. And no one would be able to declare that No. 18 is uneventful, 'barely a composition.'

Preludes 19 (E♭ major) & 20 (C minor)

Prelude 19 (E♭ major)

The E♭-major Prelude is an exquisite specimen of Chopin's 'harp' etude, similar to the earlier Etude in A♭ major, Op. 25, No. 1. The use of this Prelude in the cycle, as I have already mentioned, might be a reference to a harp in Lamartine's *Les*

---

[46]   George Sand, *Story of My Life: The Autobiography of George Sand* (Albany, NY: State University of New York Press, 1991), p. 1091.

[47]   Anne Williams, *Art of Darkness: A Poetics of Gothic* (Chicago: University of Chicago Press, 1995), p. 67.

[48]   Ibid., pp. 67, 69.

Example 5.45(a) Chopin, Prelude 19, mm. 1–8

Préludes (p. 45). The indicated tempo marking is Vivace, which most modern pianists interpret as 'fast' or 'very fast.' Traditionally, however, Vivace meant a slower tempo, and Chopin, through his teacher Joseph Elsner, was well steeped in musical traditions. For example, Leopold Mozart lists Vivace as the slowest of the fast tempos, slower than Allegretto (but faster than Moderato).[49] Jean-Jacques Rousseau also maintains in the *Dictionnaire de musique* that Vivace refers to the character of the work rather than its tempo.[50] Indeed, if the tempo of Prelude 19 (as well as that of Prelude 11 in B major, also marked Vivace) adheres to the traditional guidelines, its gentle tenderness is beguiling, and it becomes easy for the *Dies irae* motifs to emerge unhindered. In the exceedingly rapid tempo that prevails today, Prelude 19 whizzes by in a cheerful gallop.

The tranquility of Prelude 19 is interrupted, however, by two sudden, explosive crescendos (mm. 29–32 and 65–67, Examples 5.45c and 5.46) that reveal a disquieting undercurrent punctuated by the continual presence of *Dies irae*. These disconcerting crescendos are overlooked or underplayed in most performances of the Prelude.

The *Dies irae* motifs, both complete and abbreviated, are quite prominent here. The bass line provides mostly harmonic rather than thematic support, except in mm. 29–32, where it doubles in parallel thirds the upper voice (Example 5.45c), and in mm. 43–44. Here the bass goes up through all six notes of a whole-tone scale, while the melody moves down chromatically (Example 5.46).

---

[49] L. Mozart, *Versuch*, pp. 48–9.
[50] See Leta E. Miller, 'C.P.E. Bach's Sonatas for Solo Flute,' *Journal of Musicology*, 11/2 (Spring 1993), p. 210.

Example 5.45(b) Prelude 19, mm. 13–26

After an atmospheric E♭-major triad in mm. 1–2 and floating partial motifs a^3 and a in m. 3, the upper voice presents palindromically intertwined motifs a^7 and a^2, immediately followed by b^2, a^2, and e. Motif a^2 in mm. 7–8 is doubled in thirds in LH (Example 5.45a).

The second phrase of the opening period ends with c^2, e^7, and e in the treble (Example 5.45b, mm. 13–16).

In the middle section, which begins in m. 17, motifs a^2, e, a^4, e^3, and e^7 in the top voice are contrapuntally combined with d^3 and c in the middle voices (Example 5.45b). The midsection concludes with a series of b^1 motifs in parallel

Example 5.45 (c) Prelude 19, mm. 29–32

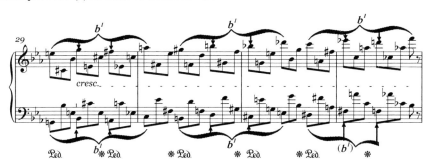

thirds (mm. 29–32). This rising sequence breaks the serene countenance of the Prelude, and not only because of the dramatic crescendo, but also because of the harsh, out-of-context, whole-tone scale outlined by the sequence (the first notes of every melodic third are E♮, F♯, G♯, B♭, C, and D; see Example 5.45c).

The conclusion of the ABA form, in addition to the whole-tone scale in the bass in mm. 43–45, brings dovetailed motifs c^1 and c^2, e, f^2, and e^4 (Example 5.46, mm. 44–9).

The coda is devoted mostly to chromatic versions of motif c. Normally, in its diatonic form, c contains a stepwise motion comprising five notes within the interval of a fifth. The chromatic variants of motif c in mm. 49–53 and 57–61 include descending pentachords, as well, but within the range of a diminished or a perfect fourth.

Motifs c in the coda are supplemented with a in a middle voice in mm. 55–56, a^1 in the middle voice in LH in mm. 64–65, and f^2 in m. 63. Another crescendo, at the conclusion of the Prelude, leads to motif a in the top voice (Example 5.46).

Links

The connecting linchpin is the last *ff* chord in No. 19; Prelude 20 opens with a *ff* chord, which in the RH part is almost identical, save for one note in the middle. The common motivic cells include the descending gesture B♭-A♮-A♭-G-F♯-E♭ in mm. 65–68 of Prelude 19 (Example 5.46), which is repeated in the bass of No. 20 in mm. 5–7 (with F♮ replacing F♯; Example 5.47). The sequence G-F-E♭/E♭-D-C in the treble in mm. 54–55 of Prelude 19 (Example 5.46) comes back in Prelude 20, on beats 3 and 4 of mm. 1–2 (Example 5.47).

Besides pitch identity, Preludes 19 and 20 introduce another kind of connector that comes into play. It involves a sequence that begins in the preceding major prelude and continues into the ensuing minor prelude. This can be defined as 'sequential continuity.'

Thus, two chromatic versions of motif c figure prominently in the coda of Prelude 19 (mm. 48–53 and 57–61). They consist of scale degrees 5-(♭)6-5-♯4-4-3

Example 5.46 Chopin, Prelude 19, mm. 43–71

in E♭ major. Prelude 20 begins with a diatonic version of the same motif, which proceeds sequentially: 5-6-5-4-3 first in C minor and then in A♭ major (Prelude 20, mm. 1–2, Example 5.47). Not surprisingly, the sequence moves down by thirds, reflecting the tonal motion from a major key to its relative minor.

Prelude 20 (C minor)

An earlier version of the C-minor Prelude consisted of only mm. 1–8 plus the final measure. After Camille Pleyel, who was one of the dedicatees of the *Préludes* and who probably commissioned the work, expressed concern that Prelude 20 ran too short, Chopin extended the piece by repeating its second phrase.[51]

A combination of block-chord texture, a *passus duriusculus* in the bass (mm. 5–6 and 9–10), and dotted rhythms generates a mixture of three genres in this Prelude: chorale, lament, and funeral march (according to Chopin's pupil Jane Stirling, the composer called the Prelude '*La Prière*'—the prayer[52]). Unlike many nineteenth-century funeral marches, including those by Chopin, the C-minor Prelude does not incorporate the pavane rhythm. Instead of the more commonly subdivided second and/or fourth beats, it is the third beat that is persistently subdivided in No. 20.

The references to the pavane rhythm, however, are not an indispensable attribute of nineteenth-century funeral marches. Beethoven's *Marcia funebre* from the *Eroica* Symphony, Alkan's *Marche funèbre*, Op. 39, No. 5, and Berlioz's *Marche funèbre pour la dernière scène d'Hamlet* do not incorporate the pavane into their rhythmic patterns.

One problematic issue in Prelude 20 is the last beat of m. 3 (Example 5.47). Should the last melodic note in that measure be E♮ or E♭? Editions and opinions remain divided. Some of Chopin's autographs, as well as the French and German first editions, do not introduce a flat on the fourth beat. Neither do one of the English first editions and the scores belonging to Chopin's pupils Camille Dubois and Marie Scherbatoff (which were annotated by the composer).

By contrast, one of Chopin's autographs, the copy of it made by George Sand, the first impression of the English first edition, and the score of Chopin's pupil Jane Stirling all show a flat added to the last quarter note.

Which version is correct? The answer is: both. The quest for a definitive solution of the E♭/E♮ dilemma is futile. Chopin often went back and forth between different textual variants, without reaching a conclusive 'best' version.[53]

---

[51]   See Eigeldinger's commentary in *Préludes Op. 28, Op. 45*, The Complete Chopin: A New Critical Edition, p. 66.

[52]   Eigeldinger, *Chopin: Pianist and Teacher*, p. 83.

[53]   See, for example, Anatole Leikin, 'The Alternative Versions of Chopin's Piano Sonatas: Sorting out the Composer's Intentions,' in *Early Music: Context and Ideas* (Cracow: Institute of Musicology, Jagiellonian University, 2003), pp. 178–83.

Example 5.47   Chopin, Prelude 20, mm. 1–8

As Jeffrey Kallberg pointed out, Chopin did not see composition as a finite process and 'allowed multiple versions of a piece to appear before the public.'[54]

Indeed, the coexistence of competing authorized versions of the same musical piece seems a blessing, not a shortcoming, for it gives performers the opportunity to choose a variant that better fits their individual interpretation.

In this particular case, a return to C minor at the end of measure 3 sounds concluding (to a certain degree), separating this measure slightly from the G-major ending of the first phrase. A touch of a diminuendo on the last two beats of m. 3 would be appropriate in this case, before resuming the crescendo in the following measure.

The C-major triad on the fourth beat of m. 3, on the contrary, immediately initiates a shift to G major, strongly propelling the music toward the forceful G-major cadence in m. 4. The choice between the two readings is best left to the pianist.

As mentioned earlier, the melodic line in the first two measures of Prelude 20 sequentially continues motifs c from the coda of Prelude 19 (mm. 49–53 and 57–61). In the C-minor Prelude, however, motifs c in mm. 1–2, 8, and 12 are abbreviated by one (last) note. This modification brings them closer to a^3, if we consider the sixteenth notes as passing tones (for example G-A♭-G-(F)-E♭). Motif e^3 follows these motifs in mm. 3–4 (Example 5.47).

In the second and third phrases (mm. 5–8 and 9–12), *Dies irae* motifs are intertwined with each other and juxtaposed contrapuntally (Example 5.47).

---

[54]   Jeffrey Kallberg, *Chopin at the Boundaries: Sex, History, and Musical Genre* (Cambridge, MA: Harvard University Press, 1996), p. 228.

Example 5.48   Chopin, Prelude 21, mm. 1–16

Preludes 21 (B♭ major) & 22 (G minor)

Prelude 21 (B♭ major)

The B♭-major Prelude is yet another 'nocturne,' the last in the set, with a busy and thematically rich accompaniment part. For this reason, as in Prelude 13 (F♯ major), the pedaling in No. 21 is reduced to a minimum—except for mm. 17–24, when the pedal, on the contrary, is held down first for two and then for six measures in a row.

The persistently reiterated descending chromatic motion in the LH part, in all probability, reflects the *passus duriusculus* from previous preludes, even though only once (in m. 38) does it descend from the first scale degree, in full accordance

Deciphering the Préludes

Example 5.49   Chopin, Prelude 21, mm. 17–32

with the tradition. The upper line in the LH part moves in the opposite direction, often outlining motifs f^3, e, and f^2 (Example 5.48).

The cantilena in mm. 1–8 consists exclusively of motifs a^5, f^2, f^4, and b^2. When the melody arrives at a half cadence in m. 13, the accompanimental bridge that leads into the next sections is based on motifs f^3 and e^7 (Example 5.48).

In the middle section, the melody incorporates only two complete *Dies irae* motifs, e^5 and e^6. The upper line in the accompaniment, however, consists of an uninterrupted string of interlocked a^6 and a^3 in mm. 17–24 and b^6 and b motifs in mm. 25–32. Visually, the upper accompanimental voice on the downbeats of mm. 26 and 28 is missing in LH. The missing G♭, however, is heard quite clearly, in spite of being written in the upper staff. Indeed, it is advisable to play it with the LH thumb so as to achieve better RH legato without the pedal (Example 5.49).

Example 5.50 Chopin, Prelude 21, mm. 33–59

Deciphering the Préludes   137

In a condensed reprise, the melodic line comprises motifs b^6 and e^2. The accompaniment part and the bridge to the coda are both based largely on the same motifs as those heard in the first section (Example 5.50). In the coda, which begins in m. 45, the reiterated bass phrase includes symmetrically interlocked motifs e^1 and e^5 (mm. 45, 47, 49, 51, and 53–4). The rising serpentine line in the bass in mm. 55–56 moves through motifs f^5 and e^1.

The Links

The connecting pitch in this dyad of preludes is B♭ in the bass—the last bass octave in LH in Prelude 21 and the first octave in Prelude 22. There are also thematic links. Thus, the gesture B♭-A-G, prominently displayed in the LH part (see the circled eighth notes in mm. 45, 47, 49, 51, and 53–54, Example 5.50), serves as a commencement of Prelude 22 (Example 5.51a). Its prominence becomes apparent not only because it is played six times. In the score belonging to his student Jane Stirling, Chopin underscored this motif by adding the upward stems and moving it to the RH part in m. 47. Then, in m. 49, Chopin's fingering in the same score suggests playing the B♭-A-G motif by sliding the thumb on the first two notes, which accentuates this gesture.[55]

Another link is the last two eighth notes in the alto in mm. 50 and 52, E♭-D. In the concluding two measures of Prelude 21, the same motif recurs in the alto, in augmentation (see notes marked by '+' in Example 5.50). Then it reappears in Prelude 22, at the beginning of the RH part (Example 5.51a).

Sequential continuity provides an additional linkage. The lone accented note in m. 57 of Prelude 21 is followed by the accented C and B♭ in the middle voice in mm. 58–59. The resulting motif, D-C-B♭, is sequentially repeated a third down at the very opening of Prelude 22 (B♭-A-G; Example 5.51a).

Prelude 22 (G minor)

The stormy G-minor Prelude is a concise octave etude. A radically condensed reprise (from m. 34) and circumvented cadences between the ABA sections contribute to the work's restlessness.

The Prelude includes several *Dies irae* motifs, in both the bass and the upper voice. In the first phrase (mm. 1–8), the bass moves up through motifs b^4 and e^7, concluding with a^2. At the same time, the treble introduces a *passus duriusculus* in mm. 5–9, G-F♯-F♮-E♮-E♭-D (Example 5.51a).

The ending of the second phrase in mm. 13–16 differs from that of the first phrase. The last third of b^4 in m. 12, D-B♭, is transposed to a higher register at the beginning of m. 13 (G-E♭) and is trailed by e^3. Simultaneously, the upper voice states a chromatic version of c, shortened by one note (Example 5.51b).

The middle section adds a few more *Dies irae* motifs to the mix: e^7, d^2, d^1, f^1, and e^5 (Example 5.52).

---

55   Fryderyk Chopin, *Préludes Op. 28, Op. 45*, ed. Jean-Jacques Eigeldinger, p. 39.

Example 5.51 (a) Chopin, Prelude 22, mm. 1–9, (b) Prelude 22, mm. 12–15

Example 5.52 Chopin, Prelude 22, mm. 17–24

Preludes 23 (F major) & 24 (D minor)

Prelude 23 (F major)

The sheer sonic beauty of widely spaced undulating major triads, often with added sixths, sevenths, or ninths, is one of the more admired hallmarks of Chopin's piano writing. Lithe chromatic interspersions, introduced in m. 4 and the LH trills, only highlight the prevailing atmospheric diatonicism of Prelude 23.

The structure of the Prelude is charmingly unsophisticated, although the period consists of an uncommon number of phrases: five. The first four-measure phrase is transposed a fifth up in mm. 5–8 and then repeated in F major but an octave higher. The third phrase (mm. 13–16) is essentially a drawn-out half cadence, leading to a return of the first phrase, this time two octaves higher.

Just as unusual is the E♭ added to the concluding F-major tonic in the last two measures of the piece (Example 5.54).

The function of the LH part is primarily harmonic and coloristic. It contains only fragments of *Dies irae* motifs, such the first three notes of a^4 or b (for example, F-A-G-[A] in m. 3 and D-B♮-C-[A] in m. 4). The lone full *Dies irae* motif in LH is one of the shortest ones, e^3 in m. 16, which imitates, in augmentation, motifs e^3 from the RH part (Example 5.53b).

In addition to e^3, the melody also includes quite a few other motifs: b^7, b, b^4, b^3, b^2, e^4, and a^7 (Examples 5.53a, b).

Example 5.53 (a) Chopin, Prelude 23, mm. 1–5 (RH), (b) Prelude 23, mm. 14–16

Example 5.54   Chopin, Prelude 23, mm. 19–22

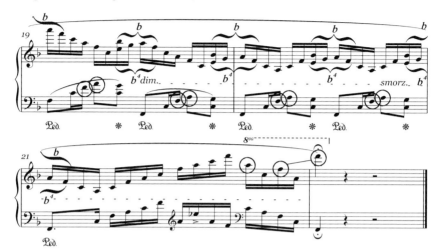

The Links

Preludes 23 and 24 are the sole pair that does not contain a single connecting pitch. Instead, we find a common motivic cell, F-A. This gesture caps the reiterated rising F-major arpeggios in LH throughout Prelude 23, including mm. 19–21 toward the end. The same two pitches top the repeated rising arpeggios in LH at the beginning of Prelude 24 (Example 5.55).

The identical motif in reverse, A-F, concludes the melodic line in Prelude 23 (see circled notes in Example 5.54). The treble in No. 24 commences with the same pitches (Example 5.55).

As in the previous two pairs of preludes, the links between the pieces are reinforced by sequential continuity. In this particular case, the LH arpeggios at the end of Prelude 23 outline the tonic fifth F-C before moving on higher to F-A. The ascending tonic fifth is sequentially transposed to D-A at the opening of Prelude 24; the F-A part of the LH arpeggio, however, remains unchanged (Example 5.55).

Prelude 24 (D minor)

Kresky adds the D-minor Prelude to 'the small list of disappointments among the preludes,' although not to the top of the list:

> The relentless bass pattern, itself an awkward formation, underlies a piece otherwise marred by an unimaginative literalness. For example, as the first harmony remains unchanged for the opening nine and a half bars, the accompaniment figure is played nineteen times in exact repetition. Similarly, a

Example 5.55 (a) Chopin, Prelude 24, mm. 1–14, (b) Prelude 24, mm. 42–43

full fourth of the total span of the piece, mm. 19–37, is given over to a wholesale replay of the first eighteen bars in transposition.[56]

I cannot dispute the critical comments listed above. What can be argued, however, is that issues like the recurrent accompaniment figure, its 'awkward formation,' and the chords that remain unchanged for several measures at a stretch should be considered within a broader context in order to be better understood.

To begin with, Prelude 24 is filled with the funeral chant's motifs. In the melody, besides detached motifs e^5, e, a^3, b, f^3, and a, some continuous strings of the *Dies irae* motifs are heard, often intricately interwoven with each other. Thus, in mm. 9–12, a chain of motifs comprises e, c, c^3, and a; in mm. 60–62, motifs a, f^3, b^1, and f^3 follow each other in succession (Examples 5.55a, b, 5.56).

In the LH part, the most prominent focal points are the two notes at the top of the arpeggios. Ascending melodic thirds, formed by these notes, dominate the thematic facet of the accompaniment. When this pattern changes, however, motifs a^1 and b^5 occasionally emerge (Examples 5.55a, b; see also mm. 17–18 and 35–6).

Example 5.56   Chopin, Prelude 24, mm. 60–62 (RH)

As for the long stretches of unchanging chords, both Preludes 23 and 24 display an obsession with protracted, pedaled triad sonorities. The difference between the two is that in Prelude 23, the focus is on the exquisitely rippling, translucent major triads. In Prelude 24, the mostly minor triads (as well as other chords) are placed in a low, harsher, and more aggressively sounding register.

'Awkward' heaving in the accompaniment, as well as powerful groundswells in the melody, possibly allude to Canto V from Lamartine's *Les Préludes*, which depicts a terrifying storm at sea. Parallels with roaring waves and fierce squalls are magnified by continuous pedaling that often lasts for up to four measures in a row.

Kresky also disapprovingly describes the Prelude's ending, arguing that 'the funeral bell that tolls so starkly at the end may impress more as a clumsy cliché than with real drama.' Actually, the impression of the final three bell strikes can vary widely, from a stark repetition of low D to an awe-inspiring, horrifying rumble. The difference lies in the pedaling.

Chopin's final pedal indication in the Prelude comprises five measures, with no release marking in the end, leaving to the performer's discretion the decision

---

[56] Kresky, *A Reader's Guide*, p. 125.

Example 5.57   Chopin, Prelude 24, mm. 73–77

about when to lift the pedal after the piece ends (Example 5.57). The pedal blends together a dissonant cluster of six notes (D, E, F, G, A, and B♭) over a six-octave span.

This pedaling may appear overindulgent, just as in the B♭-minor Prelude; by the same token, Chopin's pedaling in other preludes, such as the A-minor and F♯-major, may seem too scant. I cannot stress enough, though, that Chopin was exceptionally meticulous in his pedal markings: no matter how peculiar his pedaling may seem, it always proves, eventually, to be purposeful and meaningful.

Regrettably, most pianists choose to ignore the composer's pedal marking in the end of Prelude 24, replacing it with much cleaner and more 'elegantly sounding' pedaling—perhaps trying to avoid being accused of inartful use of the pedal.[57] As a result, the originally intended thunderous, profoundly reverberating, apocalyptic bell tolling quickly fizzles, ending in a blandly reiterated solitary bass note. The main point of the Prelude's ending, however, is not elegance. It is horror.

In Gothic horror literature, 'castles and abbeys are more often than not haunted and bells are wont to be tolled by ghosts at midnight. … Such bells always herald some horrifying event, … harbingers of dreadful occurrences.'[58] The question remains, though: why does the bell strike three times? Neither Chopin nor his students ever clarified the matter.

One possible explanation for the triple tolling of the bell, heralding a dreadful occurrence, may be found in a centuries-old Catholic tradition. Durandus of Saint-Pourçain (ca. 1275–1332), a renowned theologian and philosopher, directed that when someone was *in extremis* (at the point of dying), a bell ought to be tolled twice for a woman, thrice for a man, and more times for a cleric (depending on the orders the cleric had received).[59]

At the end of Opus 28, Chopin, tellingly, tolls the bell thrice.

---

[57]   One extremely rare exception to this tendency is Mikhail Pletnev's performance of the D-minor Prelude at a concert in Moscow in 2009.

[58]   Élizabeth Durot-Boucé, 'Midnight Trysts: "Minuit est la plus belle heure du jour,"' *Études anglaises*, 57 (2004/3), p. 300.

[59]   *The Catholic Encyclopedia: An International Work of Reference on the Constitution, Doctrine, Discipline, and History of the Catholic Church* (New York: Encyclopedia Press, 1913), vol. 2, p. 421.

Chapter 6
Further Thoughts

The *Dies irae* Spills Over

Chopin's obsession with the funeral plainchant, described by George Sand,[1] brought about a remarkable proliferation of the *Dies irae* motifs in the *Préludes*. A logical question is, did Chopin limit his preoccupation with the chant exclusively to Opus 28?

In addition to the *Préludes*, Chopin completed Ballade in F major, Op. 38, in the Carthusian monastery in Mallorca. The opening section of the Ballade is often described as bucolic—in part because of the *siciliano* rhythm, traditionally associated with bucolic scenes and melancholy emotions, and in part because F major is customarily considered to be a pastoral key.[2]

Other features contributing to the simple, pastoral charm of the Andantino are its plain four-part chorale texture; the unadorned, unpedaled tone of the piano (the sustaining pedal in this section covers only the repeated C in the first two measures and the concluding arpeggio 42 measures later); and a mostly repetitive melodic line, often merely gyrating within a narrow range.

Beneath this unsophisticated surface, however, we find a dense motivic construction enriched by polyphonic interchanges. At the heart of this construction is the opening, hallmark motif of the *Dies irae* and its symmetrical transmutations. Motif a^3 first appears in the alto in mm. 3–4 and then is imitated in the soprano in mm. 6–7. Immediately afterward, a^3 is repeated with a short passing note in mm. 7–9, contrapuntally combined with a^6 in the tenor (Example 6.1a). At the end of the Andantino section comes a double entry of motif a (Example 6.1b).

All in all, motif a and its variants are stated 35 times in the Andantino sections throughout the Ballade, which is hardly coincidental.

In the stormy fast sections, a quadruple statement of b in mm. 177–178 and 181–182 may perhaps be considered fortuitous (Example 6.2a). But when a, consisting of exactly the same pitches as the A-minor entries of that motif in Prelude 2 (C-B-C-A in mm 157–164), is played persistently no fewer than 30 times in a row, it is close to impossible to contend that the use of a here is unintentional (Example 6.2b).

---

[1] George Sand, *Histoire de ma vie*, trans. Dan Hofstadter (New York: Harper & Row, 1979), p. 410.

[2] Jonathan D. Bellman, *Chopin's Polish Ballade: Op. 38 as Narrative of National Martyrdom* (Oxford: Oxford University Press, 2010), pp. 33–4 and 153.

Example 6.1 (a) Chopin, Ballade, Op. 38, mm. 3–10, (b) Ballade, Op. 38, mm. 38–42

Motif *a* can be discerned in another piece composed in Valldemossa, Polonaise in C minor, Op. 40, No. 2. It is evident, however, only four times in the entire composition: E♭-D-E♭-C in mm. 6, 43, and 104, and C-B♭-C-A♭ in m. 61. Even if the use of *a* here is deliberate, its presence in the Polonaise is somewhat negligible.

There is another Polonaise, though, written seven years later, *Polonaise-fantaisie*, Op. 61, in which motif *a* not only is tangible, but it also plays a commanding role in this work's thematic makeup.

Polonaise-fantaisie is shaped as a sonata form with an introduction, a vast exposition (mm. 22–213), a short development (mm. 214–241), and a severely compressed recapitulation (mm. 242–288). The first conspicuous thematic attribute reminiscent of Opus 28 is an oscillating, trill-like melodic gesture. It permeates both the principal and secondary sections. And, as in the *Préludes*, this gesture is closely connected with motif *a*.

In the principal section (mm. 22–66), *a* is integrated into both the melody and the bass line (Example 6.3). Motif *a* is restated multiple times, and not merely in the principal section at the beginning of the form (mm. 44–49) but also in the transition, when the principal theme is recalled (see mm. 94–97, 98–103, and 108–113), and in the recapitulation (mm. 242–249).

Although the secondary theme is also based on an oscillating melodic figure, motif *a* makes only a brief but notable appearance during a modulation from A♯ major to B minor and B major (C𝄪-C♯-C𝄪-A♯, C𝄪-C♯-D♮-B, and D♯-C𝄪-D♯-B in Example 6.4).

Chopin's Ballade, Op. 38 and *Polonaise-fantaisie*, Op. 61 amply demonstrate that the composer's fascination with the somber plainchant was by no means confined to the *Préludes*.

Example 6.2 (a) Chopin, Ballade, Op. 38, mm. 177–182, (b) Ballade, Op. 38, mm. 157–166

Example 6.3 Chopin, *Polonaise-fantaisie*, Op. 61, mm. 24–31

Example 6.4 Chopin, *Polonaise-fantaisie*, Op. 61, mm. 166–168

Echoes of *Winterreise*

Chopin's Opus 28 bears influences of many outside sources—musical, literary, and ambient. It is therefore difficult to imagine that, while working on the *Préludes* during a harsh winter in Mallorca, the composer quelled any thoughts of the only other existing cycle of 24 pieces that reflected—in one way or another—a bleak winter journey.

Franz Schubert's *Winterreise*, written in 1827 and published the following year, is a cycle of 24 songs that Schubert himself called 'horrifying.'[3] It is indeed a unified cycle rather an assorted collection, integrated not only poetically but musically as well.

---

[3] Susan Youens, *Retracing a Winter's Journey: Schubert's* Winterreise (Ithaca, NY: Cornell University Press, 1991), p. 27.

Example 6.5 Schubert, *Winterreise*, 'Gefrorne Tränen,' (a) mm. 22–24, (b) mm. 26–28

One common thematic thread is an assembly of melodic gestures consisting of minor-scale degrees ♯7, 1, 2, and 3, which outline the interval of a diminished fourth. This poignant melodic formation is by no means limited to the *Winterreise*. Perhaps the most notable diminished-fourth theme before Schubert was the subject of Bach's C♯-minor Fugue from the first book of the *Well-Tempered Clavier* (C♯-B♯-E-D♯). Schubert evidently paid homage to this Bach theme by employing it, in various keys, in the overture to the opera *Fierrabras* (1823), in the 'Agnus Dei' from his Mass in E♭ major, D. 950 (1828), and in the piano part of his song 'Der Doppelgänger' (1828).

In *Winterreise*, this theme materializes only in 'Gefrorne Tränen' (Examples 6.5a, b).

In the other songs, the minor-scale degrees ♯7, 1, 2, and 3 are assembled into various motivic configurations, as shown in Examples 6.6a–f, regardless of whether the songs are written in major or minor keys. Only four out of the 24 songs do not include this particular melodic formation: 'Die Post,' 'Die greise Kopf,' 'Der stürmische Morgen,' and 'Mut.'

One important attribute that can be gleaned from Examples 6.5 and 6.6 is that in the vast majority of cases, the four pitches generate a tetrachord consisting of alternating half-whole-half-whole steps (see Examples 6.6b, e, h). The only exceptions to this formation are found in the songs 'Die Krähe' and 'Im Dorfe,' in which the second scale degree is lowered (for example, E♭-D♭-C-B♮ in C minor at the end of 'Die Krähe').

Example 6.6 (a) 'Gute Nacht,' (b) 'Erstarrung,' (c) 'Der Lindenbaum,' (d) 'Auf dem Flusse,' (e) 'Rückblick,' (f) 'Irrlicht,' (g) 'Einsamkeit,' (h) 'Täuschung'

(a)

(b)

(c)

(d)

(e)

(f)

(g)

(h)

The tetrachord alternating half and whole steps is distinctive by virtue of being one half of the octatonic scale. Of the two types of the octatonic scale, the one that begins with a whole step consists of two diatonic minor tetrachords

Example 6.7 (a) Octatonic scale (diatonic tetrachords), (b) Dorian scale, (c) Octatonic scale (chromatic tetrachords)

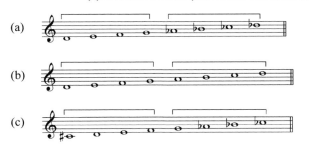

(Example 6.7a). If the same tetrachords are put together a whole step apart, they form the Dorian mode (Example 6.7b). It is only the placement of the two Dorian (or minor) tetrachords at a half-step distance that produces an octatonic scale.

The other type of the octatonic scale, however, consists of two identical chromatic rather than diatonic tetrachords that both can, therefore, be defined as octatonic (Example 6.7c). While Schubert does not expand his octatonic tetrachords to the full extent of a scale (save for a whole step added occasionally on either side of the tetrachord, turning it into an octatonic pentachord), these archetypes of a full scale acquire a specific octatonic flavor.

In Chopin's *Préludes*, melodic segments built on octatonic tetrachords sound in 14 of the 24 pieces: Nos. 4, 5, 6, 8, 10, 11, 12, 13, 14, 15, 16, 18, 20, and 22.[4] Bach's 'octatonic' theme surfaces in No. 8 (see the last two beats in the melody in mm. 1 and 2, Example 5.21). Other examples include the treble line in m. 8 of Prelude 6 (Example 5.17) and in m. 22 of Prelude 13 (Example 5.33); the first four sixteenths in Prelude 18 (Example 5.44a); and the bass line in mm. 1–2 in Prelude 22 (Example 5.51a). A few times, octatonic tetrachords are presented in scalar form, as in Preludes 10 and 15 (see Examples 5.26a, b and 5.37a, b). In Prelude 5, Chopin moves beyond Schubert's ♯7-1-2-3 arrangement of minor-scale degrees, instead placing an octatonic tetrachord on ♭6-5-4-3 in D major (B♭-A-G-F♯ in Example 5.16, mm. 33–5).[5]

---

[4] Dmitry Shostakovich adopted this melodic configuration for his musical signature. It consists of the first letter of his first name and the first phoneme of his surname, spelled in German as SCH (in the Cyrillic alphabet, this phoneme is indicated by only one, nonmusical letter 'Ш'): D-(e)S-C-H, or D-E♭-C-B.

[5] Chopin expanded octatonic scales beyond tetrachords in some of his compositions written both before and after the *Préludes*. In Ballade, Op. 23 (published in 1836), the lower layer of eighth notes in the RH passage in mm. 130–134 comprises an octatonic scale B♭-C♭-C♯-D-E♮-F-G-A♭-B♭, and so on. In Nocturne, Op. 27, No. 1 (also published in 1836), the conclusion of the middle section incorporates an almost complete octatonic scale in mm.

Example 6.8 Schubert, *Winterreise*, 'Gute Nacht,' (a) mm. 10–11, (b) mm. 22–23

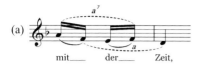

A host of melodic phrases constructed of octatonic tetrachords is not the sole thematic attribute that the *Winterreise* shares with the *Préludes*. Another common thematic element manifests itself in numerous oscillating, trill-like figures that permeate both cycles. And, as in Opus 28, these gestures in the *Winterreise* are often associated with motifs *a* from the *Dies irae*.

The question, of course, is whether Schubert purposefully introduced the *Dies irae* chant into the *Winterreise*. His set predates, by a couple of years, Berlioz's *Symphonie fantastique*, which broadly popularized the chant. There is no evidence that Schubert quoted in the *Winterreise* an extended version of the chant, cited shortly afterward by Berlioz and Alkan. But the presence of the opening and the most distinguishable *Dies irae* phrase—motifs *a*, *b*, and their permutations—is actually prodigious in Schubert's cycle.

The first song, 'Gute Nacht,' sets the tone; motif *a* concludes several melodic phrases, with motifs a^7 and *a* in Example 6.8a symmetrically interlocking (Examples 6.8a, b).

Motif *a* then reappears in all the following songs but two: 'Wasserflut' and 'Irrlicht.' In many of the songs, *a* sounds in its original form; in Examples 6.9c and 6.9e, motif *a* springs from an oscillating melodic gesture (see Examples 6.9a–f).

All the permutations of *a*, shown in Example 4.8, are present in the *Winterreise*. The most commonly used is a^2, found in eight songs (Examples 6.10a, b). Motif a^3 trails not far behind (five songs; Example 6.10c). Even symmetrically interlocked motifs occasionally appear in the cycle (Examples 6.8a, 6.11a, b). In this context, certain groups of broken thirds may be viewed as motifs *b* (Example 6.12).

Did Schubert intentionally make references to the *Dies irae* in his 'horrifying cycle of songs'? Are these references a series of subconscious allusions to that somber chant, generating thematic gestures that perfectly fit his cycle's gloomy subject matter? Or are all these numerous motifs, which permeate the *Winterreise*, mere happenstance?

To answer these questions with any degree of certainty would require a separate investigation. For my immediate purposes, however, the subject is inconsequential.

78–81: D♮-E♭-F-G♭, F-G♭-A♭-A♮. And in *Polonaise-fantaisie*, Op. 61 (1846), an octatonic scale in mm. 240–241 leads into the recapitulation (C-D♭-E♭-F♭-F♯-G-A♮-B♭, and so forth).

Example 6.9 (a) 'Gefrorne Tränen,' (b) 'Rückblick,' (c) 'Die Krähe,'
(d) 'Letzte Hoffnung,' (e) 'Im Dorfe,' (f) 'Mut'

154 *The Mystery of Chopin's* Préludes

Example 6.10 Schubert, *Winterreise*, (a) 'Erstarrung,' (b) 'Der Lindenbaum,' (c) 'Die Wetterfahne'

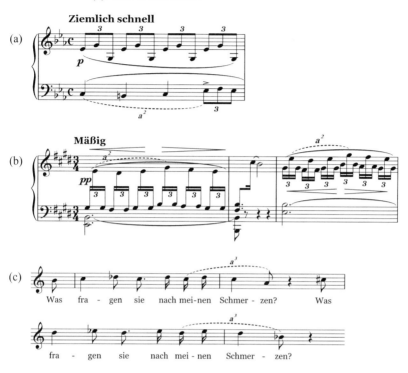

Example 6.11 Schubert, *Winterreise*, (a) 'Der greise Kopf,' (b) 'Mut'

It does not really matter whether or not Schubert purposefully drew on the *Dies irae*. Much more important is the issue of whether Chopin sensed resemblances between the *Winterreise* and the *Dies irae*, and that is entirely possible. If an

Example 6.12 Schubert, *Winterreise*, 'Der Leiermann'

ordinary musicologist like myself can hear the first phrase from the *Dies irae* (motifs *a*, *b*, and their symmetrical permutations) throughout the *Winterreise*, so could Chopin, especially since his mind, according to his intimate, George Sand, was preoccupied with the funeral chant. To a careful observer, Schubert amply demonstrates how motifs *a* and *b*—or their identical twins, entirely unrelated to the *Dies irae*—can be symmetrically elaborated and absorbed into the fabric of music. Chopin's *Préludes* fully assimilates all these developments.

More Interlinks

This book has two primary analytical foci. One is the pairings of the preludes in Chopin's Opus 28, which is comparable to the pairings of both the cantos in Lamartine's *Les Préludes* and the preludes and fugues in Bach's *Well-Tempered Clavier*. The other is the use of the *Dies irae* chant in the *Préludes* as a musical symbol of one of the more prevalent topics in the poem: death. It is clear that the chant thoroughly pervades the *Préludes* and defines most of its thematic framework, which makes Opus 28 a monothematic composition.

Yet Lamartine's poem contains other recurrent, albeit not as prevalent, images as well. For example, the wind, in its various manifestations, is one such image. It is the wind that no longer ignites a flame in the protagonist's smoldering soul ('*mais aujourd'hui mon âme, / Comme un feu dont le vent n'excite plus la flamme,*' I.5–6); the breeze that reverberates a harp ('*Harpes, que j'entendais résonner dans les airs,*' I.11) and caresses a lyre ('*Un vent caresse ma lyre,*' X.1); the thirsty zephyr that dries up her tears ('*Ah! laisse le zéphyr avide / A leur source arrêter tes pleurs;*' III.36–7); the fierce north wind throwing about a ship with no masts ('*au gré des aquilons,*' V.3); the winter winds tearing withered leaves away from an oak tree ('*Comme dans nos forêts, le chêne avec mépris / Livre aux vents des hivers ses feuillages flétris;*' V.23–4); the whispering fragrant breeze ('*le son une brise embaumée,*' IX.18); and the strong winds clattering the military flags ('*Ou le bruit des drapeaux soulevés par les vents,*' VIII.15) and then sweeping away the foul dust after the battle ('*Les vents balayeront leur poussière infectée,*' VIII.114).

Another thread that extends across the poem is flowing water. Canto III mentions a brook under the shade ('*le ruisseau sous l'ombrage,*' III.4) and a murmuring stream ('*Le flot murmurant,*' III.56). In Canto VIII, in a battle scene, streams become rivulets of blood ('*ruisseaux de sang,*' VIII.96); then, in the same canto, the river washes clean its bloodied banks ('*Le fleuve lavera sa rive ensanglantée,*' VIII.113). Cantos IX and XI return to the pastoral images of a forest river ('*Et que l'écho des bois, ou le fleuve en coulant,*' IX.11) and of the meadows interspersed with flowing creeks ('*Gazons entrecoupés de ruisseaux,*' XI.5; '*Les lits murmurant des ruisseaux,*' XI.60). Among other common themes bridging together different cantos are fire (I.6, VIII.67), waves (III.1, 48, IV.3, V.6, 26), a dove (III.6–8, III.58, XI.24), tears (III.25, 71, VI.4, XI.75), the sea and the ocean (III.43, IV.4, V.1–8), and hillsides (III.49, VIII.89, XI.2).

Likewise, Chopin's *Préludes* contain additional thematic, genre, and textural links that span the set (many of these links were described in Chapter 5):

- The first three beats of Prelude 9 (Example 5.25) mirror the chorale fragment from Prelude 2 (mm. 21–22, Example 5.6). An almost identical chord progression, but in E major, surfaces in Prelude 15 in mm. 40–41 and 56–57.
- The mazurka elements in Prelude 7, specifically the two harmonic parallel thirds on the first beats of mm. 3 and 11 (B♯/D♯-C♯/E, Example 5.20) are presented linearly during mazurka interjections in Prelude 10 in mm. 4, 12, and 15–18 (B♯-C♯-D♯-E, Examples 5.26a, b). Somewhat similarly, the melodic gesture C♯-A♯-B-D in mm. 4–6 of Prelude 7 is reflected in mm. 3–4 of Prelude 10, in a similar rhythm and nearly identical pitches, A♯-B♯-C♯-D♯ (compare Examples 5.20 and 5.26a).
- Examples 5.17 and 5.29 show that the palindromic combination of motifs a^4 and a at the beginning of Prelude 6 (B-D-C♯-D-B, in which pitches 1–4 form motif a^4, while pitches 2–5 comprise motif a) comes back, in transposition, at the opening of Prelude 12 (G♯-B-A♯-B-G♯ in the tenor).
- The descending lament pattern, in various voices and in either a diatonic or a chromatic (*passus duriusculus*) version, appears in Preludes 4, 12, 16, 17, 20, and 22.
- Preludes 1 and 8 contain melodic lines that occasionally resemble each other; both are carried by the RH thumb and are doubled in upper octaves.
- The two 'watery' preludes, Nos. 3 and 23, outline prominently a major triad with an added sixth. In Prelude 23, this creates a distinct pentatonic hue (Example 5.53a); in Prelude 3, the triad is usually filled in with passing notes (Example 5.7).
- Heavily pedaled, descending rapid-note crashes in RH, traversing almost the entire expanse of the keyboard, are placed at the conclusions of Preludes 18 and 24 (Examples 5.44c, 5.57).

Although most of these links are not as prominent as the ones that tie together the odd- and even-numbered Preludes, they are audible nonetheless.

Further Thoughts 157

Should the *Préludes* Be Played Together, or Separately?

The additional connections between the preludes, listed above, further consolidate the *Préludes* into a unified cycle. But this does not necessarily mean that Opus 28 should only be performed in its entirety. Chopin's concert-programming preferences for the preludes remain unclear. He never played the entire set in public concerts; at the same time, as far as we know, he never publicly performed merely a single prelude. The existent concert programs and reviews mention indeterminate groups of preludes. Twice, in 1841 and 1848, the number of preludes was listed on the program as four, but without specifying which preludes were performed.[6]

The fact that Chopin only played selected groups of preludes in concerts does not contradict the idea of Opus 28 as a unified cycle. The concert practice of the time did not treat symphonies, concertos, or sonatas as unbreakable, sacrosanct wholes. Selected movements from symphonies and concertos were commonly performed in public concerts in the late eighteenth and early nineteenth centuries.[7]

Beethoven, in his letter to Ferdinand Ries of 19 April 1819, offers advice regarding various possibilities for playing selected movements of his Piano Sonata, Op. 106 in concerts:

> If the Sonata should not be suitable for London, I could send you another one; or you could also omit the Largo, and begin straight away with the Fugue in the last movement; or you could use the first movement and then the Adagio, and then for the third movement the Scherzo—and omit entirely No. 4 with the Largo and Allegro risoluto. Or you could take just the first movement and the Scherzo and let them form the whole sonata. I leave this to you to do as you think best.[8]

Parisian audiences at that time (as well as audiences everywhere else) enthusiastically applauded between the movements of a symphony, often forcing the orchestra to repeat individual movements. Movements of a symphony or a concerto were habitually interspersed in concerts with other, smaller works. For example, in one concert in Paris, the first three movements of Beethoven's Ninth Symphony were separated from the choral finale by a few popular songs by Weber and Rossini.[9] Chopin himself, whether he performed works by others or

---

[6] Jean-Jacques Eigeldinger, 'Twenty-Four Preludes Op. 28: Genre, Structure, Significance,' in Jim Samson (ed.), *Chopin Studies* (Cambridge: Cambridge University Press, 1988), p. 170; William G. Atwood, *Fryderyk Chopin: Pianist from Warsaw* (New York: Columbia University Press, 1987), p. 236.

[7] Mary Sue Morrow, *Concert Life in Vienna: Aspects of a Developing Musical and Social Institution* (Stuyvesant, NY: Pendragon Press, 1989), pp. 153–4, 158.

[8] William S. Newman, *Beethoven on Beethoven: Playing His Piano Music His Way* (New York: Norton, 1988), p. 275.

[9] James H. Johnson, *Listening in Paris: A Cultural History* (Berkeley: University of California Press, 1995), pp. 199, 258–60.

158   *The Mystery of Chopin's* Préludes

his own compositions, frequently played only selected movements of concertos and sonatas.[10]

Therefore, the *Préludes* need not be performed without interruption from beginning to end. The pianist should, however, take into consideration the intrinsic bonds within the diptychs of the odd- and even-numbered preludes. Playing selected preludes in subsets of two, in which every major-mode Prelude serves as a preamble to the following minor-mode piece (a 'prelude to death'), will maximize the dramatic impact generated by each subset.

And Once Again: 'Preludes to What?'

When André Gide pondered why Chopin's pieces are titled 'preludes,' he decisively rejected the idea that the name Chopin chose for Opus 28 originated with Bach's preludes from *The Well-Tempered Clavier*.

Indeed, the two books of *The Well-Tempered Clavier*, unlike Chopin's *Préludes*, are not unified cycles. Inside Bach's two sets, however, as Gide asserted, every prelude/fugue pair merges into an integral whole. The influence of *The Well-Tempered Clavier* on Opus 28 is undeniable, yet it is rooted not only in the *Clavier*'s preludes but also in the preludes and the fugues combined. The overall structure of Opus 28 emulates Bach's binary units: every major-mode prelude in Chopin's opus introduces the subsequent minor-mode piece, through compositional procedures similar to those of *The Well-Tempered Clavier*. The minor-mode pieces in Opus 28, though, are not fugues, and although Chopin incorporates some fugal techniques into his set, he does so in both major and minor preludes.

Since Chopin's preludes are not modeled solely on Bach's preludes, it is only logical to assume that the *Préludes* were not named after the preluding portions of Bach's collection. Was Chopin's set titled, perhaps, after the early nineteenth-century preludes? That would be even less likely. The earlier preludes (see, for instance, Examples 1.1 and 1.2) were never performed publicly by themselves, either individually or in groups. Rather, these didactic pieces were typically plucked out of collections and used as preambles to concert pieces when pianists, for whatever reason, could not extemporize preludes on the spot. Moreover, the composers of published preludes encouraged pianists to introduce various changes into the text of their preludes, depending on what main composition a prelude introduced. Needless to say, Chopin's preludes have nothing in common with their earlier utilitarian namesakes, which is why Liszt and others considered Chopin's preludes to be groundbreaking, self-sufficient compositions rather than introductions to other works.

Meanwhile, Chopin's set does share a number of qualities with Lamartine's *Les Préludes*, as Liszt himself proclaimed in 1841.[11] The poem's digressive

---

[10]   Atwood, *Fryderyk Chopin*, pp. 69, 83, 87, 157.
[11]   Ibid., p. 233.

Further Thoughts 159

fantastic imagery corresponds perfectly to Schumann's description of Opus 28 as a 'wild motley' of 'strange sketches' and 'ruins' filled with 'the morbid, the feverish, the repellent.' Interconnections between the cantos of the poem, as well as its omnipresent *idée fixe*—death—are reflected in Chopin's cycle of interconnected pieces, monothematically based on the Requiem Mass chant *Dies irae*, a broadly recognized musical symbol of death. Consequently, it is entirely possible that Chopin's choice of the title for Opus 28, just as Liszt's pick of the same title for his symphonic poem several years later, was more affected by Lamartine's *Les Préludes* than by any preceding collection of utilitarian preludes.[12]

Furthermore, Chopin's *Préludes* may be considered, in a sense, an implicit precursor of later instrumental requiem music, such as David Popper's *Requiem for Three Cellos and Orchestra* (1891), Benjamin Britten's *Sinfonia da Requiem* (1940), Howard Hanson's Symphony No. 4, 'Requiem' (1943), and Toru Takemitsu's *Requiem for Strings* (1957), among many others.[13] Chopin's gripping reflections on death, saturated with the all-pervading *Dies irae*, are essentially an instrumental requiem—a piano requiem in 24 movements.

---

[12] Incidentally, it takes almost as much time to recite the poem as to perform the *Préludes*.

[13] An extensive list of instrumental requiems is compiled in Robert Chase, *Dies Irae: A Guide to Requiem Music* (Lanham, MD: The Scarecrow Press, 2003), pp. 313 and 686–7.

Appendix

XVI: Les Préludes
Nouvelles Méditations Poétiques
Alphonse de Lamartine

XVI: The Preludes
New Poetic Meditations
English Translation: Tamah Swenson

LES PRÉLUDES

LES PRÉLUDES

CANTO I

CANTO I

1	La nuit, pour rafraîchir la nature embrasée,		1	The night, to refresh the blaze of nature,
2	De ses cheveux d'ébène exprimant la rosée,		2	Takes repose on the hilltops, wringing out the dew
3	Pose au sommet des monts ses pieds silencieux,		3	From her ebony tresses, her feet silent,
4	Et l'ombre et le sommeil descendent sur mes yeux:		4	And shadow and sleep descend on my eyes:
5	C'était l'heure où jadis … mais aujourd'hui mon âme,		5	This was a time before … but today my soul,
6	Comme un feu dont le vent n'excite plus la flamme,		6	Like a fire from which the wind no longer excites a flame,
7	Fait pour se ranimer un inutile effort,		7	Rekindled to ignite a futile endeavor,
8	Retombe sur soi-même, et languit et s'endort.		8	Collapses on itself, languishes and smolders.
9	Que ce calme lui pèse! O lyre! ô mon génie!		9	How much this calm weighs! O lyre! O my Genius!
10	Musique intérieure, ineffable harmonie,		10	Music of the soul, ineffable harmony,
11	Harpes, que j'entendais résonner dans les airs,		11	Harps, which I heard reverberating from above,
12	Comme un écho lointain des célestes concerts;		12	Like a distant echo of heavenly concerts;
13	Pendant qu'il en est temps, pendant qu'il vibre encore,		13	While there is still time, while it is resounding,
14	Venez, venez bercer ce cœur qui vous implore.		14	Come, come and comfort this heart that beseeches you.
15	Et toi, qui donnes l'âme à mon luth inspiré,		15	And you, who gives a soul to my inspired lute,
16	Esprit capricieux, viens, prélude à ton gré!		16	Capricious Spirit, come, prelude as you like!

CANTO II

1 Il descend! il descend! la harpe obéissante
2 A frémi mollement sous son vol cadencé,
3   Et de la corde frémissante
4 Le souffle harmonieux dans mon âme a passé.

CANTO III

1 L'onde qui baise ce rivage,
2 De quoi se plaint-elle à ses bords?
3 Pourquoi le roseau sur la plage,
4 Pourquoi le ruisseau sous l'ombrage
5 Rendent-ils de tristes accords?

6 De quoi gémit la tourterelle
7 Quand, dans le silence des bois,
8 Seule auprès du ramier fidèle,
9 L'Amour fait palpiter son aile,
10 Les baisers étouffent sa voix?

11 Et toi, qui mollement te livres
12 Au doux sourire du bonheur,
13 Et du regard dont tu m'enivres
14 Me fais mourir, me fais revivre,
15 De quoi te plains-tu sur mon cœur?

CANTO II

1 He descends! he descends! the obedient harp
2 Trembled indolently under its cadenced flight,
3   And from the vibrating string
4 Harmonious inspiration has entered my soul.

CANTO III

1 The wave that caresses this shore,
2 About what does it complain to its banks?
3 Why does the reed on the beach,
4 Why does the brook under the shade
5 Render such mournful harmonies?

6 About what does the turtledove moan
7 When, in the wood's silence,
8 Alone near the faithful ring-pigeon,
9 Love makes its wing flutter,
10 Kisses smother its voice?

11 And you, who softly surrender
12 To the gentle smile of happiness,
13 And through your intoxicating look
14 You destroy me, you revive me,
15 What complaint do you place on my heart?

16	Plus jeune que la jeune aurore,
17	Plus limpide que ce flot pur,
18	Ton âme au bonheur vient d'éclore,
19	Et jamais aucun souffle encore
20	N'en a terni le vague azur.
21	Cependant, si ton cœur soupire
22	De quelque poids mystérieux,
23	Sur tes traits si la joie expire,
24	Et si tout près de ton sourire
25	Brille une larme dans tes yeux,
26	Hélas! c'est que notre faiblesse,
27	Pliant sous sa félicité
28	Comme un roseau qu'un souffle abaisse,
29	Donne l'accent de la tristesse
30	Même au chant de la volupté.
31	Ou bien peut-être qu'avertie
32	De la fuite de nos plaisirs,
33	L'âme en extase anéantie
34	Se réveille et sent que la vie
35	Fuit dans chacun de nos soupirs

16	Younger than the new dawn,
17	More limpid than this pure wave,
18	Your soul has just blossomed with joy,
19	And never has any breath yet
20	Tarnished its faint azure.
21	However, if your heart sighs
22	From some inexplicable weight,
23	If joy vanishes from your face,
24	And if near your smile
25	A teardrop glistens in your eye,
26	Alas! It is that our weakness,
27	Folding under its blissfulness
28	Like a reed bent by a breeze,
29	Gives an accent of sadness
30	Even to the song of delight.
31	Or even perhaps warned
32	Of the flight of our pleasures,
33	The soul in overwhelming ecstasy
34	Wakes and feels that life
35	Flees with each breath we take.

36	Ah! laisse le zéphyr avide	36	Ah! Allow the thirsty zephyr
37	A leur source arrêter tes pleurs;	37	To dry up your tears at their source;
38	Jouissons de l'heure rapide:	38	Let us enjoy the fading hour:
39	Le temps fuit, mais son flot limpide	39	Time flies, but its limpid stream
40	Du ciel réfléchit les couleurs.	40	Reflects the colors of the sky.
41	Tout naît, tout passe, tout arrive	41	All is born, all proceeds, all arrives
42	Au terme ignoré de son sort:	42	At the unknown hour of its fate:
43	A l'Océan l'onde plaintive,	43	To the Ocean the plaintive wave,
44	Aux vents la feuille fugitive,	44	To the winds the fugitive leaf,
45	L'aurore au soir, l'homme à la mort.	45	The dawn to evening, man to death.
46	Mais qu'importe, ô ma bien-aimée!	46	But of what importance, oh my beloved!
47	Le terme incertain de nos jours?	47	Is the uncertain length of our days?
48	Pourvu que sur l'onde calmée,	48	Given that on the calmed wave,
49	Par une pente parfumée,	49	Along a redolent hillside,
50	Le temps nous entraîne en son cours;	50	Time carries us in its stream;
51	Pourvu que, durant le passage,	51	Given that, on this journey,
52	Couché dans tes bras à demi,	52	Lying enfolded in your arms,
53	Les yeux tournés vers ton image,	53	My eyes turned toward your image,
54	Sans le voir, j'aborde au rivage	54	Without seeing it, I approach the shore.
55	Comme un voyageur endormi.	55	Like a sleeping traveler.

56	Le flot murmurant se retire
57	Du rivage qu'il a baisé,
58	La voix de la colombe expire,
59	Et le voluptueux zéphire
60	Dort sur le calice épuisé.

61	Embrassons-nous, mon bien suprême,
62	Et sans rien reprocher aux dieux,
63	Un jour de la terre où l'on aime
64	Évanouissons-nous de même
65	En un soupir mélodieux.

66	Non, non, brise à jamais cette corde amollie!
67	Mon cœur ne répond plus à ta voix affaiblie.
68	L'amour n'a pas de sons qui puissent l'exprimer:
69	Pour révéler sa langue, il faut, il faut aimer.
70	Un seul soupir du cœur que le cœur nous renvoie,
71	Un œil demi-voilé par des larmes de joie,
72	Un regard, un silence, un accent de sa voix,
73	Un mot toujours le même et répété cent fois,
74	O lyre! en disent plus que ta vaine harmonie
75	L'amour est à l'amour, le reste est au génie
76	Si tu veux que mon cœur résonne sous ta main
77	Tire un plus mâle accord de tes fibres d'airain

56	The murmuring wave recedes
57	From the shore that it has caressed,
58	The song of the dove fades away,
59	And the voluptuous zephyr
60	Lies asleep, exhausted, on the calyx.

61	Let us embrace each other, my dearest,
62	And with nothing to blame the gods,
63	A day on the earth where one loves
64	Let us vanish just the same way
65	In a melodious sigh.

66	No, no, break this weakened string forever!
67	My heart no longer answers your enfeebled voice.
68	Love has no sounds that can express it:
69	To reveal its language, one must, one must love.
70	A single sigh of the heart that the heart returns to us,
71	An eye partially veiled by tears of joy,
72	A look, a silence, a tone of voice,
73	A word, always the same and repeated a hundred times,
74	O lyre saying more than your vain harmony!
75	Love is to love, the rest is to the Genius
76	If you want my heart to resound beneath your hand,
77	Call forth a more virile harmony from your bronze strings.

CANTO IV

1 J'entends, j'entends de loin comme une voix qui gronde;
2 Un souffle impétueux fait frissonner les airs,
3   Comme l'on voit frissonner l'onde,
4 Quand l'aigle, au vol pesant, rase le sein des mers.

CANTO V

1 Eh! qui m'emportera sur des flots sans rivages?
2 Quand pourrai-je, la nuit, aux clartés des orages,
3 Sur un vaisseau sans mâts, au gré des aquilons,
4 Fendre de l'Océan les liquides vallons!
5 M'engloutir dans leur sein, m'élancer sur leurs cimes,
6 Rouler avec la vague au fond des noirs abîmes!
7 Et revomi cent fois par les gouffres amers,
8 Flotter comme l'écume au vaste sein des mers!
9 D'effroi, de volupté, tour à tour éperdue,
10 Cent fois entre la vie et la mort suspendue,
11 Peut-être que mon âme, au sein de ces horreurs,
12 Pourrait jouir au moins de ses propres terreurs;
13 Et, prête à s'abîmer dans la nuit qu'elle ignore,
14 A la vie un moment se reprendrait encore,
15 Comme un homme, roulant des sommets d'un rocher,
16 De ses bras tout sanglants cherche à s'y rattacher.
17 Mais toujours repasser par une même route,
18 Voir ses jours épuisés s'écouler goutte à goutte;
19 Mais suivre pas à pas dans l'immense troupeau

CANTO IV

1 I hear, I hear a faraway voice that thunders;
2 An impetuous breath that makes the air tremble,
3   As one sees the wave ripple,
4 When the eagle, in weighted flight, skims the sea's breast.

CANTO V

1 Hey! Who will carry me on these seas without shores?
2 When shall I, the night, illuminated by storms,
3 On a ship without masts, at the north wind's mercy,
4 Splitting the Ocean into liquid valleys!
5 Plunging me to their breast, hurling me to their crests,
6 Rolling with the wave to the bottom of chasms' black depths!
7 And disgorged a hundred times by the acrid abyss,
8 Floating like foam to the vast open ocean!
9 By terror, by delight, alternately overcome,
10 A hundred times suspended between life and death,
11 Perhaps my soul, in the midst of these horrors,
12 Could at least relish its own terrors;
13 And, ready to be lost in the night that it ignores,
14 In the next moment would take up life again,
15 Like a man, rolling down a rocky summit,
16 With bloodied arms attempting cling to it.
17 But always retracing the same route,
18 Seeing his spent days trickling away drop by drop;
19 But following step by step within the immense herd

20	Ces générations, inutile fardeau,
21	Qui meurent pour mourir, qui vécurent pour vivre,
22	Et dont chaque printemps la terre se délivre,
23	Comme dans nos forêts, le chêne avec mépris
24	Livre aux vents des hivers ses feuillages flétris;
25	Sans regrets, sans espoir, avancer dans la vie
26	Comme un vaisseau qui dort sur une onde assoupie;
27	Sentir son âme usée en impuissant effort,
28	Se ronger lentement sous la rouille du sort;
29	Penser sans découvrir, aspirer sans atteindre,
30	Briller sans éclairer, et pâlir sans s'éteindre:
31	Hélas! tel est mon sort et celui des humains!
32	Nos pères ont passé par les mêmes chemins.
33	Chargés du même sort, nos fils prendront nos places.
34	Ceux qui ne sont pas nés y trouveront leurs traces.
35	Tout s'use, tout périt, tout passe: mais, hélas!
36	Excepté les mortels, rien ne change ici-bas!

CANTO VI

1	Toi qui rendais la force à mon âme affligée,
2	Esprit consolateur, que ta voix est changée!
3	On dirait qu'on entend, au séjour des douleurs,
4	Rouler, à flots plaintifs, le sourd torrent des pleurs.
5	Pourquoi gémir ainsi, comme un souffle d'orage,
6	A travers les rameaux qui pleurent leur feuillage?
7	Pourquoi ce vain retour vers la félicité?

20	These generations, useless burden,
21	Who die so as to die, who live so as to live,
22	And from which each spring the earth frees itself,
23	As in our forests, the oak tree disdainfully
24	Delivers its withered leaves to the winter winds;
25	Without regret, without hope, to move through life
26	Like a vessel that sleeps on a quieted wave;
27	Feeling its soul worn out by powerless work,
28	Slowly eating away at itself under the rust of fate;
29	Thinking without discovering, hoping without result,
30	Shining without lighting, dimming without extinguishing:
31	Alas! such is my fate and the fate of mankind!
32	Our fathers have traveled along the same paths.
33	Burdened with the same fate, our sons will take our places.
34	Those who are not yet born will find their footprints there.
35	Everything wears away, perishes, passes: but, alas!
36	Except for mortals, nothing changes here!

CANTO VI

1	You who restored strength to my afflicted soul,
2	Consoling Spirit, how your voice is changed!
3	One would say one hears, in the midst of pain,
4	Rolling, with plaintive waves, the muted flood of tears.
5	Why wail thus, like a wind of a storm,
6	Through the branches weeping their foliage?
7	Why the vain return toward bliss?

8	Quoi donc! ce qui n'est plus a-t-il jamais été?		8	What! That which is no longer, did it ever exist?
9	Faut-il que le regret, comme une ombre ennemie,		9	Must regret, like an enemy shadow,
10	Vienne s'asseoir sans cesse au festin de la vie,		10	Come sit tirelessly at life's banquet,
11	Et d'un regard funèbre, effrayant les humains,		11	And with a look of death, frightening all mankind,
12	Fasse tomber toujours les coupes de leurs mains?		12	Always push the cup from their hands?
13	Non: de ce triste aspect que ta voix me délivre!		13	No: your voice releases me from this doleful view!
14	Oublions, oublions: c'est le secret de vivre.		14	Let us forget, let us forget: this is the secret of living.
15	Viens; chante, et du passé détournant mes regards,		15	Come; sing, and from the past, diverting my eyes,
16	Précipite mon âme au milieu des hasards!		16	Plunge my soul into the midst of danger!

CANTO VII

1	De quels sons belliqueux mon oreille est frappée!		1	With what bellicose sounds is my ear assaulted!
2	C'est le cri du clairon, c'est la voix du coursier;		2	It is the cry of the bugle, it is the neigh of the courser;
3	La corde de sang trempée		3	The blood-soaked string
4	Retentit comme l'épée		4	Resounds like the sword
5	Sur l'orbe du bouclier.		5	On the sphere of the shield.

CANTO VIII

1	La trompette a jeté le signal des alarmes:		1	The trumpet sounded the alarm:
2	Aux armes! et l'écho répète au loin: Aux armes!		2	To arms! and the distant echo repeats: To arms!
3	Dans la plaine soudain les escadrons épars,		3	On the plain, suddenly the squadrons scatter,
4	Plus prompts que l'aquilon, fondent de toutes parts,		4	Faster than the north wind, charge in all directions,
5	Et sur les flancs épais des légions mortelles,		5	And on the wide flanks of deadly legions,
6	S'étendent tout à coup comme deux sombres ailes.		6	Extending unexpectedly like two dark wings.
7	Le coursier, retenu par un frein impuissant,		7	The charger, held back by a soft bit,
8	Sur ses jarrets pliés, s'arrête en frémissant.		8	Rears up and hesitates on quivering haunches.

9	La foudre dort encore, et sur la foule immense,
10	Plane, avec la terreur, un lugubre silence:
11	On n'entend que le bruit de cent mille soldats,
12	Marchant comme un seul homme au-devant du trépas;
13	Les roulements des chars, les coursiers qui hennissent,
14	Les ordres répétés qui dans l'air retentissent,
15	Ou le bruit des drapeaux soulevés par les vents,
16	Qui, sur les camps rivaux flottant à plis mouvants,
17	Tantôt semblent, enflés d'un souffle de victoire,
18	Vouloir voler d'eux-même au-devant de la gloire,
19	Et tantôt retombant le long des pavillons,
20	De leurs funèbres plis couvrir leurs bataillons.
21	Mais sur le front des camps déjà les bronzes grondent,
22	Ces tonnerres lointains se croisent, se répondent;
23	Des tubes enflammés la foudre avec effort
24	Sort, et frappe en sifflant comme un souffle de mort;
25	Le boulet dans les rangs laisse une large trace.
26	Ainsi qu'un laboureur qui passe et qui repasse,
27	Et sans se reposer déchirant le vallon,
28	A côté du sillon creuse un autre sillon:
29	Ainsi le trait fatal dans les rangs se promène
30	Et comme des épis les couche dans la plaine.
31	Ici tombe un héros moissonné dans sa fleur,
32	Superbe, et l'œil brillant d'orgueil et de valeur.
33	Sur son casque ondulant, d'où jaillit la lumière,
34	Flotte d'un coursier noir l'ondoyante crinière:
35	Ce casque éblouissant sert de but au trépas;

9	The lightning still sleeps, and on the immense crowd,
10	Floats, with terror, a lugubrious silence:
11	One hears only the beat of a hundred thousand soldiers,
12	Marching like a single man toward the chasm of death;
13	The chariots' rolling, the neighing of chargers,
14	The repeated orders resounding on the air,
15	Or the clattering of flags carried on the wind,
16	That on the rival's camps float with billowing folds,
17	And, at times, seem swollen by a breath of victory,
18	Wanting to carry themselves toward glory,
19	And other times falling back along the pole,
20	With funeral folds to cover their battalions.
21	But already on the front line, cannons thunder,
22	These distant thunderclaps meet and reply;
23	From flaming tubes lightning bursts out
24	And hits whistling like a breath of death;
25	The shell leaves a broad track through the ranks.
26	Like a ploughman who passes and passes again,
27	And without resting, tearing apart the valley,
28	Next to the furrow he ploughs another furrow:
29	So the fatal line runs through the ranks
30	And like the wheat puts them to rest in the plain.
31	Here falls a hero, harvested in his prime,
32	Glorious, and eye beaming with pride and valor.
33	On his swaying helmet, from which light springs,
34	Floats the billowing mane of the black charger:
35	This dazzling helmet serves as death's target;

36	Par la foudre frappé d'un coup qu'il ne sent pas,
37	Comme un faisceau d'acier il tombe sur l'arène;
38	Son coursier bondissant qui sent flotter la rêne,
39	Lance un regard oblique à son maître expirant,
40	Revient, penche sa tête et le flaire en pleurant.
41	Là tombe un vieux guerrier qui, né dans les alarmes,
42	Eut les camps pour patrie, et pour amours, ses armes.
43	Il ne regrette rien que ses chers étendards,
44	Et les suit en mourant, de ses derniers regards …
45	La mort vole au hasard dans l'horrible carrière:
46	L'un périt tout entier; l'autre, sur la poussière,
47	Comme un tronc dont la hache a coupé les rameaux,
48	De ses membres épars voit voler les lambeaux,
49	Et, se traînant encor sur la terre humectée,
50	Marque en ruisseaux de sang sa trace ensanglantée.
51	Le blessé que la mort n'a frappé qu'à demi
52	Fuit en vain, emporté dans les bras d'un ami:
53	Sur le sein l'un de l'autre ils sont frappés ensemble
54	Et bénissent du moins le coup qui les rassemble.
55	Mais de la foudre en vain les livides éclats
56	Pleuvent sur les deux camps; d'intrépides soldats,
57	Comme la mer, qu'entr'ouvre une proue écumante,
58	Se referme soudain sur sa trace fumante,
59	Sur les rangs écrasés formant de nouveaux rangs,
60	Viennent braver la mort sur les corps des mourants! …
61	Cependant, las d'attendre un trépas sans vengeance,
62	Les deux camps, à la fois (l'un sur l'autre s'élance),

36	Struck by lightning with a blow he does not feel,
37	Like a steel beam, he falls in the arena;
38	His leaping charger feeling its rein float,
39	Casts a sidelong glance at its dying master,
40	Returns, leans its head and sniffs him crying in sorrow.
41	There falls an old warrior who, born at the call to arms,
42	Had the camps for country, and for lovers, his weapons.
43	He regrets nothing but his beloved standards,
44	And he follows them dying, with his last look …
45	Death flies at random in this horrible career:
46	One perishes whole; the other, in the dust,
47	Like a trunk whose limbs have been axed off,
48	From his scattered members sees the scraps flying,
49	And, still dragging himself on the moistened ground,
50	Marks his bloodied trail in streams of blood.
51	The wounded one that death struck only with half force
52	Flees in vain, carried in the arms of a friend:
53	They are struck united breast to breast
54	And bless at least the blow that brings them together.
55	But in vain lightning's livid flashes
56	Rain on the two camps; intrepid soldiers,
57	As the sea, that opens partially to a foaming prow,
58	Suddenly closes again on its steaming wake,
59	Creating new ranks on crushed ranks,
60	Brave death on the bodies of the dying! …
61	However, tired of awaiting a death without vengeance,
62	The two armies, in unison (rush toward each other),

63	Se heurtent, et, du choc ouvrant leurs bataillons,
64	Mêlent en tournoyant leurs sanglants tourbillons.
65	Sous le poids des coursiers les escadrons s'entr'ouvrent,
66	D'une voûte d'airain les rangs pressés se couvrent,
67	Les feux croisent les feux, le fer frappe le fer;
68	Les rangs entre-choqués lancent un seul éclair:
69	Le salpêtre, au milieu des torrents de fumée,
70	Brille et court en grondant sur la ligne enflammée,
71	Et d'un nuage épais enveloppant leur sort,
72	Cache encor à nos yeux la victoire ou la mort.
73	Ainsi quand deux torrents dans deux gorges profondes
74	De deux monts opposés précipitant leurs ondes,
75	Dans le lit trop étroit qu'ils vont se disputer
76	Viennent au même instant tomber et se heurter,
77	Le flot choque le flot, les vagues courroucées
78	Rejaillissent au loin par les vagues poussées,
79	D'une poussière humide obscurcissent les airs,
80	Du fracas de leur chute ébranlent les déserts,
81	Et portant leur fureur au lit qui les rassemble,
82	Tout en s'y combattant leurs flots roulent ensemble.
83	Mais la foudre se tait. Écoutez: … des concerts
84	De cette plaine en deuil s'élèvent dans les airs:
85	La harpe, le clairon, la joyeuse cymbale,
86	Mêlant leurs voix d'airain, montent par intervalle,
87	S'éloignent par degrés, et sur l'aile des vents
88	Nous jettent leurs accords, et les cris des mourants …
89	De leurs brillants éclats les coteaux retentissent,

63	Collide, and, from the shock opening their battalions,
64	Mix swirling in bloody eddies.
65	Under the weight of the chargers the squadrons gape,
66	The closed ranks are covered by a bronze vault,
67	Fire crosses fire, iron strikes iron;
68	The colliding ranks discharge a single flash:
69	Saltpeter, amid the hazy torrents of smoke,
70	Shimmers and runs roaring on the ignited fuse,
71	And the obscuring cloud that envelops their fate,
72	Still hides from our eyes the victory or the dead.
73	Thus when two torrents in two deep gorges
74	Of two opposing hills hurling down their waves,
75	In a bed so narrow they are destined to compete
76	Arrive at the same moment, falling and colliding
77	Wave hits wave, the angry swells
78	Thrust up from afar by the forceful swells,
79	Obscure the sky by a wet mist,
80	From the impact of their fall they jar the deserts,
81	And carrying their fury to the bed that binds them,
82	While fighting, their waves roll in together there.
83	But the thunder falls silent. Listen: … in the air
84	Concerts arise from this grieving battlefield:
85	The harp, the bugle, the joyful cymbal,
86	Combining their bronze voices, rise by intervals,
87	Separate by degrees, and on the wings of the winds
88	Throw us their chords, and the cries of the dying …
89	The hillsides ring with their brilliant outbursts,

90	Le cœur glacé s'arrête, et tous les sens frémissent,
91	Et dans les airs pesants que le son vient froisser
92	On dirait qu'on entend l'âme des morts passer!
93	Tout à coup le soleil, dissipant le nuage,
94	Éclaire avec horreur la scène du carnage;
95	Et son pâle rayon, sur la terre glissant,
96	Découvre à nos regards de longs ruisseaux de sang,
97	Des coursiers et des chars brisés dans la carrière,
98	Des membres mutilés épars sur la poussière,
99	Les débris confondus des armes et des corps,
100	Et les drapeaux jetés sur des monceaux de morts.

101	Accourez maintenant, amis, épouses, mères;
102	Venez compter vos fils, vos amants et vos frères;
103	Venez sur ces débris disputer aux vautours
104	L'espoir de vos vieux ans, les fruit de vos amours!
105	Que de larmes sans fin, sur eux vont se répandre;
106	Dans vos cités en deuil, que de cris vont s'entendre,
107	Avant qu'avec douleur la terre ait reproduit,
108	Misérables mortels! ce qu'un jour a détruit!
109	Mais au sort des humains la nature insensible
110	Sur leurs débris épars suivra son cours paisible:
111	Demain, la douce aurore, en se levant sur eux,
112	Dans leur acier sanglant réfléchira ses feux;
113	Le fleuve lavera sa rive ensanglantée,
114	Les vents balayeront leur poussière infectée
115	Et le sol engraissé de leurs restes fumants,
116	Cachera sous des fleurs leurs pâles ossements!

90	The frozen heart stops, and all senses shudder,
91	And in the heavy air creased by the sound
92	One would think one hears souls of the dead pass!
93	Without warning the sun, dissipating the cloud,
94	Illuminates this horrible scene of carnage;
95	And its pale filament, over the slippery ground,
96	Unveils to our sight long streams of blood,
97	The chargers and chariots destroyed in duty,
98	Mutilated members scattered over the dust,
99	The mixed debris of armaments and bodies,
100	And of flags thrown over the piles of dead.

101	Hasten now, friends, wives, mothers.
102	Come tally your sons, your lovers and your brothers;
103	Come to these remains over which vultures fight
104	The hope of your golden years, the fruit of your love!
105	Over them endless tears will be shed;
106	In your mourning cities, how the cries will be heard,
107	Before the ground can re-create,
108	Miserable mortals! what a day has destroyed!
109	But to the fate of man indifferent nature
110	Sets its peaceful course over their scattered remains:
111	Tomorrow, the soft dawn, while rising over them,
112	Will reflect its rays in their blood-covered sabers;
113	The river will wash clean its ensanguined banks,
114	The winds will sweep away the contaminated dust,
115	And the soil made rich by their steaming remains,
116	Will conceal their pale bones under the flowers!

CANTO IX

1 Silence, esprit de feu! mon âme épouvantée
2 Suit le frémissement de ta corde irritée,
3 Et court en frissonnant sur tes pas belliqueux,
4 Comme un char emporté par deux coursiers fougueux;
5 Mais mon œil attristé de ces sombres images
6 Se détourne en pleurant vers de plus doux rivages;
7 N'as-tu point sur ta lyre un chant consolateur?
8 N'as-tu pas entendu la flûte du pasteur,
9 Quand seul, assis en paix sous le pampre qui plie,
10 Il charme par ses airs les heures qu'il oublie,
11 Et que l'écho des bois, ou le fleuve en coulant,
12 Portent de saule en saule un son plaintif et lent?
13 Souvent pour l'écouter, le soir, sur la colline,
14 Du côté de ses chants mon oreille s'incline,
15 Mon cœur, par un soupir soulagé de son poids,
16 Dans un monde étranger se perd avec la voix;
17 Et je sens, par moments, sur mon âme calmée,
18 Passer avec le son une brise embaumée,
19 Plus douce qu'à mes sens l'ombre des arbrisseaux,
20 Ou que l'air rafraîchi qui sort du lit des eaux.

CANTO X

1 Un vent caresse ma lyre:
2 Est-ce l'aile d'un oiseau?
3 Sa voix dans le cœur expire,
4 Et l'humble corde soupire
5 Comme un flexible roseau.

CANTO IX

1 Silence, Spirit of fire! my terrified soul
2 Follows the quivering of your angry string,
3 And runs trembling in your bellicose footsteps,
4 As a chariot driven by two fiery chargers;
5 But my view saddened by these somber visions
6 Is diverted weeping toward gentler shores;
7 Have you no consoling song on your lyre?
8 Did you not hear the flute of the shepherd,
9 When alone, sitting peacefully under the bending vine,
10 With his tunes, he charms the hours that he forgets,
11 And the echo from the wood, or the flowing river,
12 Carry slow and peaceful tones from willow to willow?
13 Often to hear it, in the evening, on the hill,
14 I turn my ear toward the songs,
15 An unburdening sigh relieves my heavy heart,
16 Lost in an alien world, with its voice;
17 And I feel, at times, over my quieted soul,
18 Passing with a whisper of a fragrant breeze,
19 Sweeter to my senses than the shade of the trees,
20 Or cool air that escapes from the riverbeds.

CANTO X

1 A wind caresses my lyre:
2 Is it the wing of a bird?
3 Its song fades away in the heart,
4 And the meek string sighs
5 Like a pliable reed.

CANTO XI

1	Ô vallons paternels! doux champs, humble chaumière,
2	Au bords penchant des bois suspendus aux coteaux,
3	Dont l'humble toit, caché sous des touffes de lierre,
4	Ressemble au nid sous les rameaux;

5	Gazons entrecoupés de ruisseaux et d'ombrages,
6	Seuil antique où mon père, adoré comme un roi,
7	Comptait ses gras troupeaux rentrant des pâturages,
8	Ouvrez-vous! ouvrez-vous! c'est moi

9	Voilà du dieu des champs la rustique demeure.
10	J'entends l'airain frémir au sommet de ses tours;
11	Il semble que dans l'air une voix qui me pleure
12	Me rappelle à mes premiers jours.

13	Oui, je reviens à toi, berceau de mon enfance,
14	Embrasser pour jamais tes foyers protecteurs;
15	Loin de moi les cités et leur vaine opulence,
16	Je suis né parmi les pasteurs!

17	Enfant, j'aimais, comme eux, à suivre dans la plaine
18	Les agneaux pas à pas, égarés jusqu'au soir;
19	A revenir, comme eux, laver leur tendre laine
20	Dans l'eau courante du lavoir.

CANTO XI

1	O paternal valleys! gentle fields, humble cottage,
2	Leaning at the edge of the wood suspended on the hillside,
3	Whose humble rooftop, hidden under the ivy vines,
4	Resembles a nest under the branches;

5	Meadows interspersed with streams and shadows
6	Ancient threshold where my father, adored like a king,
7	Counted his fatted herds returning from the pastures,
8	Open the door! open the door! it's me

9	There sits the rustic home of the god of the fields.
10	I hear the bell trembling from its tower;
11	It seems that in the air a voice cries out to me
12	Reminds me of my youngest days.

13	Yes, I return to you, cradle of my childhood,
14	To embrace your protective hearths forever.
15	Far away from the cities and their vain opulence,
16	I was born among the shepherds!

17	As a child, I loved, like them, to follow on the plain
18	The lambs step by step, straying until evening;
19	Returning, like them, to wash their delicate wool
20	In the running water of the washhouse.

21	J'aimais à me suspendre aux lianes légères,
22	A gravir dans les airs de rameaux en rameaux,
23	Pour ravir, le premier, sous l'aile de leurs mères,
24	Les tendres œufs des tourtereaux.

25	J'aimais les voix du soir dans les airs répandues,
26	Le bruit lointain des chars gémissant sous leur poids,
27	Et le sourd tintement des cloches suspendues
28	Au cou des chevreaux, dans les bois.

29	Et depuis, exilé de ces douces retraites,
30	Comme un vase imprégné d'une première odeur,
31	Toujours loin des cités, des voluptés secrètes
32	Entraînaient mes yeux et mon cœur.

33	Beaux lieux, recevez-moi sous vos sacrés ombrages!
34	Vous qui couvrez le seuil de rameaux éplorés,
35	Saules contemporains, courbez vos longs feuillages
36	Sur le frère que vous pleurez.

37	Reconnaissez mes pas, doux gazons que je foule,
38	Arbres, que dans mes jeux j'insultais autrefois;
39	Et toi qui, loin de moi, te cachais à la foule,
40	Triste écho, réponds à ma voix.

21	I loved to suspend myself from the light creepers,
22	To swing in the air, from branch to branch,
23	To grab, first, under the wing of their mothers,
24	The fragile eggs of the turtledoves.

25	I loved the scattered evening voices in the air,
26	The distant sound of the carts groaning under their weight,
27	And the muted tinkling in the woods
28	Of bells hanging from the young goats' necks.

29	And since, exiled from these sweet retreats,
30	Like a vase infused with its first perfume,
31	Always far from the cities, these secret pleasures
32	Carry away my eyes and my heart.

33	Fair places, receive me in your sacred shadows!
32	You who cover the threshold with weeping branches,
35	Willows of today, bend your long foliage
36	Over the brother you mourn.

37	Recognize my steps, soft grasses on which I tread,
38	Trees, that I insulted in my games long ago,
39	And you who, far from me, hid yourself in the crowd,
40	Sad echo, answer my voice.

41	Je ne viens pas traîner, dans vos riants asiles,		41	Within your cheerful refuge, I do not come to drag through,
42	Les regrets du passé, les songes du futur:		42	The regrets of the past, the dreams of the future:
43	J'y viens vivre; et, couché sous vos berceaux fertiles,		43	I come there to live; and, laid under your fertile cradles,
44	Abriter mon repos obscur.		44	To shelter my obscure repose.

45   S'éveiller, le cœur pur, au réveil de l'aurore,
46   Pour bénir, au matin, le dieu qui fait les jours;
47   Voir les fleurs du vallon sous la rosée éclore
48   Comme pour fêter son retour;

45   To wake, the heart pure, at the break of dawn,
46   To thank, in the morning, the god who made the days;
47   To see the dew-laden buds blossom in the vale
48   As to celebrate his return;

49   Respirer les parfums que la colline exhale,
50   Ou l'humide fraîcheur qui tombe des forêts;
51   Voir onduler de loin l'haleine matinale
52   Sur le sein flottant des guérets;

49   To breathe the fragrances that the hillside exhales,
50   Or the damp coolness that falls from the forests;
51   To view from afar the undulating morning breath
52   Floating on the bosom of fallow fields;

53   Conduire la génisse à la source qu'elle aime,
54   Ou suspendre la chèvre au cytise embaumé,
55   Ou voir ses blancs taureaux venir tendre d'eux-même
56   Leur front au joug accoutumé,

53   To lead the young heifer to the wellspring she likes,
54   Or to tie the goat to the fragrant cytisus,
55   Or to see the white bulls come tether themselves
56   Their brow accustomed to the yoke,

57   Guider un soc tremblant dans le sillon qui crie,
58   Du pampre domestique émonder les berceaux,
59   Ou creuser mollement, au sein de la prairie,
60   Les lits murmurants des ruisseaux;

57   To drive a trembling ploughshare that screeches in the furrow,
58   To prune the vine climbing on the trellis,
59   Or to dig quietly, in the heart of the field,
60   The streambeds murmuring;

61	Le soir, assis en paix au seuil de la chaumière,
62	Tendre au pauvre qui passe un morceau de son pain;
63	Et, fatigué du jour, y fermer sa paupière
64	Loin des soucis du lendemain;
65	Sentir, sans les compter, dans leur ordre paisible,
66	Les jours suivre les jours, sans faire plus de bruit
67	Que ce sable léger dont la fuite insensible
68	Nous marque l'heure qui s'enfuit;
69	Voir, de vos doux vergers, sur vos fronts les fruits pendre;
70	Les fruits d'un chaste amour dans vos bras accourir;
71	Et, sur eux appuyé, doucement redescendre:
72	C'est assez pour qui doit mourir.
73	Le chant meurt, la voix tombe: adieu, divin génie!
74	Remonte au vrai séjour de la pure harmonie:
75	Tes chants ont arrêté les larmes dans mes yeux.
76	Je lui parlais encore … il était dans les cieux.

61	In the evening, sitting at peace on the cottage threshold,
62	To offer a piece of his bread to the poor one passing by;
63	And, tired from the day, closing his eyes
64	Far from the cares of tomorrow;
65	To feel, without counting them, in their quiet march,
66	Days following days, without making more of a sound
67	Than this light grain of sand's unperceived flight from which
68	We note the hour escapes;
69	See, from your sweet orchards, the fruit hanging over your heads;
70	The fruit of a pure love rushing into your arms;
71	And, leaning on them, gently walk back down:
72	It's enough for those who must die
73	The song fades away, the voice falls: goodbye, divine Genius!
74	Take up again the true sojourn of pure harmony:
75	Your songs have stopped the tears in my eyes.
76	I was still speaking to him … he was in heaven.

Bibliography

Albrechtsberger, Johann Georg, *Methods of Harmony, Figured Base, and Composition*, trans. Arnold Merrick (London: R. Cocks & Co., 1834), vols 1 and 2.

Atwood, William G., *Fryderyk Chopin: Pianist from Warsaw* (New York: Columbia University Press, 1987).

Bauçà de Mirabò Gralla, Concepció, *La Real Cartuja de Jesús de Nazaret de Valldemossa* (Salzburg: Institut für Anglistik und Amerikanistik, Universität Salzburg, 2008).

Beebe, Richard W.O., and Deborah L. Funk, *Fundamentals of Emergency Care* (Albany, NY: Delmar, 2001), vol. 1.

Bellman, Jonathan D., *Chopin's Polish Ballade: Op. 38 as Narrative of National Martyrdom* (Oxford: Oxford University Press, 2010).

Berkowitz, Aaron, *The Improvising Mind: Cognition and Creativity in the Musical Moment* (Oxford: Oxford University Press, 2010).

Birkett, Mary Ellen, *Lamartine and the Poetics of Landscape* (Lexington, KY: French Forum, 1982).

Boczkowska, Ewelina, 'Chopin's Ghosts,' *19th-Century Music*, 35/3 (Spring 2012), 204–23.

Boelcke, Andreas, 'Chopin's *24 Préludes*, Opus 28: A Cycle Unified by Motion between the Fifth and Sixth Scale Degrees' (DMA thesis, University of Cincinnati, 2008).

Bonner, Andrew, 'Liszt's *Les Préludes* and *Les Quatre Élémens*: A Reinvestigation,' *19th-Century Music*, 10/2 (Autumn 1986), 95–107.

Botting, Fred, *Gothic (The New Critical Idiom)* (London: Routledge, 1996).

Boyd, Malcolm, 'Dies Irae: Some Recent Manifestations,' *Music & Letters*, 49/4 (1968), 347–56.

Branson, David, *John Field and Chopin* (New York: St. Martin's Press, 1972).

The Catholic Encyclopedia: An International Work of Reference on the Constitution, Doctrine, Discipline, and History of the Catholic Church (New York: Encyclopedia Press, 1913), vol. 2.

Ceron, Christina, 'Manfred, The Brontës, and the Byronic Gothic Hero,' in Peter Cochran (ed.), *The Gothic Byron* (Newcastle upon Tyne: Cambridge Scholars Publishing, 2009), pp. 165–77.

Chase, Robert, *Dies Irae: A Guide to Requiem Music* (Lanham, MD: The Scarecrow Press, 2003).

Cherubini, Luigi, *A Course of Counterpoint and Fugue*, trans. J.A. Hamilton (London: R. Cocks & Co., 1841, originally published in 1835), vol. 1.

180 *The Mystery of Chopin's* Préludes

Chomiński, Jósef, *Preludia Chopina* (Cracow: PWM, 1950).

Chopin, Fryderyk, *Preludes Opp. 28, 45*, ed. Jan Ekier (Warsaw: PWM, 2000), Source Commentary by Jan Ekier.

———, *Preludes, Opus 28*, ed. Thomas Higgins. Norton Critical Scores (New York: W.W. Norton, 1973).

———, *Preludes*, ed. Ignacy J. Paderewski, 30th edn (Cracow: PWM, 2001).

———, *Préludes Op. 28, Op. 45*, edited, with preface and critical commentary, by Jean-Jacques Eigeldinger. The Complete Chopin: A New Critical Edition (London: Edition Peters, 2003).

Chopin's Letters, collected by Henryk Opienski (New York: Vienna House, 1971).

Clark, Steve, 'Graveyard School,' in Marie Mulvey-Roberts (ed.), *The Handbook to Gothic Literature* (New York: New York University Press, 1998), pp. 107–8.

Claudon, Francis, 'Chopin et Lamartine ou l'Élégie moderne,' in Irena Poniatowska (ed.), *Chopin and His Work in the Context of Culture* (Cracow: Musica Iagellonica, 2003), vol. 2, pp. 183–94.

Clery, E.J., 'The Genesis of "Gothic" Fiction,' in Jerrold E. Hogle (ed.), *The Cambridge Companion to Gothic Fiction* (Cambridge: Cambridge University Press, 2002), pp. 21–40.

Cochran, Peter, 'Byron Reads and Rewrites Gothic,' in Peter Cochran (ed.), *The Gothic Byron* (Newcastle upon Tyne: Cambridge Scholars Publishing, 2009), pp. 1–78.

Colosimo, Jennifer Driscoll, 'Schiller and the Gothic—Reception and Reality,' in Jeffrey L. High, Nicholas Martin, and Norbert Oellers (eds), *Who Is This Schiller Now? Essays on His Reception and Significance* (Rochester, NY: Camden House, 2011), pp. 287–301.

Correspondance de Frédéric Chopin, ed. Bronislas É. Sydow (Paris: Richard-Masse, 1981), vol. 2.

Cortot, Alfred, *In Search of Chopin*, trans. Cyril and Rena Clarke (New York: Abelard Press, 1952).

Curbet, Joan, '"Hallelujah to Your Dying Screams of Torture": Representations of Ritual Violence in English and Spanish Romanticism,' in Avril Horner (ed.), *European Gothic: A Spirited Exchange 1760–1960* (Manchester: Manchester University Press, 2002), pp. 161–82.

Czerny, Carl, *A Systematic Introduction to Improvisation on the Pianoforte* [*Systematische Anleitung zum Fantasieren auf dem Pianoforte*], Op. 200, trans. and ed. Alice L. Mitchell (New York: Longman, 1983).

David, Johann Nepomuk, *Das Wohltemperierte Klavier: Der Versuch einer Synopsis* (Göttingen: Vandenhoeck & Ruprecht, 1962).

Davis, Richard, 'The Music of J.N. Hummel: Its Derivations and Development,' *The Music Review*, 26 (1965), 169–91.

Dembowski, Karol, *Deux ans en Espagne et en Portugal, pendant la guerre civile 1838–1840* (Paris: Charles Gosselin, 1841).

Durot-Boucé, Élizabeth, 'Midnight Trysts: "Minuit est la plus belle heure du jour,"' *Études anglaises*, 57 (2004/3), 297–309.

Bibliography 181

Eddie, William Alexander, *Charles-Valentin Alkan: His Life and His Music* (Aldershot: Ashgate Publishing, 2007).

Eigeldinger, Jean-Jacques, 'Twenty-Four Preludes Op. 28: Genre, Structure, Significance,' in Jim Samson (ed.), *Chopin Studies* (Cambridge: Cambridge University Press, 1988), pp. 167–94.

———, *Chopin: Pianist and Teacher as Seen by His Pupils* (Cambridge: Cambridge University Press, 1990).

———, 'Placing Chopin: Reflections on a Compositional Aesthetics,' in John Rink and Jim Samson (eds), *Chopin Studies 2* (Cambridge: Cambridge University Press, 1994), pp. 102–39.

Eisler, Benita, *Chopin's Funeral* (New York: Alfred A. Knopf, 2003).

Ferrà, Bartolomé, *Chopin and George Sand in Majorca*, trans. James Webb (Palma de Mallorca: Edicions la Cartoixa, 1936).

Gamer, Michael, *Romanticism and the Gothic: Genre, Reception, and Canon Formation* (Cambridge: Cambridge University Press, 2000).

Gide, André, *Notes on Chopin*, trans. Bernard Frechtman (New York: Philosophical Library, 1949).

Goertzen, Valerie Woodring, 'By Way of Introduction: Preluding by 18th- and Early 19th-Century Pianists,' *The Journal of Musicology*, 14/3 (Summer 1996), 299–337.

———, 'Setting the Stage: Clara Schumann's Preludes,' in Bruno Nettl and Melinda Russell (eds), *In the Course of Performance: Studies in the World of Musical Improvisation* (Chicago: University of Chicago Press, 1998), pp. 237–60.

Goldberg, Halina, *Music in Chopin's Warsaw* (Oxford: Oxford University Press, 2008).

Graves, Robert, 'Historical Summary,' in George Sand, *Winter in Majorca*, trans. and annotated by Robert Graves, 2nd edn (Chicago: Academy Chicago Publishers, 1992), pp. 175–85.

Gregory, Robin, 'Dies Irae,' *Music & Letters*, 34/2 (1953), 133–9.

Hale, Terry, *'Frénétique* School,' in Marie Mulvey-Roberts (ed.), *The Handbook to Gothic Literature* (New York: New York University Press, 1998), pp. 58–63.

———, *'Roman noir,'* in Marie Mulvey-Roberts (ed.), *The Handbook to Gothic Literature* (New York: New York University Press, 1998), pp. 189–95.

———, 'French and German Gothic: The Beginnings,' in Jerrold E. Hogle (ed.), *The Cambridge Companion to Gothic Fiction* (Cambridge: Cambridge University Press, 2002), pp. 63–84.

———, 'Translation in Distress: Cultural Misappropriation and the Construction of the Gothic,' in Avril Horner (ed.), *European Gothic: A Spirited Exchange 1760–1960* (Manchester: Manchester University Press, 2002), pp. 17–38.

Hamilton, Kenneth, *After the Golden Age: Romantic Pianism and Modern Performance* (Oxford: Oxford University Press, 2008).

182 *The Mystery of Chopin's* Préludes

Haraszti, Émile, 'Genèse des préludes de Liszt qui n'ont aucun rapport avec Lamartine,' *Revue de Musicologie*, vol. 35, no. 107/108 (December 1953), 111–40.

Higgins, Thomas, 'Chopin Interpretation: A Study of Performance Directions in Selected Autographs and Other Sources' (PhD dissertation, University of Iowa, 1966).

Howard, V.A., 'On Musical Quotation,' *The Monist*, 58/2 (1974), 307–18.

Huneker, James, *Chopin: The Man and His Music* (New York: C. Scribner's Sons, 1900; rpt. 1923).

Johnson, James H., *Listening in Paris: A Cultural History* (Berkeley: University of California Press, 1995).

Jonson, George Charles Ashton, *A Handbook to Chopin's Works*, 2nd edn (London: W. Reeves, 1908).

Kallberg, Jeffrey, 'Small "Forms": In Defence of the Prelude,' in Jim Samson (ed.), *The Cambridge Companion to Chopin* (Cambridge: Cambridge University Press, 1992), pp. 124–44.

———, *Chopin at the Boundaries: Sex, History, and Musical Genre* (Cambridge, MA: Harvard University Press, 1996).

———, 'Chopin's March, Chopin's Death,' *19th-Century Music*, 25/1 (Summer 2001), 3–26.

Keller, Hermann, *The Well-Tempered Clavier by Johann Sebastian Bach*, trans. Leigh Gerdine (London: George Allen & Unwin Ltd, 1976).

Kirnberger, Johann Philipp, *Die Kunst des reinen Satzes in der Musik* (facsimile of the original edition of 1771–1779) (Hildesheim: Georg Olms Verlagsbuchhandlung, 1968), part 1.

Kollmann, August Friedrich Christopher, *An Introduction to the Art of Preluding and Extemporizing in Six Lessons for the Harpsichord or Harp*, Op. 3 (London: R. Wonum, 1792).

Korespondencja Fryderyka Chopina z George Sand i z jej dziećmi, ed. Krystyna Kobylańska (Warsaw: Państwowy Instytut Wydawniczy, 1981), vol. 1.

Korsyn, Kevin, *Decentering Music: A Critique of Contemporary Musical Research* (Oxford: Oxford University Press, 2003).

Kramer, Lawrence, *Music and Poetry: The Nineteenth Century and After* (Berkeley: University of California Press, 1984).

———, *Music as Cultural Practice, 1800–1900* (Berkeley: University of California Press, 1990).

———, 'Chopin at the Funeral: Episodes in the History of Modern Death,' *Journal of the American Musicological Society,* 54/1 (Spring 2001), 97–125.

Kresky, Jeffrey, *A Reader's Guide to the Chopin Preludes* (Westport, CT: Greenwood Press, 1994).

Krutov, V.V., and L.V. Shvetsova-Krutova, *Mir Rakhmaninova: temy i variatsii* [*Rachmaninov's World: Themes and Variations*] (Tambov: Shusharin Y.M., 2004), vol. 1.

Bibliography

Lagerberg, Steven, *Chopin's Heart: The Quest to Identify the Mysterious Illness of the World's Most Beloved Composer* (CreateSpace, 2011).

Lamartine, Alphonse de, *Les Préludes*, in *Nouvelles méditations poétiques* (Paris: Urbain Canel, 1823).

———, *Selected Poems from Premières et Nouvelles Méditations*, edited, with biographical sketch and notes, by George O. Curme (Boston: D.C. Heath & Co., 1896).

———, *Méditations*, ed. Fernand Letessier (Paris: Garnier Frères, 1968).

———, *Méditations poétiques*, ed. Marius-François Guyard (Paris: Editions Gallimard, 1981).

Laurens, J.B., *Souvenirs d'un voyage d'art à l'île de Majorque* (Paris: Arthus Bertrand, 1840).

Leikin, Anatole, 'Genre Analysis in the Music of Chopin,' presented at the Joint Meeting of the Pacific Southwest and Northern California Chapters of the American Musicological Society, Santa Barbara, California, 28 April 1985.

———, 'The Dissolution of Sonata Structure in Romantic Piano Music (1820–1850)' (PhD dissertation, University of California, Los Angeles, 1986).

———, 'The Sonatas,' in Jim Samson (ed.), *The Cambridge Companion to Chopin* (Cambridge: Cambridge University Press, 1992), pp. 160–87.

———, 'Chopin's A-minor Prelude and its Symbolic Language,' *International Journal of Musicology*, 6 (1997), 149–62.

———, 'The Alternative Versions of Chopin's Piano Sonatas: Sorting out the Composer's Intentions,' in *Early Music: Context and Ideas* (Cracow: Institute of Musicology, Jagiellonian University, 2003), pp. 178–83.

Lombard, Charles M., *Lamartine* (New York: Twayne Publishers, 1973).

Lovecraft, Howard Phillips, *Supernatural Horror in Literature* (New York: Dover Publications, 1973).

Main, Alexander, 'Liszt after Lamartine: "Les Preludes,"' *Music & Letters*, 60/2 (April 1979), 133–48.

Majka, Lucyna, Joanna Gozdzik, and Michal Witt, 'Cystic Fibrosis – A Probable Cause of Frédéric Chopin's Suffering and Death,' *Journal of Applied Genetics*, 44/1 (2003), 77–84.

Meyer, Leonard B., *Emotion and Meaning in Music* (Chicago: Chicago University Press, 1956).

Mickiewicz, Adam, *Forefathers*, trans. Count Potocki of Montalk (London: The Polish Cultural Foundation, 1968).

Miller, Leta E., 'C.P.E. Bach's Sonatas for Solo Flute,' *Journal of Musicology*, 11/2 (Spring 1993), 203–249.

———, 'C.P.E. Bach and Friedrich Ludwig Dülon: Composition and Improvisation in late 18th-Century Germany,' *Early Music*, 23/1 (February 1995), 65–81.

Morrow, Mary Sue, *Concert Life in Haydn's Vienna: Aspects of a Developing Musical and Social Institution* (Stuyvesant, NY: Pendragon Press, 1989).

Mozart, Leopold, *Versuch einer gründlichen Violinschule* (Augsburg: Johann Jacob Lotter, 1756).

Müller-Reuter, Theodor, *Lexikon der Deutschen Konzertliteratur* (New York: Da Capo Press, 1972); first published in Leipzig (C.F. Kahnt, 1909).

Myasoedov, Andrei, *O garmonii russkoy muzyki* [*On Harmony in Russian Music*] (Moscow: Prest, 1998).

Newman, William S., *Beethoven on Beethoven: Playing His Piano Music His Way* (New York: Norton, 1988).

Niecks, Frederick, *Frederick Chopin as a Man and Musician* (London: Novello and Company, 1902), vol. 2.

O'Shea, John G., 'Was Frédéric Chopin's Illness Actually Cystic Fibrosis?' *Medical Journal of Australia*, 147 (1987), 586–9.

———, *Music and Medicine: Medical Profiles of Great Composers* (London: J.M. Dent, 1990); 2nd edn published as *Was Mozart Poisoned? Medical Investigations into the Lives of the Great Composers* (New York: St. Martin's Press, 1991).

Raabe, Peter, *Franz Liszt*, 2nd edn (Tutzing: Hans Schneider, 1968), vol. 2.

Reuber, Alexandra Maria, 'Haunted by the Uncanny – Development of a Genre from the Late Eighteenth to the Late Nineteenth Century' (PhD dissertation, Louisiana State University, 2004).

Samson, Jim, *The Music of Chopin* (London: Routledge & Kegan Paul, 1985).

———, *Chopin* (New York: Schirmer Books, 1997).

Sand, George, *Histoire de ma vie*. Œuvres autobiographiques (Paris: Gallimard, 1971), vols 1 and 2.

———, *Histoire de ma vie*, trans. Dan Hofstadter (New York: Harper & Row, 1979).

———, *Story of My Life: The Autobiography of George Sand*, group trans., ed. Thelma Jurgrau (Albany, NY: State University of New York Press, 1991).

———, *Winter in Majorca*, trans. and annotated by Robert Graves, 2nd edn (Chicago: Academy Chicago Publishers, 1992).

Schachter, Carl, 'The Triad as Place and Action,' *Music Theory Spectrum*, 17/2 (Fall 1995), 149–69.

Schenker, Heinrich, *Free Composition*, trans. and ed. Ernst Oster (New York: Longman, 1979).

Selected Correspondence of Fryderyk Chopin, trans. and ed. Arthur Hedley (New York: McGraw-Hill, 1963).

Shakespeare, William, *King Richard II* (Cambridge, MA: Harvard University Press, 1956).

Shelley, Percy Bysshe, *Adonais: An Elegy on the Death of John Keats* (London: Reed Pale Press, 1935).

Small, Helen, 'Madness,' in Marie Mulvey-Roberts (ed.), *The Handbook to Gothic Literature* (New York: New York University Press, 1998), pp. 152–7.

Smith, Charles J., 'On Hearing the Chopin Preludes as a Coherent Set: A Survey of Some Possible Structural Models for Op. 28,' *In Theory Only*, 1/4 (1975), 5–16.

Sobaskie, James William, 'Precursive Prolongation in the *Préludes* of Chopin,' *Journal of the Society for Musicology in Ireland*, 3 (2007–2008), 25–61.

Sposobin, Igor, *Elementarnaya teoriya muzyki* [*Foundations of Music Theory*] (Moscow: Gosmuzizdat, 1959).

———, *Lektsii po kursu garmonii* [*Lectures on Harmony*], ed. Y. Kholopov (Moscow: Muzyka, 1969).

Subotnik, Rose Rosengard, 'Romantic Music as Post-Kantian Critique: Classicism, Romanticism, and the Concept of the Semiotic Universe,' in Kingsley Price (ed.), *On Criticizing Music: Five Philosophical Perspectives* (Baltimore, MD: Johns Hopkins University Press, 1981), pp. 87–95.

Szulc, Tad, *Chopin in Paris: The Life and Times of the Romantic Composer* (New York: A Lisa Drew Book/Scribner, 1998).

Werker, Wilhelm, *Studien über die Symmetrie im Bau der Fugen und die motivische Zusammengehörigkeit der Präludien und Fugen des "Wohltemperierten Klaviers" von Johann Sebastian Bach* (Leipzig: Breitkopf und Härtel, 1922).

Williams, Anne, *Art of Darkness: A Poetics of Gothic* (Chicago: University of Chicago Press, 1995).

Wood, Charles W., *Letters from Majorca* (London: Richard Bentley & Son, 1888).

Youens, Susan, *Retracing a Winter's Journey: Schubert's* Winterreise (Ithaca, NY: Cornell University Press, 1991).

Index

Aladro-Font, Jordi, xiii
Albrechtsberger, Johann Georg, 61, 64
Alkan, Charles-Valentin, 55–6, 59, 63–4, 132, 152
Arlincourt, Charles-Victor Prévost d', 19
Atwood, William, 7, 11n, 79n, 157n

Bach, Johann Sebastian, 1, 6, 47–50, 52, 67, 111, 149, 151, 155, 158
Balzac, Honoré de, 13
Bauçà de Mirabó, Concepció, xiii, 35, 39
Beckford, William, 20
Beebe, Richard W.O., 78n
Beethoven, Ludwig van, 57, 64, 76, 98, 100, 132, 157
Bellman, Jonathan, xiii, 44, 145n
Berkowitz, Aaron, 3n
Berlioz, Hector, 55–6, 59, 63, 132, 152
Birkett, Mary Ellen, 32n
Blair, Robert, 17
Boczkowska, Ewelina, 36n
Boelcke, Andreas, 3n, 10, 67n
Bonner, Andrew, 53
Botting, Fred, 32
Boyd, Malcolm, 56, 59
Branson, David, 57n
Britten, Benjamin, 159
Bülow, Hans von, 1, 54n, 78
Byron, Lord George Gordon, 17n, 18–20, 21n, 24

Calafell Alemany, Enric, xiii, 39
Capilonch Ferrà, Rosa, xiii
Ceron, Christina, 18n, 19n
Chase, Robert, 159n
Cherubini, Luigi, 61, 63n, 64
Chomiński, Jósef, 10
Chopin, Fryderyk,
    Andante spianato et Grande polonaise brillante, Op. 22, 7, 8
    Ballade, Op. 23, 44, 151
    Ballade, Op. 38, 44, 145–7
    Ballade, Op. 47, 8
    Cello Sonata, Op. 65, 58
    Etude, Op. 10 No. 5, 7
    Etude, Op. 25 No. 1, 44
    Fantaisie, Op. 49, 47, 76
    Impromptu, Op. 29, 102
    Impromptu, Op. 36, 7
    Mazurka from 'Notre temps' No. 2, 47
    Mazurka, Op. 24 No. 2, 47
    Nocturne, Op. 15 No 3, 44, 76
    Nocturne, Op. 27 No. 1, 76, 100, 151n
    Nocturne, Op. 37 No. 1, 76
    Nocturne, Op. 48 No. 1, 7, 76, 98
    Nocturne, Op. 48 No. 2, 44
    Nocturne, Op. 55 No. 1, 76
    Prelude, Op. 45, 9
    Polonaise-Fantaisie, Op. 61, 76, 146, 148, 151n
    Préludes, Op. 28, xiii, xiv, 1, 3, 6–11, 16, 21, 40, 45–7, 51–2, 54–6, 59–60, 63–4, 66, 145–6, 152, 155, 158–9
    Prelude 1 (C major), 10, 51, 54, 67–71, 76, 100
    Prelude 2 (A minor), 40, 51, 54, 55, 68–78, 85, 87, 100–1, 143
    Prelude 3 (G major), 51, 64, 78–82
    Prelude 4 (E minor), 40, 51, 55, 80–8
    Prelude 5 (D major), 40, 89–90, 98
    Prelude 6 (B minor), 52, 55, 60, 89–92, 104
    Prelude 7 (A major), 7, 9, 40, 51, 52, 76n, 92–4
    Prelude 8 (F♯ minor), 7, 51, 94–8
    Prelude 9 (E major), 41, 52, 98–101

Prelude 10 (C♯ minor), 9, 41, 45,
101–2
Prelude 11 (B major), 51, 102–4,
128
Prelude 12 (G♯ minor), 45, 51, 60,
104–8
Prelude 13 (F♯ major), 108–11,
113, 143
Prelude 14 (E♭ minor), 9, 41,
111–13
Prelude 15 (D♭ major), 9, 64,
113–16
Prelude 16 (B♭ minor), 41, 45, 51,
115–2, 143
Prelude 17, (A♭ major), 16, 51, 52,
121–5
Prelude 18 (F minor), 41, 51, 52,
125–7
Prelude 19 (E♭ major), 45, 51,
127–33
Prelude 20 (C minor), 7, 8, 51, 55,
76n, 130–4
Prelude 21 (B♭ major), 51, 134–7
Prelude 22 (G minor), 45, 51,
137–8
Prelude 23 (F major), 139–40
Prelude 24 (D minor), 45, 140–3
Scherzo, Op. 20, 43, 56
Scherzo, Op. 31, 8, 43, 47
Sonata, Op. 35, 45, 75–6, 111
Waltz, Op. 64 No. 2, 65
Waltz, Op. 70 No. 2, 47
Waltz, Op. 70 No. 3, 58
Cichy, Wojciech, 29
Clark, Steve, 16n, 17n
Claudon, Francis, 13n
Clementi, Muzio, 3, 46
Clery, Emma J., 16n
Cochran, Peter, 17n, 18, 21n
Corri, Philip Antony, 3
Cortot, Alfred, 58n
Cramer, Johann Baptist, 3, 8
Cruveilhier, Jean Baptiste, 28–9
Curbet, Joan, 24n
Czerny, Carl, 4, 46, 48

David, Johann Nepomuk, 48
Davis, Richard, 57n

Debussy, Claude, 1
Dembowski, Karol, 26
Dies irae chant, 55–66
in Alkan's '*Morte*', 55–6, 59
in Berlioz's *Symphonie fantastique*,
55–6, 59
in Chopin's
Ballade, Op. 38, 145–7
Polonaise-Fantaisie, Op. 61,
146–8
Préludes, Op. 28, 55, 59–68,
71–80, 85–9, 90–142
in Liszt's *Totentanz*, 55–6, 63–4,
in Schubert's *Winterreise*, 152–5
Driscoll Colosimo, Jennifer, 18n
Dubois, Camille, 16, 121, 123
Durandus of Saint-Pourçain, 143
Durot-Boucé, Élizabeth, 20n, 31, 37n,
143n
Dussek, Jan, 4

Eddie, William Alexander, 56n
Eigeldinger, Jean-Jacques, 3n, 8n, 10,
16n, 40, 41, 43n, 46, 48n, 51,
55, 70n, 73n, 74n, 81n, 83, 85,
100, 116, 123n, 121, 132n 137n,
157n
Eisler, Benita, 30n
Ekier, Jan, 70, 74n, 100n
Elsner, Joseph, 60–1, 128
Ezerova, Maria, xiii, 36–8

Ferrà, Bartomeu, 34, 35n
Field, John, 57
Fontana, Julian, 24, 27, 35
Funk, Deborah L., 78n

Gamer, Michael, 21n
Gaubert, Pierre-Marcel, 23
Gautier, Théophile, 24
Gide, André, 1, 53, 71, 158
Goethe, Johann Wolfgang von, 19
Goldberg, Halina, 61n
Gothic fiction, 16–21, 24, 31–2, 36–7, 39,
43, 56, 77, 123, 125, 127, 143
Gozdzik, Johanna, 29
Graves, Robert, 26n, 28n, 39, 40n
Gray, Thomas, 17

Index 189

Gregory, Robin, 56
Grétry, André Ernest Modeste, 3
Grzymala, Wojciech, 24, 28
Gutmann, Adolf, 44
Guyard, Marius-François, 14, 15n

Hale, Terry, 18n, 19n
Hamilton, Kenneth, 1n, 7n
Hannon, Colin, 2n
Hanson, Howard, 159
Haraszti, Émile, 53
Harris, Peter, xiii
Haslinger, Tobias, 3
Haydn, Franz Joseph, 64
Heine, Heinrich, 13
Hervey, James, 17
Hewitt, James, 3
Higgins, Thomas, 1n, 6n, 55, 74n, 92n, 100
Hoffmann, E.T.A., 18–19
Hofmann, Josef, 2, 8n
Hofstadter, Dan, 60n
Howard, V.A., 77n
Hugo, Victor, 13
Hummel, Johann Nepomuk, 3–6, 8, 46–8, 52, 57
Huneker, James, 71n, 78

Janin, Jules, 19–20
Johnson, James H., 157n
Jonson, George Charles Ashton, 71n

Kalkbrenner, Frédéric, 3, 46
Kallberg, Jeffrey, 7–9, 36n, 52, 133n
Keller, Hermann, 48–9, 51
Kelly, Isabella, 16
Kirnberger, Johann Philipp, 61, 64, 68, 76
Kollmann, August Friedrich Christopher, 3n
Korsyn, Kevin, 10
Kramer, Lawrence, 10, 73n, 77
Kresky, Jeffrey, 10, 51, 73n, 79, 116, 125, 140, 142
Krutov, Vladimir, 1n

Lagerberg, Steven, 29

Lamartine, Alphonse de, xiii, 11, 13–17, 19–21, 23n, 32, 39, 44, 46–7, 52–5, 78n, 79, 127, 142, 155, 158–9, 161
Latouche, Henri de, 20
Laurens, Jean-Joseph Bonaventure, 26, 32–3, 35
Lenz, Wilhelm von, 44, 48
Lewis, Matthew, 18, 24
Liszt, Franz, 1, 6–7, 11, 46, 53–6, 59, 63–5, 113, 158–9
Lombard, Charles M., 13n, 17n, 19n
Lovecraft, Howard Phillips, 17n

Mahler, Gustav, 76
Main, Alexander, 20n, 53
Majka, Lucyna, 29
Mallefille, Félicien, 23
Maturin, Charles, 18, 24, 125
Mendelssohn, Felix, 121
Mendizábal, Juan Álvares, 31
Mérimée, Prosper, 24
Meyer, Leonard B., 73n
Miller, Leta, 1n, 128n
Mickiewicz, Adam, 13, 44, 78
Morrow, Mary Sue, 157n
Moscheles, Ignaz, 3, 8, 57
Mozart, Leopold, 100, 128
Müller, Friederike, 48
Müller-Reuter, Theodor, 54n
Myasoyedov, Andrei, 47n

Newman, William S., 157n
Niecks, Frederick, 25n, 113
Nodier, Charles, 19
octatonic tetrachords/scales,
    in Chopin's works, 101, 151
    in Schubert's *Winterreise*, 149–51

O'Shea, John, 29

Paderewski, Ignacy, 16, 70, 117, 121
Parnell, Thomas, 17
Plater, Ludwik, 43
Pletnev, Mikhail, 143n
Pleyel, Camille, 8, 132
Popper, David, 159
Potocki, Jan, 24

190   *The Mystery of Chopin's* Préludes

Quadrado, José María, 26

Raabe, Peter, 53
Rachmaninov, Sergei, 1
Radcliffe, Ann, 18–19, 125
Ratay, Beth, xiii
Reeves, Clara, 16
Reuber, Alexandra Maria, 17n, 19n
Rhynsburger, Mark, xiii
Ries, Ferdinand, 157
Ritzarev, Marina, 99n
roman/école frénétique, 19–20, 56
roman noir, 19
Rosengard Subotnik, Rose, 73n, 78n
Rossini, Gioachino, 157
Rousseau, Jean-Jacques, 128
Rubinstein, Anton, 1, 45

Samson, Jim, 7n, 10n, 57n, 67n, 73n, 92n
Sand, George, 6, 13, 19–20, 23–8, 30–3,
    35, 37–41, 54, 56, 59, 60n, 74, 113,
    127n, 145, 154
Sand, Maurice, 24, 40, 113
Sand, Solange, 24, 39–40
Sandeau, Jules, 23
Schachter, Carl, 82–3
Schauerroman, 18
Schenker, Heinrich, 73n
Schiller, Friedrich von, 18–20
Scherbatoff, Marie, 68, 132
Schoenberg, Arnold, 66
Schubert, Franz, 44, 58, 79, 89, 98, 148–9,
    151–2, 154
Schumann, Clara, 2, 121
Schumann, Robert, 1–2, 9–11, 45–6, 57,
    158

Shakespeare, William, 17
Shelley, Percy Bysshe, 78
Shostakovich, Dmitry, 1, 151n
Shvetsova-Krutova, Lidiya, 2n
Scriabin, Alexander, 1
Słowacki, Juliusz, 13
Small, Helen, 125n
Smith, Charles J., 51
Sobaskie, James William, 46
Sposobin, Igor, 47n
Stirling, Jane, 28, 132, 137
Sue, Eugène, 19–20
Swenson, Tamah, xiii, 13n, 161
Szulc, Tad, 13n, 19n, 23n, 36n
Szymanowska, Maria, 3

Takemitsu, Toro, 159
Tchaikovsky, Pyotr, 57

Walpole, Horace, 16–18, 125
Warner, Richard, 16
Weber, Carl Maria von, 157
Werker, Wilhelm, 48
Williams, Anne, 18, 21n, 127n
Witt, Michal, 29
Wojciechowski, Tytus, 43
Wood, Charles William, 34–5
Wood, John Muir, 7
Woodring Goertzen, Valerie, 2n, 3n
Woodworth, Mark, xiii
Würfel, Wilhelm, 3, 46

Youens, Susan, 148n
Young, Edward, 17

Zywny, Adalbert, 48